THE ATTITUDE OF AGNOSTICISM

We often describe ourselves as agnostic on a wide range of topics, such as does God exist, is string theory true, or will the president win re-election? But what, precisely, does it mean to be agnostic? This monograph employs the tools and techniques of analytic philosophy to offer a broad account of what it means to be agnostic in both theological and non-theological contexts, and offers a critical discussion of the major descriptive accounts of agnosticism in the contemporary analytic philosophical literature. Unlike most other volumes on the subject, which approach the question from a theological point of view, this is the first book-length discussion of agnosticism from a purely philosophical point of view. It serves as a natural starting point for students and specialists in philosophy and anyone who is interested in the topic of agnosticism through the lens of analytic philosophy.

AVERY ARCHER is Associate Professor of Philosophy at George Washington University, Washington, DC. He has published articles in several academic journals, including *Philosophical Studies*, *Synthese*, and *Analysis*.

THE ATTITUDE
OF AGNOSTICISM

AVERY ARCHER

George Washington University

Shaftesbury Road, Cambridge CB2 8EA, United Kingdom

One Liberty Plaza, 20th Floor, New York, NY 10006, USA

477 Williamstown Road, Port Melbourne, VIC 3207, Australia

314–321, 3rd Floor, Plot 3, Splendor Forum, Jasola District Centre, New Delhi – 110025, India

103 Penang Road, #05–06/07, Visioncrest Commercial, Singapore 238467

Cambridge University Press is part of Cambridge University Press & Assessment, a department of the University of Cambridge.

We share the University's mission to contribute to society through the pursuit of education, learning and research at the highest international levels of excellence.

www.cambridge.org
Information on this title: www.cambridge.org/9781009214728

DOI: 10.1017/9781009214759

© Avery Archer 2024

This publication is in copyright. Subject to statutory exception and to the provisions of relevant collective licensing agreements, no reproduction of any part may take place without the written permission of Cambridge University Press & Assessment.

First published 2024
First paperback edition 2025

A catalogue record for this publication is available from the British Library

Library of Congress Cataloging-in-Publication data
NAMES: Archer, Avery, editor.
TITLE: The attitude of agnosticism / edited by Avery Archer, George Washington University, Washington DC.
DESCRIPTION: Cambridge ; New York, NY : Cambridge University Press, 2024. | Includes bibliographical references and index.
IDENTIFIERS: LCCN 2023039290 (print) | LCCN 2023039291 (ebook) | ISBN 9781009214735 (hardback) | ISBN 9781009214728 (paperback) | ISBN 9781009214759 (epub)
SUBJECTS: LCSH: Agnosticism.
CLASSIFICATION: LCC B808 .A88 2024 (print) | LCC B808 (ebook) | DDC 211/.7–DC23/eng/20240129
LC record available at https://lccn.loc.gov/2023039290
LC ebook record available at https://lccn.loc.gov/2023039291

ISBN 978-1-009-21473-5 Hardback
ISBN 978-1-009-21472-8 Paperback

Cambridge University Press & Assessment has no responsibility for the persistence or accuracy of URLs for external or third-party internet websites referred to in this publication and does not guarantee that any content on such websites is, or will remain, accurate or appropriate.

For Averlyn

Contents

Acknowledgements		*page* x
1	Introduction	1
	1.1 Overview	1
	1.2 Chapter Descriptions	2
	1.3 A Unique Perspective	4
2	Criteria for a Satisfactory Account of Agnosticism	6
	2.1 Introduction	6
	2.2 Non-Belief and Friedman's Criteria	7
	2.3 The Possibility of Doxastic Inconsistency	12
	2.4 Examples of Doxastic Inconsistency	16
	2.5 Alternatives to the Inconsistent Attitudes Explanation	18
	2.6 Agnosticism-Involving Doxastic Inconsistency	21
	2.7 The Impossibility of Agnosticism-Involving Inconsistency	23
	2.8 Attitudinal Accounts and Wagner's Criteria	32
	2.9 Conclusion	39
3	Competing Attitudinal Accounts of Agnosticism	41
	3.1 Introduction	41
	3.2 Russell's Metacognitive Account	41
	3.3 Crawford's Metacognitive Account	43
	3.4 Masny's Metacognitive Account	48
	3.5 Raleigh's Metacognitive Account	50
	3.6 Wagner's Endorsed-Indecision Account	52
	3.7 Friedman's Sui Generis Account	54
	3.8 Conclusion	57
4	The Questioning-Attitude Account of Agnosticism	59
	4.1 Introduction	59
	4.2 Defining Key Terms	59
	4.3 Agnosticism as Question-Directed	61
	4.4 Agnosticism as Proposition-Directed	66
	4.5 Agnosticism Attitude-Ascriptions	71

	4.6 Agnosticism as Sui Generis	74
	4.7 Applying the Seven Criteria	79
	4.8 Conclusion	81
5	**Agnosticism and the Inquiring State of Mind**	83
	5.1 Introduction	83
	5.2 Defining Inquiry	84
	5.3 The Inquiry-Entails-Agnosticism Thesis	86
	5.4 The Agnosticism-Entails-Inquiry Thesis	91
	5.5 The Unanswerable Questions Objection	92
	5.6 My Argument against the Descriptive Thesis	95
	5.7 My Argument against the Normative Thesis	101
	5.8 Conclusion	105
6	**The Act-Attitude Account of Doxastic Neutrality**	107
	6.1 Introduction	107
	6.2 McGrath's Tripartite Account of Neutrality	108
	6.3 The Mongrel Concept Objection	112
	6.4 Negative versus Positive Neutrality	118
	6.5 Interrogative and Anti-interrogative Attitudes	126
	6.6 Conclusion	131
7	**On the Non-existence of Practical Agnosticism**	132
	7.1 Introduction	132
	7.2 The Appropriateness Norms for Belief	133
	7.3 The Appropriateness Norms for Intention	134
	7.4 Agnosticism, Picking, and Buridan's Ass	138
	7.5 Is Indifference Practical Agnosticism?	142
	7.6 Agnosticism, Acceptance, and the Truth-Aim	145
	7.7 Conclusion	149
8	**Agnosticism and Pragmatic Reasons**	151
	8.1 Introduction	151
	8.2 Agnosticism and Transparency	151
	8.3 Agnosticism and Pragmatic Considerations	155
	8.4 Schroeder's Belief Sufficiency Principle	158
	8.5 Agnosticism and Evidentialism	164
	8.6 Conclusion	169
9	**Agnosticism, Permissivism, and Peer Disagreement**	171
	9.1 Introduction	171
	9.2 Agnosticism-Involving Permissivism	172
	9.3 Nickel's Argument for Permissivism	175
	9.4 Objections to Permissivism	180
	9.5 The Requirements for Epistemic Peerhood	188
	9.6 An Argument for the Agnostic Response	196

	9.7	Palmira's Objection to the Agnostic Response	197
	9.8	Conclusion	201
10	**Conclusion**		203
	10.1	Agnosticism as Sui Generis Attitude	204
	10.2	Agnosticism's Rational Appropriateness	205
	10.3	Giving Agnosticism Its Due	207

References   209
Index   214

Acknowledgements

This book has benefited significantly from the aid and support of several individuals. I am especially indebted to Christopher Whalin and Usha Nathan, both of whom read and provided invaluable feedback on my book manuscript. If there are any gross philosophical errors in the pages that follow, they are solely and entirely to blame. I am also grateful to Jane Friedman, Matthew McGrath, Lisa McCune, Jeanie Schreiber, Christine Susienka, and Katja Vogt for helpful discussions.

Several of the arguments in Chapter 2 of this monograph are recycled from my paper 'Agnosticism-Involving Doxastic Inconsistency', in the journal *Erkenntnis*,[1] Chapter 4; 'The Questioning-Attitude Account of Agnosticism', is a revised version of a journal article by the same name published in *Synthese*;[2] and Chapter 5 borrows heavily from my article 'Agnosticism, Inquiry, and Unanswerable Questions' published in *Disputatio*.[3] I am grateful to these journals for granting me permission to reuse this material.

I have presented portions of this book to audiences in the philosophy departments of Portland State University, Rice University, University of Vermont, Virginia Tech, and the University of Wisconsin-Madison, as well as the audiences at the 2017 meeting of the Indiana Philosophical Society, the 2019 meeting of the Northwest Philosophy Conference, and the 2020 meeting of the Central American Philosophical Association. The feedback I received from these venues greatly improved the arguments and ideas contained in the pages that follow. I am also grateful to my colleagues in the George Washington University Philosophy Department who graciously conspired to shoulder a disproportionate amount of the service-related administrative responsibilities within the department so that I would have the time needed to complete this monograph. Special thanks are due to David DeGrazia, who served as both a mentor and guide from the

[1] Archer (2023). [2] Archer (2022). [3] Archer (2019).

inception of the writing process up until my securing of a book contract with Cambridge University Press. This book would not exist today without his generous input and guidance. Most of all, thanks to my feline companion, Xanthippe, for her unwavering emotional support throughout the writing process.

CHAPTER I

Introduction

1.1 **Overview**

In the popular imagination, an agnostic is someone who holds that the existence of a god is unknown or unknowable.[1] However, unlike the term atheist, with which it is often associated, the term agnostic is routinely used in a non-theological way, as when someone, after being asked for their opinion on whether a certain candidate will win the presidential elections or regarding the truth of string theory, announces that they are agnostic on the matter. This book will be interested in the term in its broad usage, one that includes its application to theological and non-theological subject matter.

The most widely discussed contemporary account of agnosticism is that of Jane Friedman, who conceives of it as a sui generis mental attitude – that is, one that cannot be reduced to belief or some other mental attitude. Recently, however, sui generis views have come under fire by the likes of Michal Masny (2020) and Thomas Raleigh (2021), who hold that agnosticism may be reduced to a higher-order belief and intention (Masny) or a metacognitive belief (Raleigh). Moreover, Raleigh observes that Friedman's sui generis account is currently 'the only fleshed out version of the view'.[2] Consequently, theorists who are attracted to a sui generis conception have found themselves short on options. The present monograph aims to fill this lacuna by offering a fully developed alternative version of the sui generis view that not only avoids the now widely litigated shortcomings of Friedman's account, but also exposes and improves upon several weaknesses in the competing views of Masny, Raleigh, and others. The central thesis of this book is that agnosticism is best conceived of as the rationally appropriate attitudinal response to some proposition, **P**, in

---

[1] See and cf. Huxley (1889). [2] Raleigh (2021: 2454).

cases in which one's competently considered evidence is insufficient to establish both the truth and falsity of **P**.

1.2 Chapter Descriptions

The Attitude of Agnosticism will have two major tasks. The first task will be to provide a critical survey of the most influential theoretical approaches to agnosticism within contemporary analytic philosophy – including the accounts of Sean Crawford (2004), Friedman (2013a, 2013b, 2013c, 2017a), Whitney Lilly (2019), Errol Lord (2020; 2021), Michal Masny (2020), Matthew McGrath (2021), Thomas Raleigh (2021), and Verena Wagner (2021) – and highlight their relative strengths and weaknesses. The second task will be to articulate and defend a novel version of the sui generis account of agnosticism, employing the aforementioned accounts of agnosticism as foils for my own.

Here is the plan. In Chapter 2, I vet various criteria for a satisfactory account of agnosticism that have been proposed in the literature. This includes criteria like Friedman's requirement that one only be agnostic about a matter one has considered (which I endorse) and Wagner's requirement that one can be agnostic about a matter only if one is undecided with respect to that matter (which I reject). I also offer a sustained defence of what is arguably the most controversial criterion for a satisfactory account of agnosticism: preserving the possibility of a subject being doxastically inconsistent by believing some proposition, **P**, at some time, t, and being agnostic towards **P** at t.

In Chapter 3, I apply the criteria vetted in Chapter 2 to the accounts of Russell, Crawford, Masny, Raleigh, Wagner, and Friedman. I demonstrate that each account fails to satisfy one or more of the criteria for a satisfactory descriptive account of agnosticism. This will clear the way for my own proposed view.

In Chapter 4, I advance a non-reductive, proposition-directed, sui generis account of agnosticism called the *questioning-attitude account*. The questioning-attitude account is non-reductive because it denies that agnosticism is reducible to other mental states like belief, desire, or intention. It is a proposition-directed account because it holds that the object of agnosticism is a proposition, as opposed to a question or another mental state. It is a sui generis account because it holds that unlike belief, which involves an affirming stance towards a proposition, or disbelief, which involves a denying stance towards a proposition, agnosticism involves a distinct questioning stance towards a proposition. I conclude by demonstrating that the questioning-attitude account is able to satisfy the various criteria for a satisfactory account of agnosticism set forth in Chapter 2.

In Chapter 5, I mount a sustained argument against Friedman's claim that one is agnostic about whether **P** if and only if one is in an inquiring state of mind about whether **P**. I reject the claim that an inquiring state of mind entails agnosticism on the grounds that it fails to accommodate cases in which an agent inquires with the aim of ratcheting up an instance of (justified) believing to the status of knowledge or an instance of knowledge to the status of complete certainty. I reject the claim that agnosticism entails being in an inquiring state of mind on the grounds that it fails to accommodate cases in which a subject is agnostic towards **P** but is unmotivated to inquire about whether **P** because they believe or know that the question of whether **P** is unanswerable. I conclude that the raison d'être of agnosticism is not to facilitate inquiry or an inquiring state of mind, but rather to constitute a rationally appropriate doxastic response to one's competently considered evidence being insufficient to establish both the truth and falsity of a proposition.

In Chapter 6, I advocate for a *bipartite act-attitude account* of doxastic neutrality, according to which the mental act of withholding judgement stands to the attitude of agnosticism as the mental act of judging stands to the attitude of belief. My proposed account stands in contrast with that of Matthew McGrath, who argues that there are at least three distinct ways of being neutral – namely agnosticism, refraining from judgement, and suspension of judgement. I argue that suspension of judgement, as conceived of by McGrath, is not a distinct way of being neutral. This leaves only the mental act of refraining from judgement (or what I call 'withholding judgement') and the mental state of agnosticism as the two genuine ways of being doxastically neutral.

In Chapter 7, I contend that there is no practical attitude that stands to intending to do **X** and intending not to do **X** as agnosticism towards **P** stands to believing **P** and disbelieving **P**. In short, there is no practical analogue to agnosticism. Call this the *non-existence thesis*. I defend the non-existence thesis against potential objections and highlight some of its implications for the norms governing belief and intention.

In Chapter 8, I defend the thesis that there may be pragmatic reasons to be agnostic. Given that agnosticism is one of the possible outcomes of *doxastic deliberation* – that is, deliberation about whether to believe **P** – it follows that pragmatic considerations may determine the outcome of doxastic deliberation. However, while I hold that pragmatic considerations may be reasons to refrain from belief, I deny that they may be reasons to believe.

According to *uniqueness theorists*, there is only one rationally permissible doxastic attitude available to an agent given a certain body of evidence. *Permissivists* reject this claim. In Chapter 9, I defend a weak version of permissivism, according to which there are cases in which it is rationally permissible to either believe **P** based on some evidence, *e*, or be agnostic about **P**, given *e*. What makes this version of permissivism more modest than standard formulations of the thesis is that it is not committed to there being cases in which it is rationally permissible to either believe **P** or disbelieve **P** based on *e*. I also defend the thesis that agnosticism is the rationally appropriate response to cases of revealed peer disagreement. Call this thesis the *Agnostic Response*. I respond to Michele Palmira's objection to the Agnostic Response, which alleges that it cannot accommodate cases in which one of the parties to the disagreement is already agnostic. Let us refer to cases of revealed peer disagreement in which one of the parties to the disagreement is agnostic as *agnostic disagreement*. Contra Palmira, I argue that in cases of agnostic disagreement, the agnostic party is rationally justified in retaining her attitude of agnosticism.

Chapter 10, the Conclusion, summarises the central theses defended in my monograph and explains how they fit together to provide us with a more complete picture of the nature and normative significance of agnosticism.

1.3 A Unique Perspective

One of the main selling points of any monograph is the unique perspective of its author. As such, a brief description of the personal significance of agnosticism and of how the attitude has featured in my biography seems fitting. My very first career was that of an evangelical Christian minister and church pastor in the twin-island republic of Trinidad and Tobago. Early in my tenure as a pastor, I began to experience doubts about the existence of God which culminated in the adoption of an agnostic position on the question of God's existence. The public revelation of my agnosticism about God's existence resulted in my losing my ministerial position, my excommunication from the church, my estrangement from many of my friends and family, and my being forced to relocate to the United States to begin a new life. Throughout this ordeal, I wrestled over whether the inconclusiveness of my available evidence with regard to the existence of God was sufficient reason to embrace an agnostic position given the significant personal cost attached to doing so. Was such a life-changing

1.3 A Unique Perspective

question to be settled by the state of my evidence alone? Did the practical benefits of remaining within my religious community constitute reasons to continue believing? Did the significant emotional, social, and professional cost of agnosticism constitute a reason not to be agnostic? For me, at the time, these questions were not merely theoretical. They were pressing, urgent, and had literally reshaped the course of my life.

Being forced to wrestle with a question in a high-stakes situation can inspire a certain seriousness and focus that is difficult to replicate if said question is merely one of academic curiosity. Take for example the debate over whether non-evidential considerations may be reasons to transition from an attitude of agnosticism to belief. It would be all too easy to have such a question settled by how neatly a particular answer fits with other aspects of whatever theoretical account one happens to favour. However, in my case, a positive answer to this question would seem to have the implication that the significant personal price I paid in the name of intellectual honesty was a needless, and perhaps altogether misguided, sacrifice. This would make such a view unpalatable in ways it would not be otherwise. Moreover, my awareness of this biographical detail should caution me against being too hasty in dismissing the possibility of pragmatic reasons for belief and/or agnosticism.

The preceding anecdote illustrates one of the many ways in which the specific circumstances that have led to my interest in the topic of agnosticism may have shaped (both wittingly and unwittingly) the account of agnosticism defended in this monograph. While I actively defend the thesis that there may be pragmatic reasons to be agnostic, I am careful to distinguish this from the thesis that there may be pragmatic reasons to move from agnosticism to belief, the latter being a view I reject. Such subtleties may initially seem like mere theoretical fastidiousness. But since holding that there may be pragmatic reasons to be agnostic is consistent with the evaluation that I made the right call in leaving my ministerial past behind while the view that there may be pragmatic reasons to believe potentially is not, the practical import of the distinction between the two views is difficult to overstate. In sum, the perspective reflected in this volume is that of someone who is intimately familiar with the potentially far-reaching implications of our conception of agnosticism and of when the attitude is demanded of us.

CHAPTER 2

Criteria for a Satisfactory Account of Agnosticism

2.1 Introduction

Epistemologists have long recognised that belief and disbelief do not exhaust the possible commitment-involving mental stances we may take towards a given proposition. A third, neutral, commitment-involving mental stance is also possible. This third neutral mental stance has been variously referred to as *suspension of judgement, withholding judgement*, or *agnosticism*.[1] (For the sake of simplicity, I will largely restrict myself to the use of the term 'agnosticism' in this book.) Furthermore, there is a great deal of disagreement about how agnosticism is best characterised. In this chapter, I discuss seven criteria for a satisfactory descriptive account of agnosticism. I will begin with an examination of the four criteria derived from the work of Jane Friedman that have contributed to the almost universal rejection of non-attitudinal accounts of agnosticism among analytic philosophers. I then offer a defence of the most controversial Friedman-inspired criterion: namely that a satisfactory descriptive account of agnosticism must preserve the possibility of someone being doxastically inconsistent by simultaneously believing and being agnostic towards the same proposition. This will be important since allowing for the possibility of agnosticism-involving doxastic inconsistency will be one of the most distinctive features of the descriptive account of agnosticism offered in this book. I conclude by considering three additional criteria due to Verena Wagner. The goal of this chapter is to introduce and vet these criteria, which I will be applying to the major competing contemporary accounts of agnosticism in Chapter 3.

---

[1] An example of an author who employs the terms 'suspension of judgement' and 'agnosticism' to refer to metaphysically distinct phenomenon is Matthew McGrath (2021). In Section 6.4.1, I make the case for continuing the now standard practice of employing the terms 'suspension of judgement' and 'agnosticism' interchangeably.

2.2 Non-Belief and Friedman's Criteria

Let us take as our point of departure the conception of agnosticism of Roderick Chisholm (1976) and Bergmann (2005), who hold that being agnostic towards **P** is simply not believing **P** and not believing ¬**P**. Following Friedman (2013a), let us describe an agent who neither believes nor disbelieves **P** as being in a state of *non-belief* towards **P** and let us call the descriptive account of agnosticism that equates being agnostic with non-belief as *Non-Belief*:

Non-Belief: One is agnostic towards **P** at t if and only if one is in a state of non-belief with respect to **P** at t.

Non-Belief is an example of a non-attitudinal account of agnosticism. According to non-attitudinal accounts, while both believing and disbelieving involve a mental stance towards a proposition (affirming and denying, respectively), agnosticism is merely the absence of an affirming or denying mental stance towards a proposition.

Friedman has argued (I believe, convincingly) that being in a state of non-belief is neither sufficient nor necessary for agnosticism.[2]

Against the *sufficiency* claim, Friedman observes that cavemen neither believed nor disbelieved that the Large Hadron Collider would find the Higgs boson. Nevertheless, it is false that they were agnostic about whether the Large Hadron Collider would find the Higgs boson, the question being one they simply never considered. The takeaway from Friedman's example is that one cannot be agnostic towards some proposition (or question) if one has never been in cognitive contact with that proposition (or question). Hence, we arrive at the first criterion that a satisfactory descriptive account of agnosticism must satisfy:

> **Cognitive Contact Criterion**
> A descriptive account of agnosticism is satisfactory only if it precludes the possibility of someone being agnostic towards a proposition (or a question) if she has not considered the proposition (or question).

Against the claim that being in a state of non-belief is *necessary* for agnosticism, Friedman observes that it seems possible for someone to be irrational by being agnostic about **P** at some time t while also believing **P** at t.[3] If this is right, then a satisfactory descriptive account of agnosticism should leave

---

[2] Recent critics of Non-Belief include: Friedman (2013), Atkins (2017), Rosa (2019), Masny (2020), McGrath (2020), and Raleigh (2021).
[3] See and cf. Friedman (2017: 305).

room for agnosticism-involving doxastic inconsistency. This yields a second potential criterion for a satisfactory descriptive account of agnosticism:

Inconsistency Criterion
A descriptive account of agnosticism is satisfactory only if it preserves the possibility of someone being rationally inconsistent by simultaneously believing and being agnostic towards a proposition (or question).

Many theorists reject the Inconsistency Criterion.[4] I believe this is a mistake. However, a full-throated defence of this criterion is yet to appear in print. I will attempt to fill this lacuna in the literature in Sections 2.3–2.7, where I offer a sustained defence of the Inconsistency Criterion.

While the Inconsistency Criterion remains controversial, most theorists agree that the Cognitive Contact Criterion is a legitimate requirement for a satisfactory descriptive account of agnosticism. A defender of the non-attitudinal accounts who also wishes to satisfy this criterion may modify Non-Belief so that it includes a consideration-condition. This yields what we may call *Non-Belief + Consideration*:

Non-Belief + Consideration: One is agnostic towards **P** at t if and only if one has considered **P** by t and is in a state of non-belief with respect to **P** at t.[5]

Contra Non-Belief + Consideration, Friedman argues that having considered **P** is neither sufficient nor necessary for being agnostic towards **P**. Against the *sufficiency* claim, we can imagine someone with late-stage Alzheimer's who previously considered **P** but who is no longer cognitively equipped to grasp **P**. Such an agent may be in a position of non-belief with respect to **P** at t, and may have also considered **P** by t, but is nevertheless not agnostic towards **P** at t. The lesson of examples like this, according to Friedman, is having previously performed the cognitive act of considering **P**, where **P** is the object of one's non-belief, does not guarantee that one is agnostic post-consideration. Against the *necessity* claim, we can imagine someone who arrives at agnosticism towards **P** via some non-standard means, like hypnosis. This leads her to conclude that a descriptive account of agnosticism should leave room for agnosticism that is not preceded by considering **P**. The upshot is that the Non-Belief + Consideration should be rejected.

The rejection of the consideration condition entails the rejection of any kind of deliberation condition – to wit, a satisfactory descriptive account of

---

[4] These include Wagner (2021).
[5] This is the sort of picture we get from Hájek (1998) and Wedgwood (2002). See and cf. Zinke (2021: 4).

agnosticism must leave room for the possibility of agnosticism that is not preceded by deliberation. This is important since, inter alia, we want to preserve the intelligibility of the kind of radical scepticism about the past proposed by Russell and Full (1921):

> There is no logical impossibility in the hypothesis that the world sprang into being five minutes ago, exactly as it then was, with a population that 'remembered' a wholly unreal past.[6]

Given that it is possible that we all sprang into existence five minutes ago with all of our memories and mental states remaining qualitatively as they are (at least from an introspective point of view), it follows that our having all of our current doxastic attitudes must be consistent with this possibility. Since our current doxastic attitudes include not only believing and disbelieving but also agnosticism, it follows that it should be conceptually possible for us to have the agnostic states we currently enjoy without engaging in prior deliberation. Otherwise, we could refute radical scepticism about the past by merely observing that we have doxastic attitudes. However, it is a sad fact that radical scepticism about the past is not so easily refuted. The preceding observations yield our third Friedman-inspired criterion for a satisfactory descriptive account of agnosticism, which we may call the *Spontaneity Criterion*:

Spontaneity Criterion
A descriptive account of agnosticism is satisfactory only if it preserves the possibility of someone being agnostic towards a proposition (or question) they have not previously considered or deliberated about.

There may initially appear to be some tension between the Cognitive Contact and Spontaneity criteria. After all, does not being in cognitive contact with a proposition involve considering (in some minimal but important sense) that proposition? I believe we may mollify the apparent tension between Cognitive Contact and Spontaneity by disambiguating between two things we may mean when we say that someone has considered whether **P**. We may use the expression 'consider whether **P**' to simply mean that someone has entertained a question in the manner necessary for grasping what is being asked. Call this sense 'weakly considering'. We may also use the expression 'consider whether **P**' to mean that an agent is entertaining a question with the aim or intention of figuring out the answer to it. Call this sense 'strongly considering'.

---

[6] Russell and Full (1921: 159–160).

I believe it is possible to weakly consider some question, **Q**, without strongly considering **Q**. Take for example, the following, question:

(1) Have the Dallas Cowboys won more than four Super Bowls?

Since I have zero interest in American football, I have no desire to find out the answer to (1). Nor do I have the aim or intention to figure out the answer to (1). Hence, while I have entertained (1) in the manner necessary for grasping what is being asked, my lack of desire to know the answer to (1) means that I have not considered (1) with the aim or intention of answering it. In short, while I have weakly considered (1), I have not strongly considered (1). Moreover, weakly considering (1) is not a sufficient condition for deliberating about or inquiring into (1). I have neither inquired into nor deliberated about whether the Dallas Cowboys won more than four Super Bowls. Hence, if we understand the kind of consideration implicated by the Cognitive Contact Criterion as 'weakly considering', then the criterion does not require inquiry or deliberation.

While deliberation about whether **P** is not a prerequisite for being agnostic towards **P**, it remains true that deliberation about whether **P** often terminates in being agnostic towards **P**. This point is echoed by Friedman in the following passage:

> Suspending judgment then can be thought of as one way of terminating a deliberative process and (other things equal) moving into a more settled state, viz., a state of suspended judgment or agnosticism. Suspending then is (other things equal) a way of (at least temporarily) terminating a deliberative process that is sufficient for getting into a state of agnosticism. Either this way of terminating a deliberative process is a matter of forming or coming to have an attitude towards the proposition under consideration or it is not.[7]

The just-cited passage hints that not every case in which an agent's deliberation about whether **P** fails to culminate in either believing or disbelieving **P** qualifies as a case of being agnostic about **P**. An agent may stop deliberating about whether **P** prematurely due to disinterest, distraction, or death. Cases in which we stop deliberating about whether **P** prematurely due to disinterest, distraction, or death differ from ones in which our deliberation culminates in agnosticism towards **P**. This observation yields the following Friedman-inspired criterion for a satisfactory account of agnosticism:

---

[7] Friedman (2013b: 179).

Termination Criterion
A descriptive account of agnosticism is satisfactory only if it is able to explain the difference between subjects who close deliberation by suspending and those who either drop out prematurely or close deliberation in some other way than by suspending.[8]

Insofar as one fails to both believe and disbelieve **P** in cases in which one prematurely stops deliberating about whether **P** due to disinterest, distraction, or death, it follows that all such cases would qualify as being agnostic towards **P**, according to Non-Belief. Hence, Non-Belief is unable to satisfy the Termination Criterion. This remains true even when we add the consideration-condition since deliberating about whether **P** entails having considered **P**, even if said deliberation ends prematurely. Hence, accepting the Termination Criterion as a requirement for a satisfactory descriptive account of agnosticism provides us with additional grounds for rejecting Non-Belief + Consideration.

Moreover, it may be argued that the Termination Criterion is an insurmountable obstacle for any otherwise plausible non-attitudinal account of agnosticism. Consider, for example, non-attitudinal accounts that include the requirement that in addition to non-belief towards **P**, one must be resistant to believing **P** and disbelieving **P** in order to qualify as being agnostic towards **P**. Call this proposal *Non-Belief + Resistance*:

Non-Belief + Resistance: One is in a state of being agnostic towards **P** at t if and only if one is in a state of non-belief and belief resistance with respect to both **P** and ¬**P** at t.[9]

An agent who prematurely abandons deliberation about whether **P** due to disinterest may conceivably also be belief-resistant with respect to both **P** and ¬**P**. This may, for example, be true of Friedman's arachnophobe, who is resistant to thinking about or forming any opinion regarding the eyesight of spiders. When presented with the question as to whether spiders have good eyesight, such an individual may quickly terminate their deliberation because of the anxieties produced by their phobia. Moreover, said anxieties may make them resistant to both believing and disbelieving that spiders have good eyesight since they find any mental attitudes towards the proposition unpalatable. Insofar as such an individual is both in a state of non-belief and is also belief-resistant with respect to both **P**

---

[8] See and cf.: Wagner (2021: 3–4).
[9] Sylvan (2016) has something along the lines of the present resistance condition in mind when he writes: 'agnosticism consists in settled resistance to belief on the evidence' (1653).

and ¬**P**, they would qualify as being agnostic towards **P**, according to Non-Belief + Resistance. However, we would not ordinarily consider an agent who simply avoided forming any attitudes about the eyesight of spiders because of their irrational fears as being agnostic about the question at hand. Hence, Non-Belief + Resistance also fails to satisfy the Termination Criterion.

Admittedly, there are versions of the non-attitudinal account that seem able to satisfy the Termination Criterion. Consider, for example, the non-attitudinal account that combines Non-Belief with the requirement that the agent's non-belief be grounded in epistemic reasons.

Non-Belief + Reasons: One is in a state of suspending judgment about **P** at t if and only if one is in a state of non-belief with respect to **P** at t for epistemic reasons.

The defender of Non-Belief + Reasons may point out that someone who stops deliberating about whether **P** prematurely due to disinterest, distraction, or death is not in a state of non-belief with respect to **P** for epistemic reasons. Hence, according to Non-Belief + Reasons, such an agent would not qualify as being agnostic towards **P**. Non-Belief + Reasons therefore satisfies the Termination Criterion.

However, Friedman points out that there are independent reasons to reject Non-Belief + Reasons. For example, someone could be agnostic for non-epistemic reasons (e.g. an avid sports fan may think it is good luck to be agnostic about whether her team will win) or irrationally continue to be agnostic towards **P** even if she recognises she has more reason to believe **P** or ¬**P** (e.g. the insecure teen who continues to be in doubt about whether her crush likes her despite abundant evidence that he does). Hence, the Termination Criterion may be seen as presenting the defender of the non-attitudinal account with a dilemma: a given non-attitudinal account will either (1) fail to distinguish between deliberation that culminates in agnosticism and deliberation that ends prematurely due to disinterest, distraction, or death or (2) preserve said distinction by proposing an implausible requirement for someone to be agnostic. It is doubtful that there is any version of the non-attitudinal account that escapes this dilemma.

2.3 The Possibility of Doxastic Inconsistency

I believe that the most comprehensive objection to non-attitudinal accounts of agnosticism is their failure to satisfy the Inconsistency Criterion. However, as I noted in Section 2.2, the Inconsistency Criterion remains

2.3 The Possibility of Doxastic Inconsistency

the most controversial of the Friedman-inspired criteria for a satisfactory descriptive account of agnosticism. In the next two sections, I limn a sustained argument in support of the Inconsistency Criterion. I begin, in this section, with a discussion of doxastic inconsistency involving believing **P** and disbelieving **P**, the possibility of which most theorists accept, and describe the cognitive mechanism that psychologists claim makes such inconsistency possible. I then argue, in Section 2.4, that the aforementioned cognitive mechanism is equally capable of facilitating doxastic inconsistency involving believing **P** at t and being agnostic towards **P** at t or disbelieving **P** at t and being agnostic towards **P** at t. I conclude that if one accepts the possibility of the first kind of doxastic inconsistency, then parity of reasoning requires that one accepts the second.

There is fairly widespread consensus among philosophers that although rationally incompatible, believing **P** and disbelieving **P** (or believing ¬**P**) are nevertheless compossible. Indeed, having inconsistent doxastic attitudes is a regrettably ubiquitous phenomenon. In their popular book, *Brain Briefs*, the psychologists Art Markman and Bob Duke attempt to shed light on why inconsistent doxastic attitudes are such a widespread phenomenon. They observe that our brain 'associates beliefs with specific situations and makes it easier to retrieve those beliefs in the situations with which they are associated'.[10] Hence, our belief that **P** may have been first formed in some situation S_1 and thereafter becomes associated with S_1 and situations that are saliently similar to S_1. Establishing this association when a belief is first formed makes it easier to call it to mind when we find ourselves in situations like S_1 on future occasions. For example, I may be able to recall that one my students, Taylor, self-identifies as non-binary whenever they enter my classroom dressed in jeans and T-shirt because my belief that they self-identify as non-binary is associated with certain visual experiences – for example, seeing Taylor in my classroom wearing non-gender-specific clothing – and undergoing this visual experience cues the retrieval of my belief about Taylor's self-identification. Let us call this aspect of belief formation and recall *associative belief retrieval*.

One consequence of associative belief retrieval is that a given belief may only come to mind when we find ourselves in situations that are saliently similar (from our perspective) to the one in which a belief was first formed. Furthermore, Markman and Duke observe that 'if you learn some new fact that turns out to be inconsistent with something else you know, there are no automatic mechanisms in your brain that point out the inconsistency

[10] Markman and Duke (2016: 216).

and force you to resolve it. Instead, you simply end up with two different beliefs that are not consistent.'[11] Hence, having formed the belief that **P** in S_1, we may later form the belief that ¬**P** in some situation, S_2, that is not saliently similar to S_1, and our belief that ¬**P** remains associated with S_2 and situations that are saliently similar to S_2. This may ultimately leave us with a pair of inconsistent beliefs that fail to come into cognitive contact with each other because each is associated with very different situations. For example, we can imagine that if I were to run into Taylor at the supermarket wearing a dress, the novel set of visual cues generated would lead me to form the belief that Taylor self-identifies as female, without my recognition that this belief conflicts with my previously formed belief that Taylor self-identifies as non-binary. Moreover, both beliefs may persist without my recognising the inconsistency, if the belief that Taylor identifies as non-binary only comes to mind when I see Taylor wearing non-gender-specific clothing in class and my belief that Taylor identifies as female only comes to mind when I encounter Taylor wearing a dress outside the classroom. Let us refer to the phenomenon just described – where a pair of inconsistent doxastic attitudes are allowed to persist undetected because they are each associated with disparate situations – as *mental compartmentalisation*.[12]

Our capacity for mental compartmentalisation notwithstanding, there may be times when a pair of conflicting beliefs are both forced to the forefront of our thinking, making the previously undetected inconsistency apparent. Leon Festinger (1957) coined the term 'cognitive dissonance' to describe our awareness of such cognitive conflict. Festinger observed that cognitive dissonance often results in feelings of mental discomfort or anxiety and theorised that mental compartmentalisation is a subconscious psychological defence mechanism aimed at avoiding the discomfort caused by cognitive dissonance. Hence, according to Festinger, our failure to recognise inconsistent doxastic attitudes in cases of mental compartmentalisation is not merely a passive side effect of associative belief retrieval, but may also involve an active subconscious process that keeps potentially inconsistent attitudes from coming to the forefront of our awareness at the same time.

---

[11] Markman and Duke (2016: 215).
[12] What I am calling 'mental compartmentalisation' appears to be the same cognitive phenomenon many philosophers refer to as 'fragmentation'. However, like many terms of art, 'fragmentation' is conceived of differently or put to different use by different philosophers. (See, e.g., Greco [2015], McGrath [2020], Bendaña and Mandelbaum [2021], and Elga and Rayo [2021, 2022].) Since I do not wish to endorse one or more of these differing conceptions, I have opted to employ my own label for the cognitive phenomenon described by Markman and Duke.

2.3 The Possibility of Doxastic Inconsistency

The picture suggested by the aforementioned research is at odds with a certain naïve conception of our cognitive architecture. According to the naïve conception, the mind is like a single large warehouse in which all our beliefs are housed and accessible. According to this metaphor, we may conceive of beliefs like clearly labelled boxes containing propositions, stacked inside the warehouse. If one of the boxes contains some proposition, **P**, then it follows that one believes **P**. If the proposition, ¬**P**, is in one of the belief boxes, then one believes ¬**P**. In the case in which one is agnostic about **P**, neither **P** nor ¬**P** is in one's belief box. Hence, in this view, being agnostic towards **P** entails not believing **P** and not believing ¬**P**. Call this the *mind-as-warehouse model*.[13]

The empirical research of Markman and Duke suggests that a better metaphor for the mind is that of a long corridor with doors. Each door leads to a room with boxes. The boxes are a metaphor for various doxastic attitudes and the closets are a metaphor for the situational context in which the attitude was first formed and with which the attitude remains associated. Call this the *mind-as-hallway model*. The mind-as-hallway model portrays mental compartmentalisation as a fundamental part of our cognitive architecture. There is no single vantage point from which all of our beliefs (or propositional attitudes in general) are accessible. According to the mind-as-hallway model, when we find ourselves in a situational context that is saliently similar to the one in which a doxastic attitude was initially formed, this triggers the opening of the relevant closet door. Having a door opened and the content of one of the closets be visible from the hallway represents an agent's conscious awareness of the corresponding attitudes. For example, when I am in class and I see Taylor in a jeans and t-shirt, this triggers the opening of the door to the 'Taylor dressed in non-gender-specific clothing' situational closet, and my belief box with the proposition, 'Taylor self-identifies as non-binary' becomes the object of my conscious awareness. However, behind another doorway is a closet containing the belief-box with the proposition, 'Taylor self-identifies as female'. However, since this belief-box is only visible from the hallway when the closet containing it is triggered by my being in a situational context similar to that of seeing Taylor dressed in a dress outside of class, I never realise that I have a pair of inconsistent beliefs. This is the sort of possibility that the phenomenon of mental compartmentalisation represents.

---

[13] The mind-as-warehouse model is one way of capturing the idea that all our 'beliefs are stored in a single database' (Bendaña and Mandelbaum [2021]).

The mind-as-hallway model also sheds light on the feature of our cognitive architecture that Bendaña and Mandelbaum (2021) refer to as 'redundancy'. Redundancy is where a representational state with a certain content – like the belief that **P** – occurs more than once within a single cognitive system. Bendaña and Mandelbaum describe one of the clearest pieces of evidence in favour of redundancy in the following passage:

> Say a dog forms an association between food and the ringing of a bell in a particular spatial context, A. The association is then extinguished in context B, typically by repeatedly presenting one of the previously associated stimuli without the other, say the bell without the food. Eventually, the dog will stop salivating at the sound of the bell in context B. However, when the dog is returned to context A, the bell will once again produce a salivary response. There is nothing special about dogs – the same effect holds for (e.g.) humans.[14]

Even when countervailing evidence leads us to give up the belief that **P** in one context (or relative to one set of associations), a second instantiation of the belief that **P** may persist in some other context (or relative to a second set of associations). Or, to put it in terms of our mind-as-hallway model, we may dispose of the belief box containing **P** in one closet and there may nevertheless be another belief box containing **P** stored in some other closet. Hence, the mental phenomenon of redundancy may further illuminate how doxastic inconsistency is possible. In sum, even after we have taken the appropriate steps to update our doxastic attitudes relative to one set of associations, we may overlook other, redundant, instances of said attitude that are linked to some other set of associations.

2.4 Examples of Doxastic Inconsistency

A friend, Lisa, once related the experience of rummaging through her desk looking for her cell phone while engrossed in a conversation on the very cell phone she was looking for. She complained to the person on the other line that she could not locate her phone, and for well over a minute neither she nor the person she was talking to spotted her error. There was clearly a sense in which my friend knew that her cell phone was in her hand. After all, she was using it. However, there was also a sense in which she regarded it as an open question where her phone was located and was consequently motivated to look for it. Hence, my friend appears to have had conflicting

---

[14] Bendaña and Mandelbaum (2021).

attitudes towards the location of her phone; both believing (indeed, knowing) that it was located in her hand but also regarding it as an open question where the phone was located. (Ironically, it was the distraction afforded by her use of the cell phone that helped maintain the mental compartmentalisation necessary to prevent her belief/knowledge of the phone's location from coming into view.)

Lisa's experience is far from an isolated incident. Indeed, I have had first-hand experience with the phenomenon of mental compartmentalisation, and how it may facilitate the adoption of inconsistent commitments. As a faculty member at the University of Tennessee, Knoxville, I was tasked with organising a one-day philosophy conference which was to be held on a Saturday. The morning of the conference began with me showering and getting dressed, while also attempting to finalise the delivery of lunch boxes with a caterer. The fact that most of the on-campus facilities were closed on Saturdays made arranging the delivery of the boxes especially fraught and at several points I came to regret scheduling the conference on a Saturday as a result. However, one upside to its being Saturday was the fact that there was a shuttle that ran from the street in front of my house in downtown Knoxville to the University of Tennessee campus. Since the shuttle only ran on Saturdays, I took solace in the fact that at least I would not have to walk to campus. However, as I was getting dressed and finalising arrangements with the caterer, I noticed it was unusually quiet for a Saturday morning. This made me begin to wonder if it was not Saturday but rather Sunday, since downtown Knoxville tended to be quietest on Sunday mornings. I ventured over to my living room window to investigate, and noticed that the streets were completely empty. Seeing the empty streets led me to conclude that it could not be Saturday but must instead be Sunday. My next thought was that since the campus shuttle did not run on Sundays, I would need to walk up to campus – something I would have preferred to avoid since doing so would involve a 20-minute walk uphill and I feared I would be sweaty by the time I arrived at the conference venue. However, believing I had no other option, I set out to campus on foot. It was only when, about 10 minutes into my walk, a shuttle drove pass me, that my conflicting attitudes – that is, my belief that it was Saturday and my belief that it was not Saturday – were forced to the forefront of my awareness.

Markman's and Duke's research sheds light on how the preceding instance of inconsistent doxastic commitments was possible. My belief that it was Saturday was associated with one set of considerations – that is, the fact that it was the day of the conference – while my belief it was not

Saturday was associated with another set of considerations – that is, my inference from the observation that the streets were unusually empty for a Saturday morning to the conclusion that the campus shuttle was not running. To draw on the hallway metaphor, we may say that the proposition, 'today is Saturday', was in a belief-box in the closet containing my explicitly conference-related attitudes, and the proposition, 'today is not Saturday', was in the belief box in the closet containing my explicitly shuttle-related attitudes. Since the two chains of thought were associated with different sets of considerations, they never came in cognitive contact with each other in the manner necessary for me to recognise that they were indeed inconsistent with each other. It was this mental compartmentalisation that allowed both for the formation and persistence of my inconsistent doxastic attitudes regarding it being Saturday.

The attribution of inconsistent doxastic attitudes to an agent has important psychological and normative explanatory value. Let us refer to the precise moment I decided to walk to campus as my 'time of decision' (or t_d for short). Psychologically speaking, the attribution of inconsistent attitudes to me at t_d helps us to make sense of why I decided to walk to campus at t_d. On the one hand, the reason I decided to walk *to campus* (as opposed to somewhere else) at t_d is because I believed it was Saturday (i.e. the day of the conference). On the other hand, the reason I decided *to walk* to campus (as opposed to taking the shuttle) at t_d is because I believed it was not Saturday (i.e. the day on which the campus shuttle was running). Hence, my decision at t_d to walk to campus is explained by the fact that I both believed it was Saturday and believed it was not Saturday at t_d. Remove either attitude and it becomes mysterious why I would decide to walk to campus. Normatively speaking, the attribution of inconsistent attitudes to me at t_d allows us to make sense of the fact that it was irrational for me to decide at t_d to walk to campus. Given that the psychological explanation of my decision to walk to campus involves inconsistent doxastic attitudes, said decision either stems from or embodies an instance of irrationality. Remove either attitude and it becomes mysterious why my decision to walk to campus was rationally problematic. Call the just limned explanation of the scenario described in the above biographical anecdote the *inconsistent attitudes explanation*.

2.5 Alternatives to the Inconsistent Attitudes Explanation

There are two competitors to the inconsistent attitudes explanation that are worthy of mention. The first is that, in the biographical example

2.5 Alternatives to the Inconsistent Attitudes Explanation

limned above, I was shifting back and forth between believing and disbelieving that it was Saturday, with there being no temporal overlap between the two attitudes. Call this the *toggling attitudes explanation*. According to the toggling attitudes explanation, my behaviour on the morning in question is explained by my having shifting rather than inconsistent doxastic attitudes. The second alternative to the inconsistent attitudes explanation calls into question the facts of the case as I have described them by suggesting that, pace my self-report to the contrary, I either did not believe at t_d that the conference was on Saturday or I did not believe at t_d that the campus shuttle ran on Saturdays. Call this the *missing attitudes explanation*. The missing attitudes explanation grants that I did believe at t_d that it was the day of the conference and that the campus shuttle was not running. However, this still leaves it up in the air whether I believed or disbelieved it was Saturday. Hence, according to the missing attitudes explanation, we may explain why I decided to walk to campus at t_d without attributing to me inconsistent beliefs at t_d.

I shall presently argue that the inconsistent attitudes explanation is preferable to both the toggling and missing attitudes explanation. My starting place is the observation that a satisfactory account of my mental state at t_d must be able to explain the psychological reality of my deciding to walk to campus and the normative reality of my being irrational for having done so. However, this is a pair of desiderata that neither the toggling attitudes explanation nor the missing attitudes explanation is able to satisfy. Let us begin by considering the toggling attitudes explanation. According to the toggling attitudes explanation, there was no point at which I both believed and disbelieved it was Saturday. Hence, we may suppose that at time, t_1, I believed (but did not disbelieve) it was Saturday and that at some later time, t_2, I disbelieved (but did not believe) it was Saturday. Since (according to the toggling attitudes explanation) I did not disbelieve it was Saturday at t_1, there would be no reason for me to doubt at t_1 that the campus shuttle was running. Hence, there would be no motivation for me to decide to walk rather than take the shuttle. The upshot is that I would not have decided at t_1 to walk to campus. Furthermore, since (according to the toggling attitudes explanation) I did not believe it was Saturday at t_2, there would be no motivation for me to decide at t_2 to go to campus, irrespective of whether I believed the shuttle was running. The upshot is that at both t_1 and t_2 I would lack the attitudes psychologically necessary for being motivated to decide to walk to campus. Consequently, the toggling attitudes explanation leaves us without a psychological explanation of my decision to walk to campus.

The missing attitudes explanation appears to improve upon the toggling attitudes explanation by at least offering a coherent psychological explanation of my decision to walk to campus. Since the missing attitudes explanation grants that I believed it was the day of the conference at t_d and that I also believed at t_d that the shuttle was not running, it allows us to make sense of my decision at t_d to walk to campus. Where the missing attitudes explanation falls short is with respect to the normative explanation of why it was irrational for me to decide to walk to campus. If we follow the missing attitudes explanation in holding that I did not both believe and disbelieve it was Saturday at t_d, then my decision at t_d to walk to campus is no longer irrational. Instead, we are left with a pair of perfectly consistent attitudes; namely my belief that it was the day of the conference and that the campus shuttle was not running.

It should be observed that this failure on the part of the missing attitudes explanation has broader implications for our conception of the possible forms of human irrationality. The problem with the missing attitudes explanation is not simply that it calls into question my self-report with respect to the specific case. To constitute a cogent challenge to the possibility of doxastic inconsistency, it must insist that the combination of psychological states described in my biographical anecdote is psychologically impossible in all cases. Hence, the missing attitudes explanation does not only represent a challenge to my introspective beliefs and self-reports regarding the case, but it also challenges any attempt to explain human behaviour in terms of the inconsistent doxastic attitudes. This approach to the explanation of human action will inevitably run into problems since the inconsistent attitudes the missing-attitudes account claims to be missing may be necessary for explaining other aspects of an agent's behaviour. For example, my belief that it was Saturday not only featured in my evaluation that it was the day of the conference, but also in my negotiation with the caterers in light of the increased costs associated with weekend deliveries. Even if the case could be made that my belief that it was the day of the conference may have persisted despite the absence of my belief that it was Saturday, it is far more difficult to maintain that my interactions with the caterers was also consistent with the absence of the belief that it was Saturday since the fact that it was Saturday came up repeatedly in said interactions. The point is likely to generalise to most cases in which we are called upon to impute inconsistent attitudes to an agent. The need to impute such attitudes will not only reflect the need to explain the specific behaviour that is grounded on both inconsistent attitudes, but also other behaviours exhibited at the time which may also require imputing each of the conflicting attitudes to the agent. In such cases, the missing-attitudes account would fail to represent a plausible alternative explanation; it would simply leave too many of a given agent's behaviours unexplained.

In light of the preceding analysis, I conclude that neither the toggling attitudes explanation nor the missing attitudes explanation is able to preserve both the psychological and normative explanations of my irrational decision to walk to campus. Consequently, they lack the explanatory power of the inconsistent-attitudes explanation.

2.6 Agnosticism-Involving Doxastic Inconsistency

A close inspection of the biographical example of doxastic inconsistency limned in Section 2.5 reveals that it plausibly included a brief period in which I both believed and was agnostic about whether it was Saturday. Recall, while getting dressed to attend the conference, I began to wonder if it was actually Sunday rather than Saturday, owing to the fact that it seemed unusually quiet for a Saturday morning in downtown Knoxville. This prompted me to walk over to my living room window to check to see if there were any shuttles running on the street in front of my house. My checking to see if there were shuttles running reflected the fact that I regarded it as an open question whether it was Saturday. In other words, in that moment, I was agnostic about whether it was Saturday. If this is right (and I will say more about why I believe it is, shortly), then there was plausibly a point at which I both believed and was agnostic about whether it was Saturday.

My present contention is that if one accepts the possibility of doxastic inconsistency involving simultaneously believing and disbelieving **P** (as virtually all participants in the current debate do), and given the psychological mechanism identified in the empirical research of Markman and Duke that makes such inconsistency possible, there is no principled reason to deny the possibility of agnosticism-involving doxastic inconsistency. Recall, the efficacy of mental compartmentalisation is rooted in the fact that our doxastic commitments are typically formed in relation to a set of mental associations and these mental associations may differ in such a way that conflicting doxastic commitments fail to come in cognitive contact with each other in the manner necessary to make the aforementioned conflict apparent. Notice that the operation of this mechanism is blind with respect to the nature of the attitudes being compartmentalised. Hence, if mental compartmentalisation may result in the radically conflicting attitudes of believing that **P** and disbelieving **P** failing to come in cognitive contact with each other, then there is no reason to suppose that it could not also result in the slightly less conflicting attitudes of believing **P** and agnosticism towards **P** failing to come in cognitive contact with each other. In both cases, the putative mechanism would be the same – that is, the fact that one part of our mental economy is held separate from another allowing for the unwitting formation of inconsistent attitudes.

The phenomenon of mental compartmentalisation makes it easy to understand how agnosticism-involving doxastic inconsistency is possible. As far as my mental associations with the conference were concerned, my belief that it was Saturday remained constant. This explains why I continued to dress and get ready for a conference that I knew was being held on a Saturday. It also explains how I was able to repeatedly acknowledge it was Saturday as I coordinated with the conference caterers. In sum, with respect to my conference-related mental associations, I believed that it was Saturday. However, when I began to reflect on whether the shuttle was running, this gave rise to a different set of mental associations. It was with respect to this second set of associations that it remained an open question, as far as I was concerned, whether it was Saturday. In sum, with respect to the shuttle-related mental associations, I was agnostic about whether it was Saturday. Indeed, my agnosticism was sufficient to prompt me to inquire into whether it was Saturday (by walking over to my living room window), and it was my failing to see any shuttles that led me to adopt the attitude of disbelieving towards its being Saturday.

We may expand the mind-as-hallway metaphor to accommodate the possibility of agnosticism-involving doxastic inconsistency by conceiving of agnosticism as its own attitudinal box. On the present suggestion, we may make sense of the claim that agnosticism is a sui generis attitude, on par with belief and disbelief, by conceiving of the three traditional doxastic attitudes as three distinct boxes, with each box representing a different mental stance one may take towards a proposition. Rationality demands that, at any given point in time, a proposition be present in at most one of the three possible attitudinal boxes. However, agnosticism towards **P** does not require **P** being absent from the belief and disbelief boxes. One is agnostic so long as **P** is in one's agnosticism box. As with other forms of doxastic inconsistency, agnosticism-involving inconsistency is metaphysically possible though normatively/rationally prohibited. Moreover, the very mental compartmentalisation that makes simultaneously believing and disbelieving possible may also make simultaneously (dis)believing and agnosticism possible. Hence, on the picture currently on offer, agnosticism-involving doxastic inconsistency is no more psychologically unattainable than doxastic inconsistency involving belief and disbelief.

2.7 The Impossibility of Agnosticism-Involving Inconsistency

Some theorists who are open to the possibility of doxastic inconsistency involving belief and disbelief are nevertheless sceptical about agnosticism-involving doxastic inconsistency. This notably includes Feldman and Conee (2018) and Thomas Raleigh (2021). I will conclude my discussion of the possibility of agnosticism-involving inconsistency with an examination of their objections to the thesis.

2.7.1 Feldman and Conee on Agnosticism-Involving Inconsistency

Feldman and Conee (2018) diagnose Friedman's commitment to agnosticism-involving inconsistency as a natural consequence of her view that all inquiring attitudes entail agnosticism. Given that it is possible (though impermissible) to inquiry into whether **P** even if one believes **P**, it follows that it is also possible to be agnostic towards **P** even if one believes **P**. However, the thesis that all inquiring attitudes entail agnosticism is highly controversial.[15] This seems to significantly weaken Friedman's case in favour of the possibility of agnosticism-involving inconsistency. By contrast, the case for agnosticism-involving inconsistency limned above does not rely on the thesis that agnosticism is entailed by all inquiring attitudes. Rather, my argument relies on the idea that the very cognitive mechanism that facilitates simultaneously believing **P** and disbelieving **P** is equally well-placed to facilitate simultaneously believing **P** and agnosticism towards **P**. I maintain that it would be ad hoc to allow for the former kind of doxastic inconsistency while denying the latter.

Apart from their criticism of Friedman's reliance on the thesis that there is a connection between inquiry and agnosticism, the only argument Feldman and Conee (2018) offer against agnosticism-involving inconsistency is that found in the following footnote:

> [S]uspending as we understand it clearly entails not believing. Believing is judging. If one believes a proposition, then one judges it in an affirmative

---

[15] See Section 5.3 for a detailed discussion of some of the problems with Friedman's claim that being in an inquiring frame of mind towards some question entails that one is agnostic towards that question.

way. It follows that one has not suspended judgment or withheld judgment.[16]

The above argument may initially appear to prove too much since it seems to apply as much to the compossibility of believing and disbelieving as it does to the compossibility of believing and agnosticism. To wit, one may argue that since believing a proposition involves judging it in an affirmative way, it follows that one has not disbelieved the proposition or judged it in a denying way. This is because judging in an affirming way is equally at odds with judging in a denying way (i.e. disbelieving) as it is with withholding judgement. In sum, it appears as though the Feldman's and Conee's argument against the compossibility of believing and agnosticism may be applied, mutatis mutandis, to the compossibility of believing and disbelieving. Call this reply to Feldman and Conee the *proves-too-much objection*.

Feldman and Conee may sidestep the proves-too-much objection by observing that believing and disbelieving are compossible because judging in an affirming way and judging in a denying way are independent mental acts or attitudes. Agnosticism, by contrast, involves the omitting of judging in an affirming way and the omitting of judging in a denying way. Hence, while mental compartmentalisation may facilitate the possibility of both judging in an affirming way (i.e. belief) and judging in a denying way (i.e. disbelief), it cannot facilitate the possibility of judging in an affirming (i.e. belief) way and the omitting to judging in an affirming way (i.e. agnosticism). However, this strategy for responding to the proves-too-much objection not only begs the question against the advocate of the sui generis approach who holds that agnosticism is its own distinct attitude, on par with believing and disbelieving, but it also presupposes the naïve mind-as-warehouse model impugned by the empirical research of Markman and Duke. Consequently, we should find their argument unpersuasive.

2.7.2   *Raleigh on Agnosticism-Involving Inconsistency*

In his 2021 paper, Raleigh mounts the following case against the possibility of agnosticism-involving doxastic inconsistency:

> If a subject can truly be said to believe that **P**, whatever your preferred metaphysics for beliefs, then she is *not suspending judgement whether* **P** *– she* has precisely *failed* to suspend judgement concerning **P**! Suspending

---

[16] Feldman and Conee (2018): footnote 4.

2.7 The Impossibility of Agnosticism-Involving Inconsistency

judgement on some question and remaining agnostic is a difficult cognitive achievement that we humans, with our thirst to form beliefs and rush to judgement, often fail at. If a subject unconsciously believes that **P**, no matter how sincerely they avow that they are suspending judgement, or 'keeping an open mind', they cannot count as genuinely agnostic.[17]

One of Raleigh's chief aims in the just-cited paper is to impugn Sui Generis Views. Hence, when Raleigh employs the expression 'suspending judgement', he is referring to the same neutral doxastic state that defenders of Sui Generis Views are theorising about. Consequently, there can be little doubt that Raleigh has what we have been calling 'agnosticism' in mind in the cited passage.

It is worth observing, at the very outset, that Raleigh's declaration that his argument stands 'whatever your preferred metaphysics for beliefs' is false. On the contrary, Raleigh's argument appears to presuppose something akin to the mind-as-warehouse metaphor where suspending **P** entails not having **P** in either the belief or disbelief box. Recall that according to the mind-as-warehouse model, to believe that **P** entails that **P** is in one of the belief boxes and to believe that ¬**P** entails that ¬**P** is in one of the belief boxes. In the case in which one is agnostic about **P**, neither **P** nor ¬**P** is in one's belief box. Hence, in this view, believing **P** (i.e. having **P** in one of the belief boxes) straightforwardly entails that one has failed to suspend **P**, just as Raleigh insists. However, if we held that each of the three doxastic attitudes corresponded with a different kind of attitudinal box (as is the case according to the mind-as-hallway model), then having **P** in the agnosticism box is both necessary and sufficient for suspending **P**. Whether one also has **P** in the belief or disbelief box would be irrelevant. Hence, a metaphysical conception of belief that views it as part of a tri-attitudinal complex consisting of three distinct sui generis attitudes would fail to have the implication that if one believed that **P**, one ipso facto has '*failed* to suspend judgement concerning **P**'.

Raleigh's rejection of the possibility of agnosticism-involving inconsistency appears to rest on two factors: (i) linguistic considerations having to do with the literal meaning of the expression 'suspending judgement' and (ii) the alleged fact that agnosticism is a difficult cognitive achievement. I shall argue at present that neither of these considerations provides compelling grounds for rejecting the possibility of agnosticism-involving inconsistency.

---

[17] Raleigh (2021: 10).

The Argument from Agnosticism's Difficulty
Since it is the more philosophically interesting of the two, let us begin with Raleigh's second claim; the alleged fact that agnosticism is a 'difficult cognitive achievement'. This seems like an important point for Raleigh to make since his rejection of the possibility of agnosticism-involving inconsistency will be at odds with many of our self-attributions of agnosticism, including cases like the biographical example offered in Section 2.6. If agnosticism is as easily achieved as belief or disbelief, then there would be little reason not to take the aforementioned self-attributions of agnosticism at face value. After all, we would not default to a position of doubt if someone embarrassingly confessed to having inconsistent beliefs. However, if Raleigh is right that agnosticism is a difficult cognitive achievement, then we could be forgiven if we dismissed such self-attributions of agnosticism.

The claim that agnosticism is a difficult cognitive achievement may initially seem quite plausible since it is easy to call to mind examples in which an agent's eagerness to arrive at an opinion one way or another regarding some question makes it difficult to maintain an agnostic position. However, this rationale for agnosticism being difficult to achieve primarily applies to cases in which a subject has pragmatic or ideological motivations to either believe or disbelieve. Once we begin to reflect on the vast array of everyday cases in which such pragmatic or ideological motivations are absent, it becomes clear that there are many instances in which agnosticism comes more easily than either belief or disbelief. These include but are not limited to:

1. *Cases in which one lacks pragmatic or ideological motivations to believe or disbelieve and in which one's available evidence is inconclusive.* For example, suppose that Wooram knows very little about baseball and lacks any emotional investment in the sport. Hence, there is no pragmatic nor ideological motivation for him to either believe or disbelieve that the Toronto Blue Jays will win their next game. Moreover, given his general ignorance about the ranking and ability of various baseball teams, there are no evidential considerations that would make him feel psychologically compelled to form an opinion either way. When asked by a friend if he thinks the Toronto Blue Jays will win their next game, Wooram responds with a shrug: 'your guess is just as good as mine'. Thus described, Wooram would plausibly find it easier to be agnostic about whether the Toronto Blue Jays will win their next match than to either believe or disbelieve that they will.

2.7 The Impossibility of Agnosticism-Involving Inconsistency

2. *Cases in which one lacks pragmatic or ideological motivations to believe or disbelieve and in which one's available evidence indicates both outcomes are equiprobable.* For example, suppose that Jane is unable to decide which of two restaurants she should go to for dinner and resorts to flipping a coin. Jane likes both restaurants equally and lacks any pragmatic or ideological motivation to prefer one over the other. Given that Jane knows that the coin is fair, it is plausible that she would find it easier to be agnostic about whether the coin will land tails-side-up than it would be for her to either believe or disbelieve that it will land tails-side-up.

3. *Cases in which one lacks pragmatic or ideological motivations to believe or disbelieve and has pragmatic or ideological motivations to avoid knowing.* For example, suppose that Usha, an avid cricket fan, has been impatiently looking forward to the day when her two favourite cricket teams will play against each other. The day finally arrives. Usha is unable to watch the match live because she is at work and intends to watch a recording of the match when she gets home. Usha believes that she would find the viewing experience most suspenseful and fun if she does not know beforehand which team ultimately won. She therefore instructs all her co-workers to refrain from discussing the match in her presence to avoid being spoiled. When asked who she thinks would win, Usha responds: 'I honestly cannot say; both teams have equally strong records.' Thus described, Usha would plausibly find agnosticism about which team won (prior to watching the match) easier than belief or disbelief.

Each of the three cases just sketched includes a different psychological motivation for agnosticism towards some proposition, **P**. In the first, it is having inconclusive evidence to determine whether **P**; in the second, it is having evidence that **P** and ¬**P** are equiprobable; in the third, it is having pragmatic motivations for not knowing **P**. They represent a small sampling of different psychological motivations that may incline a subject towards agnosticism. What all three cases have in common is that the subject described lacks any pragmatic or ideological motivations for either believing or disbelieving. I maintain that in cases in which such extraneous motivations for belief and disbelief are absent, there is no special difficulty attached to being agnostic. The preceding examples are offered as a type of *existence proof*, aimed at establishing that there are cases in which agnosticism comes easier than (dis)belief.

The next step in my argument is to highlight that the cases in which pragmatic and ideological motivations to believe and disbelieve are present are, while common, not the norm. Admittedly, it is also easy to imagine cases in which pragmatic or ideological motivations for belief are present. However, some caution is called for when attempting to evaluate our intuitions about the relative frequency of pragmatically and ideologically motivated belief. Specifically, we must be careful not to be misled by the *availability heuristic*; the psychological tendency to evaluate the relative frequency of an event based on the ease with which examples of that event come to mind. While sometimes useful, the availability heuristic can be misleading in cases in which the ease with which something comes to mind reflects how striking, important, or memorable that thing is, rather than its relative frequency. I submit that pragmatically and ideologically motivated beliefs are such a case. Such beliefs, which commonly feature in the domains of religion and politics, tend to be some of the most striking, significant, and memorable. However, it should be clear, after a moment's reflection, that most of the attitudes we form over the course of a given day are not related to memorable topics like religion and politics. They are attitudes towards banal things like whether it will rain today, whether one's Amazon package has arrived, or whether one's pet cat is hiding in the closet or under the bed. In sum, with respect to most of the topics we form attitudes towards over the course of a given day, the ones in which we have strong pragmatic or ideological motivation to believe or disbelieve are the exceptions rather than the rule. If this is right, then the rationale Raleigh offers for thinking that agnosticism is a difficult cognitive achievement – that is, the fact that it is difficult to resist the impulse to believe – only applies in a relatively small subset of cases.

A second kind of consideration that underscores the ubiquity of agnosticism and the ease with which we often arrive at the attitude is the close connection between agnosticism and curiosity. More often than not, when an agent is curious about whether **P**, it is because they are agnostic about whether **P**. Consider the twitterholic who is curious about whether her favourite influencer has uploaded a new post. Prior to checking her phone, she neither believes nor disbelieves that her favourite social influencer has posted something new. Rather, she is curious about whether there is a new tweet precisely because she is agnostic about there being a new tweet. Or consider the enthusiastic young gamer who cannot stop wondering if his parents got him the videogame he has been dropping subtle hints about for his birthday. More likely than not, the reason he is curious about whether his parents got him the game he desires is because he is agnostic

2.7 The Impossibility of Agnosticism-Involving Inconsistency

about whether they did. For such individuals, being agnostic is no more difficult a cognitive accomplishment than their being curious.[18] Furthermore, we would hardly describe such everyday instances of curiosity as a 'difficult cognitive achievement'. There would therefore be little reason to regard the accompanying instances of agnosticism as such.

A third consideration that appears to be at odds with the claim that agnosticism is difficult to achieve in cases of insufficient evidence is the common practice of using 'I do not know' to express agnosticism or suspended judgement. More often than not, saying 'I do not know', in the context of an ordinary conversation, is not a report about the epistemic status of a belief one already possesses. Rather, it is a way of flagging that one regards the truth or falsity of a proposition to be an open question – that is, that one is withholding judgement on the matter. Consider cases in which someone responds to the following questions with 'I do not know':

(A) **Jill**: Is it supposed to snow today?
     Jack: I do not know.
(B) **Jill**: Did the babysitter arrive yet?
     Jack: I do not know.
(C) **Jill**: Was Nietzsche born in 1844?
     Jack: I do not know.

We would not typically conclude from Jack's responses to the above questions that he either believed or disbelieved 'that it is supposed to snow', 'that the babysitter did arrive', or 'that Nietzsche was born in 1844'. This is significant since saying that one does not know **P** does not literally mean or imply that one neither believes nor disbelieves **P**. Hence, our assumption that Jack does not have a settled opinion on the matter has more to do with the typical mental state of someone who says 'I do not know!' in response to a question than it does with the literal meaning of the locution. Moreover, the ubiquity of the linguistic convention of using the locution 'I do not know!' to report the absence of a belief, as opposed to an assessment of the epistemic status of a belief one already has, is not what one would expect if it were indeed true that the human rush to form judgement made agnosticism a difficult cognitive accomplishment. What this linguistic convention suggests is that suspending judgement, in the

---

[18] To be clear, I do not wish to claim that curiosity is either necessary or sufficient for agnosticism. Nevertheless, what seems undeniable is that agnosticism about whether **P** is *often* a precursor to curiosity about **P**; we are seldom curious about questions to which we already take ourselves to have the answer.

absence of the relevant information, is as much a part of ordinary life as believing and disbelieving.

Given the apparently abundant evidence against Raleigh's claim that agnosticism is difficult to achieve, one may wonder what accounts for the initial plausibility of his claim. The answer, I believe, is tied to our tendency to focus on interesting, surprising, or disturbing cases and overlook uninteresting, unremarkable, and quotidian instances. Agnosticism in the face of insufficient evidence is most difficult to achieve in cases in which someone has strong pragmatic or ideological motivations for (dis)belief. However, it just so happens that the instances in which agents have pragmatic or ideological motivations for belief often involve propositions we find interesting, surprising, or otherwise attention-holding. Consider propositions that fall under the umbrella of religion, culture, politics, and other areas that are closely tied to an agent's sense of self. If I identify as, say, a Trump supporter, I may believe that the 2020 US presidential election was stolen despite a lack of evidence in support of the claim because said proposition is widely held among members of the community to which I belong and is closely tied to my identity as a MAGA Republican. With respect to propositions for which we have strong pragmatic or ideological motivations to (dis)believe, it is indeed difficult to remain agnostic. Furthermore, since such examples tend to hold our interest, they are easy to call to mind. However, to conclude that such cases are the norm would be to fall prey to the *availability heuristic*: the tendency to estimate the frequency of a phenomenon based on how many examples readily come to mind. While beliefs for which we have pragmatic or ideological motivations may be most striking and memorable, they do not make up the majority of our beliefs. Most propositions we entertain on a daily basis are on banalities like whether it will rain today, did my Amazon package arrive, or will I run into that annoying neighbour I have been trying to avoid at the nearby Starbucks. Consequently, it would be a mistake to treat the beliefs for which we have strong pragmatic or ideological motivations for holding as paradigmatic of beliefs in general.

In summary, Raleigh's claim that agnosticism is a difficult cognitive achievement appears to rest on an overgeneralisation from a subset of cases and ignores the many instances where remaining agnostic actually comes easier or is more appealing than either belief or disbelief. If we are to properly assess the plausibility of Raleigh's claim, we should not limit ourselves to examples in which an agent has strong ideological or pragmatic motivations to believe or disbelieve. We would do well to also consider those everyday propositions whose truth we recognise we are unable to properly assess (e.g. the liberal arts freshman enrolled in a remedial calculus course), propositions about which we prefer to remain ignorant (e.g. the magic show attendee who wishes to preserve their sense of wonder), and the many propositions we feel no hesitance about reporting that we do not know.[19]

The Argument from Literal Meaning
Raleigh's argument from the literal meaning of the expression 'suspending judgement' is also uncompelling in the present context. I am opposed to the linguistic argument primarily on methodological grounds. The question of whether mental compartmentalisation can facilitate both believing that **P** at t and being agnostic towards **P** at t is an empirical one. This means that it cannot be settled by simply defining agnosticism in such a way that it is impossible to both believe **P** and be agnostic towards **P**. That would be to settle via philosophical stipulation a question that is properly settled by empirical observation. Moreover, the fact that the expression 'suspending judgment" literally implies the absence of judgement or belief is largely beside the point as far as the present contention is concerned. Consider: it would be absurd to argue that centipedes have one hundred feet based on the fact that 'centi' literally means one hundred and 'pede' literally means feet. We know from empirical observation that the average centipede has fifteen pairs of legs and such observations trump considerations relating to the literal meaning of the moniker. Likewise, it would be wrong-headed to insist that simultaneously believing that **P** and being agnostic towards **P** is psychologically impossible based on linguistic considerations having to do with the literal meaning of the expression 'suspending judgement', especially since the empirical evidence supplied by the phenomenon of mental compartmentalisation suggests otherwise. In the light of the preceding considerations, I conclude that Raleigh has

---

[19] For a very different line of argument against Raleigh's claim that agnosticism is a difficult cognitive achievement, see Lord (2020). Lord rejects Raleigh's claim that agnosticism is more cognitively demanding than belief and/or disbelief on the grounds that it 'would be surprising if the only ways animals or small children could place p in their outlooks is by believing or disbelieving – i.e., by taking a stance that involves worldly determination'(p. 139). Hence, Lord shares my scepticism about agnosticism being a difficult cognitive achievement. However, Lord's argument is part of an over-intellectualisation objection to Raleigh's metacognitive account, and does not feature as part of a discussion of the compossibility thesis. Perhaps the closest Lord gets to considering the compossibility thesis is in his repeated references to the 'Tension Test': the idea that there is a rational tension between (dis)believing and suspension. The fact that the 'Tension Test' can be applied to agnosticism suggests that Lord is committed to the compossibilty of belief and agnosticism.

failed to offer us any cogent reason to deny the compossibility of believing **P** and agnosticism towards **P**.

2.8 Attitudinal Accounts and Wagner's Criteria

Thus far, I have described the four Friedman-inspired criterion for a satisfactory account of agnosticism and I have offered a sustained defence of the single criterion that no version of the non-attitudinal account can satisfy; namely the Inconsistency Criterion. However, the move away from non-attitudinal accounts is only a first step in the attempt to arrive at a satisfactory descriptive account of agnosticism. The question that now confronts us is what are the criteria that a satisfactory attitudinal account of agnosticism must satisfy. This is the question Verena Wagner sets for herself, which ultimately leads to her proposing three additional criteria for a satisfactory descriptive account of agnosticism. These are:

Neutrality Criterion
A descriptive account of agnosticism is satisfactory only if it explains according to which feature an agnostic subject is genuinely undecided or neutral regarding some proposition (or question).[20]

Commitment Criterion
A descriptive account of agnosticism is satisfactory only if it captures the subject's commitment to indecision by means of an attitude such that the subject settles her de facto indecision regarding a proposition or question and stops further inquiry.

Revision Criterion
A descriptive account of agnosticism is satisfactory only if it is able to explain the transition from agnosticism to other doxastic states (including non-agnostic indecision) due to different kinds of defeaters.

I endorse Neutrality, but reject Commitment and Revision. Below, I explain why I think Commitment and Revision should both be rejected and propose an alternative pair of criteria in their place.

2.8.1 Wagner's Neutrality Criterion

The thesis that agnosticism towards **P** involves a certain kind of neutrality towards **P** is comparatively uncontroversial. The concept of

---
[20] Wagner (2021: 9).

agnosticism is just the concept of a neutral doxastic stance towards a proposition (or question), and this is something any satisfactory analysis of agnosticism must account for. However, different accounts will characterise this neutrality differently. Both non-belief accounts and metacognitive accounts unpack the notion of neutrality in purely negative terms – to wit, the absence of belief and disbelief. Sui generis accounts, by contrast, unpack the neutrality implicated by agnosticism in terms of some positive feature of the mental state with which agnosticism is identified.

Wagner often takes neutrality and being undecided to be roughly synonymous and complains that sui generis accounts are less parsimonious because they are committed to two different kinds of indecision – the negative indecision associated with non-belief and the positive indecision that characterises agnosticism. However, the assumption that neutrality is to be identified with indecision is controversial. For example, on many credal or degrees of belief accounts, to be neutral means having a middling credence of or around 0.5. Being undecided, by contrast, involves having no credence at all. On such views, assigning a probability of 0.5 to a proposition – is no less a decision than assigning a probability of 0.3 or 0.7. A theorist who held that agnosticism involved a middling credence would reject the charge that they are inventing a second notion of indecision since, as far as they are concerned, neutrality is not a kind of indecision. Hence, Wagner's charge that sui generis theorists are committed to two different notions of indecision begs the question; it presupposes that the sui generis theorist is committed to the claim that doxastic neutrality is a species of indecision.

2.8.2 Wagner's Commitment Criterion

It is widely held that agnosticism involves some kind of committed neutrality. However, Wagner's Commitment Criterion is distinctive in at least two respects. First, Wagner emphasises the need to distinguish between an agent's indecision and an agent's commitment or endorsement of that indecision. Compare: we may distinguish between it seeming to be true that P to a subject (such as green spinach leaves appearing red when viewed under black light) and a subject's endorsement of how things seem – that is, one taking it to be the case that the spinach leaves are red. My visual experience may represent it as being the case that the spinach leaves are red, without my believing the leaves to be red – for example, if I know that black light makes chlorophyl appear red. Hence, we may say that while my perceptual experience affirms the spinach leaves being red, it is only when I believe that the spinach leaves are red that I may be said to endorse the affirmation of the leaves being red implicated by my perceptual experience. Insofar as agnosticism is a commitment-involving attitude akin to belief, it should be possible to draw an analogous distinction between merely being indecisive or neutral with respect to some proposition, **P**, and endorsing said indecision or neutrality. On this much, I am inclined to agree with Wagner.

However, disagreements between Wagner and those who endorse a sui generis account (like yours truly) immediately arise once we begin to unpack the details of the Commitment Criterion. Wagner identifies indecision with non-belief towards a considered proposition – that is, neither believing nor disbelieving some proposition with which one has been in cognitive contact. An agent is committed to this indecision just in case they endorse their non-belief towards P as being rationally appropriate given their available evidence. Given that the identification of indecision with non-belief violates the Inconsistency Criterion, I hold that the doxastic neutrality implicated by agnosticism should not be unpacked in terms of non-belief. In Chapter 4, in which I defend my own sui generis account, I offer an alternative characterisation of doxastic neutrality. Hence, while I take the requirement that a satisfactory descriptive account of agnosticism should be able to distinguish between being neutral and being committed to said neutrality, I disagree with the identification of neutrality with Wagner's characterisation of indecision.

A second distinctive feature of Wagner's Commitment Criterion is that it views being committed to doxastic neutrality at some time, t, to entail the decision at t to forego any inquiry that may potentially remove the need for said neutrality. However, as we already noted in our analysis of Wagner's Revision Criterion, this is at odds with both our everyday conception of agnosticism and the theoretical conception of agnosticism advocated by almost all analytic philosophers currently writing on the topic. As such, I believe the clause requiring that the agnostic agent stop inquiring ought to be omitted. Hence, I proposed the following criterion in lieu of Wagner's Commitment Criterion:

> **Commitment* Criterion**
> A descriptive account of agnosticism is satisfactory only if it is able to capture the difference between a subject being neutral with respect to the truth and falsity of a proposition and the subject's commitment to the aforementioned neutrality.

2.8.3 Wagner's Revision Criterion

According to Wagner, the difference between agnosticism and non-agnostic indecision is that the latter is equivalent to non-belief towards a proposition with which one has had cognitive contact[21] while the former is equivalent to non-belief that the agent endorses and to which the agent is committed. Insofar as one should not endorse or be committed to one's non-belief towards **P** unless one has some justification for doing so, agnosticism is most naturally seen as the kind of doxastic neutrality that is the end point of inquiry and/or deliberation. Since non-agnostic indecision is not commitment-involving, it does not seem to require the same justificatory basis as agnosticism. This makes non-agnostic indecision well-poised to serve as the kind of doxastic neutrality that is (i) the pretext for inquiry and/or deliberation or (ii) the stance we adopt while inquiry and/or deliberation is still in progress. Hence, as conceived of by Wagner, agnosticism is an example of what Julia Staffel (2019) calls a *terminal attitude* – that is, 'the attitudes we reach when we have finished a deliberation or reasoning process' – while non-agnostic indecision is akin to a *transitional attitude* – that is, 'the attitudes that the agent forms at the start of and during their deliberation, before they have reached the terminal attitudes that conclude the relevant deliberation phase'.[22]

On the present picture, the need to transition from agnosticism to non-agnostic indecision would paradigmatically arise in cases in which one is (re-)opening deliberation about something one is already agnostic about. Wagner attempts to describe just such a case with the following example:

> To discuss the transition from agnosticism to mere indecision, let me introduce Marta: Marta entered the agnostic state with regard to Martian life at time t_1 for the prima facie reason that technical limitations make it impossible to determine whether there is life on Mars. At some later time, t_2, she learns about NASA's new method, which can clearly determine whether there is life on Mars. Let us assume that NASA will host a press conference later that day where the results will be released, but they are kept secret until then. Sure, Marta could just remain agnostic, but it is also plausible that Marta gives up her agnosticism in this situation and starts deliberating anew whether Martians exist while desperately waiting for the results to be released.[23]

---

[21] See and cf Wagner (2021: 8).
[22] Staffel (2019: 284). It is worth noting that since, by Wagner's lights, non-agnostic indecision is not an attitude but merely the absence of belief and disbelief towards a proposition with which one has had cognitive contact, non-agnostic indecision is not strictly speaking a transitional attitude.
[23] Wagner (2021: 16).

It is not entirely clear why the mere announcement that NASA has a new method for determining whether there is life on Mars would be sufficient to motivate Marta to deliberate anew, given that she is not privy to the evidence NASA has acquired via their new method. The evidence relevant to answering the question of whether there is life on Mars that is personally available to Marta at time t_2 – that is, after learning about the existence of the new method but prior to NASA's revelation of the results that the new method has yielded – remains the same as it was at t_1. There is no reason for Marta to begin deliberating anew at t_2 since she has no new evidence regarding whether there is life on Mars to deliberate about at t_2.

Wagner's example is puzzling not only because it fails to supply Marta with anything to deliberate about (given NASA's decision not to release the results of their new method), but also because it fails to supply Marta with any reason to give up her agnosticism about whether there is life on Mars. As with belief and disbelief, whether one should be agnostic depends on the evidence one personally has available, as opposed to evidence that exists but to which one is not privy. For example, I may be agnostic about whether the protagonist in a newly released movie I am yet to see dies by the end of the film while also recognising that since the movie is currently showing in cinemas, the information required to answer my question exists and is already available to others. My agnosticism is justified by the fact that the evidence personally available to me is insufficient to settle the question and this remains true even after the movie has been released to the general public. Likewise, the fact that the evidence for determining if there is life on Mars exists and is available to others does not change the fact that the evidence personally available to Marta is insufficient for determining if there is life on Mars. Moreover, whether Marta is justified in being agnostic depends on the evidence personally available to her. This means that if agnosticism was the rationally appropriate attitude for Marta to have at t_1 (given her total available evidence), then it is also the rationally appropriate attitude for her to have at t_2 (given her total available evidence).

Presumably, what Wagner is attempting to do is describe a case in which Marta has reason to give up her agnosticism, not because her evidence bearing on whether there is life on Mars has changed, but because she has reason to deliberate anew, and deliberation anew requires transitioning from a terminal attitude (like agnosticism) to a transitional attitude. The problem being presently highlighted is that Wagner, in his description of the case, fails to equip Marta with a reason to deliberate anew because she has no new evidence upon which to base her new

2.8 Attitudinal Accounts and Wagner's Criteria

deliberation. For Wagner's example to do the work he wants it to do, it must be supposed that NASA has not only acquired a new method for determining if there is life on Mars but also that the evidence produced by this new method has been made available to Marta. In order to remedy this weakness in Wagner's example, let us assume that Marta has read a report of the results released by NASA and is now in the process of weighing whether it establishes that there is life on Mars. By Wagner's lights, insofar as Marta has decided to deliberate anew, she justifiably transitions from agnosticism to non-agnostic indecision.

Unfortunately, even after we have strengthened Wagner's argument by making the necessary adjustments to his Marta example, there remains a major problem with his case: namely it relies on the controversial assumption that agnosticism is a purely terminal attitude. Wagner is never explicit about whether it would be rationally permissible, or even metaphysically possible, for Marta to both be agnostic and deliberate about whether there is life on Mars. However, if we did assume that deliberation about whether **P** were both metaphysically possible and rationally permissible while one were agnostic towards **P**, then this would make Wagner's conception of non-agnostic indecision functionally redundant. After all, if agnosticism towards **P** could facilitate deliberation about whether **P** just as easily as non-agnostic indecision towards **P**, then there would be no need transition from agnosticism to non-agnostic indecision. This suggests that Wagner may well be committed to the view that agnosticism towards **P** is either impossible or impermissible if one is deliberating about whether **P**. Moreover, this comports with the conception of agnosticism as an exclusively terminal attitude, with non-agnostic indecision being the appropriate doxastic state at the start of and during deliberation.

Unfortunately, denying that it is either possible or permissible to be agnostic towards **P** at t and deliberate about whether **P** at t is not only out of step with the emerging philosophical consensus, but also a radical departure from our ordinary linguistic practice regarding the attribution of agnosticism. With regard to the emerging philosophical consensus, it is worth noting that Friedman's contention that agnosticism is necessary for inquiry suggests that she sees it as primarily (if not exclusively) a transitional attitude. Most theorists have rejected this aspect of Friedman's account. However, this has led not to the rejection of the idea that agnosticism is a transitional attitude, but rather to the embracing of the idea that agnosticism is both a transitional and terminal attitude. Indeed, Staffel's entire motivation for introducing the distinction between transitional and terminal attitudes is to argue that unlike belief, which merely serves as a transitional attitude, agnosticism may serve as both.

With regard to our ordinary linguistic practice, it should be noted that we would have no problem saying that someone who was in the process of weighing the evidence for and against **P** could also be agnostic towards **P**. For example, throughout my graduate studies in theology, I regarded myself (and was regarded by my colleagues) as being agnostic about the existence of God. However, deliberation about whether God exists was a regular part of my studies in philosophical theology. The fact that this never prompted my colleagues or I to question whether I was genuinely agnostic suggests that, at least as far as my theology professors and fellow graduate students were concerned, there was no tension between being agnostic towards **P** and deliberating about whether **P**. Indeed, if agnosticism towards **P** were incompatible with deliberating about whether **P**, then philosophers could never sincerely claim to be agnostic about any of the many questions they were deliberating and debating about on an ongoing basis.

The immediately preceding observations present Wagner with a dilemma. On the one hand, if he holds that it is metaphysically impossible or normatively impermissible to be agnostic towards **P** if one is deliberating about whether **P**, then his account is not only at odds with that of most theorists, but also revisionary of our ordinary linguistic practice. While this does not imply that Wagner's theory is without merit, it does suggest that (all things being equal) it is less preferable than a theoretical account that is not revisionary in the aforementioned ways. On the other hand, if he holds that it is both metaphysically possible and normatively permissible to be agnostic towards **P** if one is deliberating about whether **P**, then he has failed to provide us with any reason to think there is a need to explain the transition from agnosticism to non-agnostic indecision. On the contrary, non-agnostic indecision turns out to be an entirely redundant mental state.

While I hold that Wagner's Revision Criterion should be rejected, the requirement presupposes a fundamental truth about agnosticism that I believe any satisfactory account of agnosticism should preserve; namely that evidential considerations may determine whether believing, disbelieving, or agnosticism is rationally permissible. Let us say that one of the three doxastic attitudes is *rationally appropriate* just in case it is rationally permissible and the remaining two doxastic attitudes not. There is wide agreement regarding the following claims about the rational appropriateness of the various doxastic attitudes: if one's evidence conclusively supports **P**, then it is rationally appropriate for one to believe **P**, if one's evidence conclusively supports ¬**P**, then it is rationally appropriate for one to disbelieve **P**, and if one's evidence is perfectly counterbalanced in its support for **P** and ¬**P**, then it is rationally appropriate for one to be agnostic towards **P**. Many theorists would go in for something stronger than the just mentioned rational appropriateness claims. They will insist that not only are believing, disbelieving, and agnosticism rationally appropriate under the specified circumstances; they are also *rationally obligatory*. However, for such claims about rational obligations to be true, we must add the qualification: insofar as one adopts any doxastic attitude at all since it would be impractical to require that we actually possess all of the doxastic attitudes warranted by our evidence.

In light of the above, I propose that we adopt the following requirement for a satisfactory descriptive account of agnosticism in lieu of the Revision Criterion:

> **Appropriateness Criterion**
> A descriptive account of agnosticism is satisfactory only if it ensures that having one's evidence be perfectly counterbalanced with respect to some proposition (or question) is a sufficient condition for the rational appropriateness of agnosticism towards that proposition (or question).

2.9 Conclusion

In this chapter, have considered the seven criteria for a satisfactory descriptive account of agnosticism proposed by Friedman and Wagner: Cognitive Contact, Inconsistency, Spontaneity, Termination, Neutrality, Commitment, and Revision. I have offered a sustained defence of Inconsistency, which remains highly controversial among theorists. Finally, I have argued that Commitment and Revision should be rejected in their current formulations and that Commitment* and Appropriateness should be accepted in their stead. I conclude that a satisfactory descriptive account of agnosticism should satisfy the following seven criteria:

> **Cognitive Contact**: A descriptive account of agnosticism is satisfactory only if it precludes the possibility of someone being agnostic toward a proposition (or a question) if she is not or never was in cognitive contact with this proposition (or question).
> **Inconsistency**: A descriptive account of agnosticism is satisfactory only if it preserves the possibility of someone being rationally inconsistent by simultaneously believing and being agnostic towards a proposition.

Spontaneity: A descriptive account of agnosticism is satisfactory only if it preserves the possibility of someone being agnostic towards a proposition (or question) they have not previously considered or deliberated about.

Termination: A descriptive account of agnosticism is satisfactory only if it is able to explain the difference between subjects who close deliberation by suspending and those who either drop out prematurely or close deliberation in some other way than by suspending.

Neutrality: A descriptive account of agnosticism is satisfactory only if explains according to which feature an agnostic subject is genuinely undecided or neutral regarding some proposition (or question).

Commitment*: A descriptive account of agnosticism is satisfactory only if it is able to capture the difference between a subject being neutral with respect to some proposition (or question) and the subject's commitment to the aforementioned neutrality.

Appropriateness: A descriptive account of agnosticism is satisfactory only if it ensures that having one's deliberation reveal that one's evidence is perfectly counterbalanced with respect to some proposition (or question) is sufficient for it to be rationally appropriate to be agnostic towards that proposition (or question).

In Chapter 3 I will apply these seven criteria to the most widely discussed contemporary attitudinal accounts of agnosticism.

CHAPTER 3

Competing Attitudinal Accounts of Agnosticism

3.1 Introduction

In Chapter 2, we identified seven criteria that a satisfactory descriptive account of agnosticism must satisfy; four Friedman-inspired criteria – Cognitive Contact, Inconsistency, Spontaneity, and Termination – and three Wagner-inspired criteria – Neutrality, Commitment, and Appropriateness. In this chapter, I will apply these criteria to six different attitudinal accounts of agnosticism: the *metacognitive accounts* of Bertrand Russell (1997), Sean Crawford (2004), Michal Masny (2020), and Thomas Raleigh (2021), the *endorsed-indecision account* of Wagner (2021), and the *sui generis* account of Friedman (2013a, 2017). I argue that all six attitudinal accounts fail to satisfy one or more of the aforementioned criteria. This will clear the path for my own positive account, which I limn in Chapter 4.

3.2 Russell's Metacognitive Account

One of the earliest versions of the attitudinal accounts found in the contemporary analytic philosophical literature is the metacognitive view of Bertrand Russell (1997):

Russell's Metacognitive Account: One is agnostic towards **P** if and only if one believes that one does not know whether **P**.

The following three claims all turn out to be true on Russell's Metacognitive Account: (1) one cannot have the metacognitive belief that one does not know whether **P** unless one has considered **P**, (2) it is possible to have the metacognitive belief that one does not know whether **P** even if one has not previously deliberated about **P**, and (3) there is a difference between deliberation that culminates in the formation of the metacognitive belief that one does not know whether **P** and deliberation that ends prior to the formation of the metacognitive belief due to distraction, disinterest, or death. It follows from (1), (2), and (3) that Russell's Metacognitive Account is able to satisfy Cognitive Contact, Spontaneity, and Termination, respectively. So far so good.

Given that one may believe that one does not know whether **P** and yet also believe or disbelieve **P**, it follows that Russell's account is able to preserve the compossibility of (dis)believing **P** and agnosticism towards **P**. Unfortunately, this is not enough to satisfy Inconsistency. Inconsistency not only posits that (dis)believing **P** and agnosticism towards **P** are compossible, but it also posits that their co-occurrence is a form of rational inconsistency. However, it is possible to believe that one does not know whether **P** and also (dis)believe **P** without thereby being guilty of rational inconsistency. For example, I believe that earth is not the only planet with life in the universe. This belief is based on: (1) the fact that earth is unexceptional when compared to the billions of earth-like planets and (2) the fact that the five chemical elements necessary for life – oxygen, carbon, hydrogen, nitrogen, and sulphur – also happen to be the most common elements in the universe. However, I also believe that I do not know that earth is not the only planet with life in the universe since such knowledge would require some kind of empirical confirmation, like the discovery of micro-organisms on one of the moons of Jupiter. In short, while I believe that earth is not the only planet with life in the universe, I also believe that I do not know that earth is not the only planet with life in the universe. However, this does not appear to make me guilty of rational inconsistency. Rather, it reflects the fact that while factors like the unexceptional nature of planet earth and the ubiquity of the chemical building blocks of life are enough to justify believing that earth is not the only planet with life in the universe, they are not enough to secure knowledge. If this is right, then believing **P** and believing that one does not know **P** (which Russell identifies with agnosticism towards **P**) does not necessarily make one rationally inconsistent. The upshot is that Russell's Metacognitive Account fails to satisfy Inconsistency.

Let us now turn to the question of whether Russell's Metacognitive Account is able to satisfy the three Wagner-inspired criteria: Neutrality, Commitment*, and Appropriateness. Russell's account plausibly satisfies Appropriateness. Consider: if one's deliberation were to reveal that one's evidence is perfectly counterbalanced with respect to **P**, this would make it rationally appropriate to believe that one does not know whether **P**. Hence, Russell's Metacognitive Account is able to preserve the intuition that having counterbalanced evidence is a sufficient condition for the rational appropriateness of agnosticism.

Unfortunately, Russell's Metacognitive Account is unable to satisfy the Neutrality and Commitment*. Russell's account unpacks the notion of doxastic neutrality in terms of the content of the metacognitive belief – to wit, that one does not know whether **P**. However, as was already alluded to above, it seems possible that one may believe that one does not know whether **P** despite the fact that one is in no way neutral on the question of whether **P**. This point is echoed by Friedman (2013b):

EVEREST SUMMIT: I may believe that Norgay reached the summit of Everest but recognise that my evidence for that belief is not quite as good as it should be and so also believe that I do not know whether Norgay made it to the top. But I am not agnostic about whether he got to the top in this case, I believe that he made it.[1]

The subject described in EVEREST SUMMIT believes that they do not know whether **P**, but is not neutral or genuinely undecided about whether **P**. Hence, Russell's Metacognitive Account fails to satisfy Neutrality. Moreover, insofar as Russell's Metacognitive Account fails to provide us with a workable conception of doxastic neutrality, it follows that it is unable to capture the difference between a subject being neutral with respect to some proposition (or question) and a subject's endorsement of or commitment to said neutrality. Consequently, Russell's Metacognitive Account also fails to satisfy Commitment*.

3.3 Crawford's Metacognitive Account

Although EVEREST SUMMIT seems successful as an objection to Russell's Metacognitive Account, it does not appear to pose a problem for all versions of the metacognitive view. Consider the structurally similar metacognitive account of Crawford (2004):

Crawford's Metacognitive Account: One is agnostic towards **P** if and only if (i) one believes that one neither believes nor disbelieves **P**, and (ii) one neither believes nor disbelieves **P**.[2]

Crawford's Metacognitive Account takes the object of the relevant metacognitive belief to be not that one fails to know whether **P** but rather that one fails to believe and disbelieve **P**. Furthermore, Crawford's account requires that the metacognitive belief be true; it must actually be the case that one neither believes nor disbelieves **P**. Since the subject described in

---

[1] Friedman (2013a:155). [2] See and cf. Bergmann (2005) and Rosenkranz (2007).

EVEREST SUMMIT believes that Norgay reached the summit, she fails to satisfy condition (ii) of Crawford's account. Consequently, EVEREST SUMMIT fails to represent a counterexample to Crawford's Metacognitive Account.

Masny argues that the following case represents a genuine challenge to Crawford's Metacognitive Account:

> DELAYED FLIGHT: Initially, Ada truly believes that she neither believes nor disbelieves that her flight will be delayed. She claims to suspend judgment about this matter. She knows that the plane is scheduled to depart in five minutes. Shortly after, Ada hears an official announcement that the plane will undergo an hour-long repair. Ada does not come to believe that her flight will be delayed. In fact, she continues to claim that she suspends judgment about it.

Once the official announcement of the flight delay has been made, Ada is rationally required to update from an attitude of agnosticism to an attitude of believing that her flight will be delayed. However, Masny claims that Crawford's Metacognitive Account is unable to explain why evidence her flight will be delayed makes Ada rationally required to give up her agnosticism. Masny puts the point as follows:

> But on Crawford's view suspension amounts to having true beliefs about one's lack of beliefs about some matter. This alone cannot rationally compel Ada to respond to relevant evidence in any way. There are lots of things that we are aware that we do not have beliefs about (how tall is the world's tallest tree?), but not in all such cases we are compelled to judge on the matter should the opportunity arise.[3]

Masny's point in the just-cited passage appears to be that having the true higher-order belief that one neither believes nor disbelieves **P** does not entail having the aim of arriving at the correct doxastic attitude towards **P** when one has been presented with the requisite evidence. The upshot is that if we buy into Crawford's Metacognitive Account, we are forced to say that when Ada hears the official announcement of the flight delay, she has no more reason to give up her agnosticism than someone who is aware that they neither believe nor disbelieve that the tallest tree is a certain height has a reason to form a judgement on the matter once the requisite evidence becomes available. Masny concludes:

> So, the DELAYED FLIGHT case exposes a shortcoming in Crawford's account. An adequate account should be able to explain why there is

[3] Masny (2020: 5024).

something faulty about claiming to suspend judgment about some matter and failing to respond to evidence that bears on it.[4]

When assessing the efficacy of Masny's objection to Crawford's Metacognitive Account, it is important to keep in mind that for a reductionist like Crawford, the norms governing agnosticism all reduce to the norms governing belief. Hence, putting aside for the time being the question of whether agnosticism should be identified with the true higher-order belief that one neither believes nor disbelieves **P**, we may simply ask what the relevant norms are governing belief in a case like DELAYED FLIGHT. Specifically, is it true that if a subject who neither believes nor disbelieves **P** is subsequently presented with evidence that is sufficient to establish the truth of **P**, that said subject is rationally permitted to continue to not believe **P** on the grounds that they did not have a prior intention to judge that **P** should the opportunity arise? I think careful consideration of cases like DELAYED FLIGHT points to a negative answer to this question.

SHOE BOX: Michal's eccentric roommate, Sean, presents him with a closed shoe box. Sean asks Michal if he believes there is a pair of black shoes in the box. Michal, who is never keen to participate in Sean's "silly games", impatiently responds that he neither believes nor disbelieves that there is a pair of black shoes in the box. Sean then opens the box to reveal a pair of black shoes in the box. Upon seeing the black shoes, Michal continues to insist that he neither believes nor disbelieves that there are a pair of black shoes in the box. Flustered, Sean asks Michal how he could possibly still not believe that there are a pair of black shoes in the box after being presented with decisive evidence that there are. Michal responds that since he did not have the intention to form a judgement on the matter should the opportunity to do so arise, he is under no rational obligation to believe now that he was presented with the requisite evidence.

The claim that one is under no rational obligation to update one's doxastic commitments when presented with evidence that warrants doing so on the grounds that one lacked the intention to form a judgement on the matter is so preposterous that Sean would be forgiven for thinking that Michal's response was not offered in good faith. Once the relevant evidence has been made available, it is too late for Michal to appeal to his supposed lack of an intention to form a judgement should the opportunity to do so arise. The lesson of SHOE BOX is that the rational obligation to adopt the beliefs that are demanded by one's evidence is not contingent on

---

[4] Masny (2020: 5024).

whether one has a standing intention to form a judgement on the matter should the opportunity arise.

In order to fully appreciate the immediately preceding point, it is helpful to distinguish between two things we could mean by the locution 'should the opportunity arise', as it features in DELAYED FLIGHT and SHOE BOX. On the one hand, the opportunity to update one's doxastic commitments with respect to some proposition, **P**, may arise because one is provided with the means to inquire into whether **P**. Call this an *inquiry-opportunity*. When presented with an inquiry-opportunity, it is a subject's rational prerogative to forego the inquiry-opportunity and remain in the state of neither believing nor disbelieving **P** should they desire to do so. For example, if Ada was invited to approach the customer service desk and inquire into whether her flight would be delayed, Ada is under no rational obligation to accept said invitation. Similarly, Michal is under no rational obligation to open the shoe box to see if there is a pair of black shoes in it should he have no interest in finding out whether there is.

On the other hand, the opportunity to update one's doxastic commitments with respect to **P** may arise because one has been presented with sufficient evidence to establish the truth of **P**. Call this a *belief-opportunity*. A belief-opportunity, unlike an inquiry-opportunity, is a case in which inquiry, if necessary at all, has been completed and one is already in possession of sufficient evidence to justify believing **P**. In such cases, it would be rationally inappropriate to not believe **P**. This is the situation that both Ada and Michal find themselves in. Upon hearing the official announcement that her flight will be delayed, Ada is in possession of sufficient evidence to establish that her flight will be delayed, and upon seeing the pair of black shoes in the opened shoe box, Michal is in possession of sufficient evidence to establish that there is a pair of black shoes in the shoe box. Once in possession of such evidence, both subjects are rationally required to form the relevant belief. Whether they had an intention to form a judgement on the matter should the opportunity arise is irrelevant to said rational obligation.

One plausible diagnosis of where Masny's analysis goes wrong is that he conflates the above two senses of what it means to have an opportunity arise to update one's doxastic commitments. Masny correctly observes that there are many propositions we neither believe nor disbelieve and about which we have no standing intention to form a judgement. We are under no obligation to form a judgement regarding such a proposition simply because an inquiry-opportunity arises. However, Masny appears to misapply this observation to cases in which we are presented with a belief-opportunity, understood as a case in which the requisite evidence has already been made available to us. Regarding such cases, Masny appears to assume that we are under no rational obligation to form the belief that our evidence warrants. However, failing to respond in the required manner to the evidence we have available is a paradigm instance of irrationality.

Two final points are worth noting with regard to Masny's analysis of DELAYED FLIGHT. First, DELAYED FLIGHT successfully elicits the intuition that Ada is engaged in something rationally inappropriate despite the fact that example never explicitly states that Ada has the intention to form a judgement on the matter should the opportunity arise. This is a hint that what is doing the heavy lifting, as far as our intuition that Ada should update her doxastic commitments is concerned, is not her intention to form such a judgement. Indeed, whether Ada had such an intention, we would still consider her stubborn refusal to update her doxastic commitments in light of the newly acquired evidence to be problematic. This, I submit, should have been Masny's first hint that he has misdiagnosed the source of Ada's apparent irrationality in DELAYED FLIGHT.

Second, what is doing the heavy lifting in the analysis of DELAYED FLIGHT, as far as Crawford's Metacognitive Account is concerned, is not condition (i) but rather condition (ii). According to condition (ii), the subject who is agnostic towards **P** neither believes nor disbelieves **P**. This means that if Ada is to qualify as being agnostic, it is not only necessary for her to have the higher-order belief that she neither believes nor disbelieves **P**, but it is also necessary that she actually not believe or disbelieve **P**. Furthermore, a subject who does not believe **P** and is subsequently presented with sufficient evidence to establish **P** is rationally required to adopt the belief that **P** once presented with said evidence. This is the position that Ada finds herself in, in DELAYED FLIGHT. After hearing the official announcement that her flight will be delayed, Ada is in possession of sufficient evidential support for believing that her flight will be delayed. Given this belief-opportunity, she is rationally required to adopt the belief warranted by the evidence she possesses. Moreover, since her not believing that the flight will be delayed is partly constitutive of her being agnostic according to Crawford's Metacognitive Account, it follows that said account not only implies that Ada is irrational for failing to update her doxastic commitments, but it also explains her irrationality in terms of the nature of her agnostic stance – that is, the fact that it is rationally inappropriate to not believe **P** if one possesses sufficient evidence to establish that **P**.

Let us now turn to the evaluation of Crawford's Metacognitive Account in terms of the criteria introduced in the previous chapter. The metacognitive belief implicated by Crawford's account allows it to satisfy Cognitive Contact, Spontaneity, Termination, and Appropriateness in very much the same way that the metacognitive belief implicated by Russell's account does. Furthermore, Crawford's Metacognitive Account unpacks the neutrality of the agnostic subject in terms of non-belief; the agnostic subject neither believes nor disbelieves **P**. Hence, Crawford's account is also able to satisfy Neutrality.

It is less obvious that Crawford's account satisfies Commitment*. The defender of Crawford's Metacognitive Account may argue that while Crawford's Metacognitive account unpacks the neutrality of the agnostic subject in terms of their neither believing nor disbelieving **P**, the agnostic subject's commitment to said neutrality is unpacked in terms of their metacognitive belief that they neither believe nor disbelieve **P**. Unfortunately, the metacognitive belief seems poorly suited to play the desired role. In this respect, it is important to distinguish between being committed to being neutral, on the one hand, and being committed to its being true that one is neutral, on the other hand. The former entails a kind of endorsement or approval. However, being committed to a certain state of affairs obtaining falls short of endorsing or approving that state of affairs. For example, I may believe that I have an irrational fear of spiders but also think that my fear is inappropriate or misplaced. Likewise, it does not follow from the fact that I believe that I neither believe nor disbelieve **P** that I consider it appropriate or endorse my neither believing nor disbelieving. If this is right, then Crawford's account fails to satisfy Commitment*. Furthermore, the very feature of Crawford's account that allows it to satisfy Neutrality – that is, the stipulation that the agnostic subject neither believes nor disbelieves **P** – renders it unable to satisfy Inconsistency. The upshot is that Crawford's Metacognitive Account ultimately proves inadequate in the face of Commitment* and Inconsistency.

3.4 Masny's Metacognitive Account

Having impugned Crawford's Metacognitive Account (at least to his own satisfaction), Masny proposes the following alternative, Crawford-inspired, metacognitive view:

Masny's Metacognitive Account: One is agnostic about whether **P** if and only (i) one believes that one neither believes nor disbelieves **P**, (ii) one neither believes nor disbelieves **P**, and (iii) one intends to judge that **P** or ¬**P**.

3.4 Masny's Metacognitive Account

Since Masny's Metacognitive Account includes both of the conditions implicated by Crawford's account, it inherits most of the strengths of Crawford's account. Specifically, Masny's account is able to satisfy Cognitive Contact, Spontaneity, Termination, and Neutrality. However, Masny's account also inherits the primary weaknesses of Crawford's account. First, while condition (ii) of Masny's account provides an account of doxastic neutrality, neither conditions (i) nor (iii) provide a plausible unpacking of what it means to endorse or be committed to said neutrality. Masny's account therefore fails to satisfy Commitment*. Second, the requirement that the agnostic subject neither believe nor disbelieve **P** violates Inconsistency.

Masny hopes that adding condition (iii) to Crawford's account would allow him to make sense of why Ada is irrational for not giving up her agnosticism in light of new evidence. As was alluded to above, Masny's motivation for adding condition (iii) seems misplaced since Crawford's Metacognitive Account can already make sense of why Ada is at fault given that it is irrational for her not to believe the flight is delayed after the official announcement that it will be.

Moreover, the addition of condition (iii) brings with it problems of its own. Specifically, condition (iii) precludes the possibility of being agnostic about whether **P** in cases in which one has no intention to arrive at a judgement that **P** or ¬**P**. This is a problem for Masny's account since not having the intention to judge **P** or ¬**P** appears to be the rationally appropriate response when we are agnostic towards a question we know or justifiably believe to be unanswerable.[5] Consider the following case:

ASTRONOMICAL BODY: Maria is investigating whether there is an astronomical body at some location, l, that is 10^{90} cubic meters away from earth. In the process of so doing, she learns that an object that is 10^{90} cubic meters away would be outside our Hubble Sphere, the spherical region surrounding an observer beyond which objects recede from that observer at a rate greater than the speed of light due to the expansion of the universe. While there remains some fact of the matter as to whether there is an astronomical body located at l, since light leaving such an object could never reach earth, it would be physically impossible for us to ever detect whether there was an astronomical object at l.

Given that her available evidence is insufficient to determine whether there is an astronomical body at location l, it is rationally appropriate for Maria to remain agnostic about whether there is an astronomical body at l.

---

[5] See Archer (2019) for an in-depth discussion of unanswerable questions as relates to the adoption of the attitude of agnosticism.

Moreover, given that Maria knows that the question of whether there is an astronomical body at *l* is unanswerable, it would be rationally inappropriate for Maria to have the intention to judge whether there is an astronomical body at *l*. In sum, it is rationally appropriate for Maria to be agnostic towards **P** at *t* and refrain from intending to judge **P** or ¬**P** at *t*. However, according to Masny's Metacognitive Account, it would be impossible for Maria to be agnostic about whether there is an astronomical body located at *l* given that she lacks the intention to form a judgement on the matter. The upshot is that Masny's proposal not only fails as a metaphysical account of agnosticism, since it implies that Maria's agnosticism would not qualify as such, but also a normative characterisation of agnosticism, since it implies that agnosticism is impossible in a situation in which it is rationally appropriate.[6] The objection may be reframed in terms of a failure of Masny's account to satisfy Appropriateness. By Masny's lights, having one's deliberation reveal that one's evidence is perfectly counterbalanced is not a sufficient condition for the rational permissibility of agnosticism since a subject with counterbalanced evidence may fail to intend to judge **P** or ¬**P**. I conclude that Masny's Metacognitive Account is inadequate since it fails to satisfy Commitment*, Inconsistency, and Appropriateness.

3.5 Raleigh's Metacognitive Account

Raleigh (2021) defends the following metacognitive account of agnosticism:

Raleigh's Metacognitive Account: One is agnostic towards **P** if and only if: (i) one believes that one cannot yet tell whether **P**, based on one's evidence, (ii) one neither believes nor disbelieves **P**, and (iii) one's belief that one cannot tell whether **P** based on one's evidence is (part of) one's reason for neither believing nor disbelieving **P**."

Like Crawford's and Masny's metacognitive accounts, Raleigh's Metacognitive Account is able to satisfy Cognitive Contact, Spontaneity, Termination, and Neutrality. Furthermore, since Raleigh's account omits the requirement that the agnostic subject have the intention to judge **P** or ¬**P**, it is not subject to the challenge posed by ASTRONOMICAL BODY to Masny's Metacognitive Account. The upshot is that Raleigh's Metacognitive Account also satisfies Appropriateness.

Wagner has argued that Raleigh's Metacognitive Account fails to satisfy Commitment*, which holds that a descriptive account of agnosticism 'has

---

[6] For a different set of criticisms of Masny's account, see Lord (2020).

3.5. Raleigh's Metacognitive Account

to capture the subject's commitment to indecision'.[7] Since there are forms of indecision that are not commitment-involving, a satisfactory account of what it means to be committed to indecision must distinguish between indecision towards a certain proposition (or question), on the one hand, and the commitment to said indecision, on the other hand. However, it is not clear that this is a desideratum that Raleigh's Metacognitive Account can satisfy. Raleigh's metacognitivism identifies the agnostic subject's indecision with respect to some proposition, **P**, with her neither believing nor disbelieving **P**. This is condition (ii) of Raleigh's Metacognitive Account. But wherein lies her commitment to said indecision? The most natural suggestion is that the agnostic subject's commitment should be identified with the higher-order belief specified in condition (i) – namely, the belief that the subject cannot yet tell whether **P** – and/or the relationship between the agnostic subject's higher-order belief and her indecision. It is at this point that Raleigh's metacognitivism appears to run into difficulty since the relationship between the agnostic subject's higher-order belief (the locus of her commitment) and her non-belief (the locus of her indecision) is not of the right kind to yield a commitment to indecision.

According to condition (iii) of Raleigh's Metacognitive Account, the meta-belief identified in condition (i) must be the motivating reason for the non-belief identified in condition (ii) if the subject in question is to qualify as genuinely agnostic: 'we want the meta-cognitive belief to be the subject's motivating reason for the doxastic neutrality and not just a merely causal-explanatory reason'.[8] For example, your belief that you cannot yet tell whether God exists may motivate you to give up your belief in God and instead adopt a position of non-belief. In such a case, the meta-belief that is the motivating reason for the indecision that is constituted by your non-belief is the psychological and/or justificatory precursor to your indecision, not your commitment to said indecision. Wagner concludes that 'the resulting state here is not a qualification of one's indecision but only indecision simpliciter. S takes the meta-belief to be a reason to become undecided by dropping the belief that **P**'.[9] The upshot, according to Wagner, is that Raleigh's account is unable to distinguish between the indecision and commitment components of agnosticism in the manner necessary to satisfy Commitment*.

The second problem Wagner identifies with Raleigh's account is that it seems unable to accommodate cases in which a subject was already in a

---

[7] Wagner (2021: 682). [8] Raleigh (2021: 2457). [9] Wagner (2021: 683).

state of non-belief prior to the deliberation that culminated in her agnosticism.[10] For example, suppose that a subject was already in a state of non-belief with respect to **P** prior to the start of her deliberation about whether **P**, and then said deliberation culminated in the subject becoming convinced that her available evidence is insufficient to determine whether **P**. In such a case, the subject's metacognitive belief that she cannot tell whether **P** would have been formed after, and consequently could not be a motivating reason for, her non-belief with respect to **P**. However, according to condition (iii) of Raleigh's Metacognitive Account, the metacognitive belief that she cannot tell whether **P** must be a subject's motivating reason for her non-belief with respect to **P**. It would seem to follow that the subject who only forms the metacognitive belief after she was already in a state of non-belief does not qualify as agnostic. The upshot is that Raleigh's Metacognitive Account appears to entail that one cannot be agnostic towards **P** if one was already in a state of non-belief with respect to **P** prior to the formation of the deliberation-inspired metacognitive belief.

Finally, like all the metacognitive accounts we have considered, Raleigh's Metacognitive Account is unable to satisfy Inconsistency. I conclude that Raleigh's Metacognitive Account is also inadequate.

3.6 Wagner's Endorsed-Indecision Account

Next, we turn to Wagner's Endorsed-Indecision Account, which emphasises that agnosticism involves two independent components: a subject's doxastic indecision and the subject's commitment to said indecision. The indecision of the agnostic subject is what is supposed to be responsible for the attitude's neutral status as compared to the non-neutral doxastic attitudes of belief and disbelief. Like the non-belief and metacognitive approaches, Wagner's Endorsed-Indecision Account unpacks doxastic neutrality in terms of the absence of belief and disbelief. However, what sets the agnostic subject apart from the merely undecided subject, according to Wagner, is that the former endorses or is committed to her indecision. To endorse or be committed to one's indecision means that one has evaluated said indecision as 'appropriate, permissible, or even obligatory'.[11] This may be because one takes one's evidence to be inadequate at that point in time or because one takes the question to be unanswerable. In either case, one's endorsement of one's indecision

[10] Wagner (2021: 684). [11] Wagner (2021: 681).

3.6 Wagner's Endorsed-Indecision Account

involves the (at least temporary) termination of further inquiry.[12] Hence, we arrive at Wagner's Endorsed-Indecision Account:

Wagner's Endorsed-Indecision Account: One is agnostic towards **P** if and only if: (i) one is or was in cognitive contact with **P**, (ii) one neither believes nor disbelieves that **P**, and (iii) one endorses (is committed to) one's neither believing nor disbelieving that **P** such that one stops inquiring into whether **P**.

Condition (i) of Wagner's Endorsed-Indecision Account aims to satisfy Cognitive Contact, condition (ii) aims to satisfy Neutrality, and condition (iii) satisfies Commitment*. Condition (iii) also ensures a distinction between subjects whose deliberation culminates in agnosticism and those whose deliberation ends prematurely due to distraction, disinterest, or death. Wagner's account therefore satisfies Termination. Furthermore, given that none of the conditions require that the subject previously deliberated about whether **P**, it follows that Wagner's account also satisfies Spontaneity.

One implication of Wagner's conception of what it means to endorse one's indecision is that it is impossible to have an attitude of committed doxastic neutrality prior to or during one's inquiry. This places Wagner's Endorsed-Indecision Account at odds with our everyday agnosticism-ascriptions. Consider the following case:

HIGGS FIELD: François is a year into a three-year research program attempting to establish the existence of the Higgs field. Unlike most of his fellow researchers, who already believe the Higgs's field exists, François claims to be agnostic on the matter. When asked why he remains agnostic about the existence of the Higgs field, François explains that he thinks that agnosticism is the only reasonable stance to take until there is direct experimental confirmation that the Higgs field exists.

Most competent English speakers would take François' self-ascription of agnosticism at face value. However, since François is currently engaged in inquiry, Wagner's Endorsed-Indecision Account implies that his self-ascription of agnosticism is false; François is not agnostic about whether the Higgs field exists. Hence, Wagner's account turns out to be at odds with our everyday agnosticism-ascriptions and Appropriateness hints at an explanation of why. Recall that according to Appropriateness, having one's evidence be perfectly counterbalanced is a sufficient condition for the rational appropriateness of agnosticism. Moreover, HIGGS FIELD illustrates

---
[12] See and cf. Staffel (2019) and Lord (2020).

that it is possible to have one's evidence with respect to **P** be counterbalanced while one is still engaged in inquiry about whether **P**. Hence, according to Appropriateness, it is not only possible, but also rationally appropriate for François to be agnostic so long as his evidence fails to establish **P** and also fails to establish ¬**P**. Hence, by holding that a subject can be agnostic only if they stop inquiring, Wagner's account implies that the rationally appropriate course of action in cases like HIGGS FIELD is actually metaphysically impossible. While not an outright contradiction of Appropriateness, this does give rise to the unhappy outcome that the rationally recommended course is metaphysically impossible, with the upshot that it would be impossible for François to do what reason demands.

3.7 Friedman's Sui Generis Account

Friedman does not offer a succinct definition of agnosticism akin to that offered by the theorists considered thus far. This may reflect the fact that she conceives of agnosticism as a primitive attitude. Indeed, Wagner complains that a sui generis account of agnosticism is inadequate for this very reason since a primitive attitude does not display the 'internal structure' needed to perform the explanatory work an attitude of agnosticism would require. Specifically, Wagner claims that a sui generis account cannot satisfy Commitment*, which requires that we distinguish between merely being doxastically neutral and one's commitment to that neutrality.

> It is problematic, however, that the primitive state of agnosticism does not have any internal structure that could explain the subject's commitment to her de facto indecision as an act of assessing her own doxastic state.[13]

However, this objection, if it were a good one, should equally apply to belief, which is also regarded as a primitive or sui generis attitude and which also involves a kind of doxastic commitment. Of course, belief is not a neutral attitude. It involves the affirmation of the truth of a proposition. However, just as we can distinguish between a subject's neutrality towards a proposition and their endorsement of or commitment to said neutral stance, we can also distinguish between an affirming (or denying) stance towards a proposition and our endorsement or commitment to said affirming (or denying) stance. If conceiving of agnosticism as a sui generis attitude were enough to preclude said analysis from accommodating

---

[13] Wagner (2021: 682).

3.7 Friedman's Sui-Generis Account 55

Commitment*, then conceiving of belief as a sui generis attitude (as all participants in the current debate in fact do) should be enough to preclude an adequate account of its being a commitment-involving attitude as well. This is sufficient to show that merely holding that agnosticism is a sui generis attitude should not be sufficient to preclude a meaningful analysis of agnosticism as a commitment-involving attitude. This, I submit, is a first hint that Wagner's criticism is on the wrong track.

The second hint that Wagner's criticism is on the wrong track is that it is simply false that holding that agnosticism is a primitive attitude implies that it has no internal structure. Again, the analogy from belief is helpful. While it is almost universally held that belief is a primitive sui generis attitude, this has not precluded various analyses of the internal structure of belief. For example, the standard description of belief as a propositional attitude implies a difference between a mental stance (i.e. the attitudinal component) and its object (i.e. the propositional component). Hence, belief, as standardly conceived, involves at least two structural features. If agnosticism is a sui generis doxastic attitude on par with belief, then we should expect it to be amenable to the same kind of analysis as belief.

This brings us to our third and final hint that Wagner's criticism is on the wrong track: to wit, neither Wagner nor any other prominent theorists writing on the topic unpacks the affirming mental stance implicated by believing **P** in terms of the absence of disbelieving or agnosticism towards **P**. Indeed, as we already noted, most theorists hold that believing **P** and disbelieving **P** are compossible. Consequently, the attempt to unpack the neutral mental stance implicated by agnosticism in terms of the absence of belief and disbelief implies that the sense in which agnosticism entails a neutral stance is different from the sense in which belief involves an affirming stance. Moreover, believing **P** entails an affirming mental stance towards **P** in virtue of properties of the attitude itself and not in virtue of the relationship in which it stands to other attitudes or the lack thereof. Hence, preserving the parity between the sense in which agnosticism is a neutral attitude and believing is an affirming attitude dictates that agnosticism should be a neutral mental stance towards **P** in virtue of proprieties of the attitude as well.

While I hold that Wagner's complaint against sui generis approaches on the whole goes too far, it is true that Friedman does not adequately fill in her proposed sui generis account for us to assess how adequately her account preserves the difference between being neutral and being committed to said neutrality. Friedman does, at various points, offer necessary and sufficient conditions for being agnostic. However, these conditions typically involve the specification of the relationship between agnosticism and other question-directed attitudes. For example, according to Friedman, one is agnostic towards some question, Q, if and only if one regards Q as an open question. This suggests one plausible candidate of what it means to say that agnosticism is a neutral attitude on Friedman's account; to wit, agnosticism is a neutral doxastic attitude because it involves regarding a question as open, unanswered, or unsettled. If this is right, then Friedman's question-directed attitude account is able to satisfy Neutrality. However, it is less clear whether Friedman's account satisfies Commitment*. Given this way of understanding doxastic neutrality, it is not immediately obvious what being committed to a question being open or unsettled amounts to. While this is not by any means an insurmountable obstacle for Friedman's account, it does highlight a lacuna in her account.

A more worrying problem with Friedman's account is that it fails to preserve Appropriateness. Recall that according to Friedman, one is agnostic towards **P** only if one is inquiring into whether **P**. This aspect of Friedman's view runs into problems accommodating cases in which a subject is agnostic towards a question they believe to be unanswerable. In cases in which one believes a question to be unanswerable, it seems rationally inappropriate to continue inquiring into that question. Moreover, there may conceivably be a case in which the evidence one has bearing on whether **P** is perfectly counterbalanced (e.g. in the case in which one has no evidence both for and against **P**) and in which one knows or justifiably believes 'whether **P**' to be unanswerable. In such a case, it would be rationally permissible to be agnostic towards **P** but not rationally permissible to inquire into whether **P**.

At times, Friedman appears to lean away from the claim that agnosticism towards **P** entails inquiring into whether **P**, instead holding that agnosticism towards **P** merely entails having an inquiring mental stance towards **P**. Having an inquiring mental stance does not entail that one engages in any of the activities typically associated with inquiry, but only involves the possession of one or more inquiring attitude(s). One of Friedman's favourite inquiring attitudes to highlight in this regard is that of curiosity. It may be rationally permissible to be curious about some question, **Q**, even in cases in which one believes **Q** to be unanswerable. Given that curiosity is an inquiring attitude, it follows that it may be rationally permissible to have an inquiring mental stance towards **Q** even if one regards **Q** as unanswerable. Hence, Friedman may plausibly deny that there are cases in which it is rationally permissible to be agnostic towards **P** but rationally impermissible to be curious (i.e. have an inquiring mental stance) towards **P**.

Unfortunately, the preceding dialectical manoeuvre is not enough to satisfy Appropriateness. Even if we grant that it is rationally permissible to be curious about an unanswerable question, it is neither metaphysically nor normatively necessary that one be curious about an unanswerable question. Thus, if we hold that having one's evidence be counterbalanced is a sufficient condition for it to be rationally appropriate to be agnostic, then there will be cases in which it is rationally appropriate to be agnostic (because one's evidence is counterbalanced) but in which it is rationally optional whether one takes an inquiring stance towards **Q**. This means that it is entirely up to the subject whether they are curious about an unanswerable question, even in cases in which the evidence bearing on the question is counterbalanced. Thus, according to Permissibility, there can (metaphysically and normatively, speaking) be cases in which a rational subject is agnostic about whether **P** but does not have an inquiring mental stance towards **P**. However, this is a possibility that Friedman's account denies. I conclude that Friedman's Sui Generis Account is at odds with Rational Appropriateness.

3.8 Conclusion

In this chapter, I have applied the criteria for a satisfactory descriptive account of agnosticism introduced in Chapter 2 to the most widely discussed attitudinal accounts of agnosticism. All of the attitudinal accounts satisfy Cognitive Contact, Spontaneity, and Termination. The following table offers a breakdown of the results for the remaining criteria: Inconsistency, Neutrality, Commitment*, and Appropriateness.

Table 3.1. *Table of Attitudinal Accounts*

Theorist	Inconsistency	Neutrality	Commitment*	Appropriateness
Russell	✗	✗	✗	✓
Crawford	✗	✓	✗	✓
Masny	✗	✗	✗	✗
Raleigh	✗	✓	✗	✓
Wagner	✗	✓	✓	✗
Friedman	✓	✓	✗	✗

As we can see from table, each of the accounts discussed in this chapter fails to satisfy one or more of the criteria for a satisfactory descriptive account of agnosticism. In Chapter 4, I offer my own positive account of agnosticism which has among its virtues the satisfaction of all seven criteria adumbrated in Chapter 2.

CHAPTER 4

The Questioning-Attitude Account of Agnosticism

4.1 Introduction

This chapter proposes a proposition-directed, sui generis account of agnosticism, according to which being agnostic about some proposition, **P**, involves a sceptical or questioning mental stance towards both the truth and falsity of **P**. Call this the *questioning-attitude account*. The questioning-attitude account contrasts with the *question-directed attitude account* of Jane Friedman, which holds that the object of agnosticism is a question rather than proposition.[1] My aim in this chapter is twofold: (i) to limn the key features of the questioning-attitude account and (ii) to demonstrate that the questioning-attitude account is preferable to its closest rival theory, the question-directed attitude account.

4.2 Defining Key Terms

Let us begin by defining some of the key terms that will feature in the analysis to follow. It is common for epistemologists and analytic philosophers of mind to distinguish between *judging*, understood as the mental act of affirming the truth of a proposition, and *belief*, understood as the mental state of affirming the truth of a proposition. This characterisation of judgement and belief comports with that advocated by Shah and Velleman (2005) in the following passage:

> [A] judgement is a cognitive mental act of affirming a proposition... It is an act because it involves occurrently presenting a proposition, or putting it forward in the mind; and it is cognitive because it involves presenting the proposition as true, or, as we have said, affirming it. A belief, by contrast, is

[1] Friedman (2013c, 2017) prefers to use the term 'suspend judgement' to refer to the neutral doxastic attitude. However, following Matthew McGrath (2020), I will use the term 'agnosticism' to refer to the attitude and 'suspend judgement' to refer to the mental act of putting off judgement. While there are important differences between my conception of the neutral doxastic attitude and Friedman's, nothing of substance will depend on this difference of terminology.

a mental state of representing a proposition as true, a cognitive attitude rather than a cognitive act.[2]

One ingredient missing from the account of belief offered in the just-cited passage is the idea that a belief is commitment-involving. The claim that belief is commitment-involving may be understood in dispositional or normative terms. Understood dispositionally, an agent being committed to the truth of **P** entails that, all things being equal, they are disposed to take it for granted that **P** is true in their deliberation and action.[3] Understood normatively, an agent being committed to the truth of **P** entails that they are subject to rational criticism if they lack sufficient evidence to establish the truth of **P** or if they were to adopt an attitude that is inconsistent with their commitment to the truth of **P**. With the preceding clarifications in mind, we may modify the account offered by Shah and Velleman in the cited passage to include the stipulation that a belief is dispositionally and normatively commitment-involving:

Believing that P $=^{def}$ the dispositionally and normatively commitment-involving mental state of affirming the truth of **P**.

Significantly, the expression 'affirming the truth of' that features in the above definition is part of a third person (or what some philosophers call a sideways-on) description of believing. There is no implication or requirement that the believing agent see themselves as affirming the truth of a proposition or that they even have the concept of 'truth'. It is the theorist describing the mental state, as opposed to the agent possessing it, that is deploying the concept of truth that features in the above definition. Hence, I do not take the content of the agent's attitude to be something like '**P** is true', since having a mental state with such a content would require the possession and deployment of the concept of truth. Neither possessing nor deploying the concept of truth is necessary for having a belief.[4]

In addition to the mental act of affirming the truth of a proposition, we may also mentally affirm the falsity of a proposition. I take both kinds of mental acts to be instances of judging. Moreover, I take judging to be commitment-involving in the dispositional and normative senses just adumbrated. Putting these ideas together, I define judging as follows:

---

[2] Shah and Velleman (2005: 503). See and cf. Cassam (2010: 81) and Raleigh (2021: 2450).
[3] See and cf. Lord (2020: 128).
[4] This comports with the view of Feldman and Conee (2018:76): 'Belief can be an attribution of truth to the proposition. But it need not employ a concept of truth. Someone's attitude toward a proposition is belief just when the attitude is inwardly accepting it as true or otherwise assenting to it.'

Judging that P $=^{def}$ the dispositionally and normatively commitment-involving mental act of endorsing the truth or falsity of **P**.

Judging a proposition to be true typically, though not always, leads to the mental state of believing, while judging a proposition to be false typically, though not always, leads to the mental state of disbelieving. We may define disbelieving as follows:

Disbelieving that P $=^{def}$ the dispositionally or normatively commitment-involving mental state of affirming the falsity of **P**.

In addition to the mental act of judging, there is also the mental act of withholding judgement. Describing withholding judgement as a 'mental act' is meant to underscore that it involves an intentional omission of judgement as opposed to the mere absence of a judgement or opinion.

The notion of a doxastic attitude is sometimes taken to include a wide range of belief-like attitudes, including accepting (e.g. Weintraub [1990: 165]), presuming (e.g. Kapitan [1986: 235]), hypothesising (e.g. Williams [1989: 124]), and having a degree of confidence in (e.g. Kaplan [1981: 310]). However, the expression, 'doxastic attitude', may be more narrowly used to refer to any member of the tri-attitudinal complex consisting in believing, disbelieving, and agnosticism.[5] It is in its narrow sense that I will be using the term in this paper. Specifically, I will be presupposing the following narrow definition of a doxastic attitude:

Doxastic Attitude $=^{def}$ any member of the tri-attitudinal complex consisting in believing that **P**, disbelieving that **P**, and agnosticism towards **P**.

Notice that the above definition takes the object of all three attitudes to be a proposition. As we shall discuss at length in Section 4.3, this is controversial since some theorists hold that the object of agnosticism is not a proposition but a question.

4.3 Agnosticism as Question-Directed

Thanks to the ground-breaking work of Jane Friedman (2013a, 2013b, 2017a), it has become increasingly fashionable among philosophers interested in the topic of agnosticism to describe it as a question-directed

---

[5] Examples of the narrow usage of the term 'doxastic attitude' include: Conee and Feldman (1985), Steup (1988), Chisholm (1989), Sosa (1991), Feldman (2002, 2003, 2007), Steup (2008), Ryan (2010), Turri (2012), and McGrath (2020). For an argument that the attitudes of believing, disbelieving, and agnosticism (or what she calls 'suspending judgement') are not reducible to degrees of belief, see Friedman (2013c).

attitude. Question-directed attitudes are so named because they have questions rather than propositions as their object.[6] Hence, while the belief that God exists has the proposition 'God exists' as its object, it is alleged that agnosticism has the question 'Does God exist?' as its object. Other putative question-directed attitudes include inquiring, wondering, and being curious about.

One indication that an attitude has a question rather than a proposition as its object is that ascriptions of the attitude take an interrogative complement, like 'who', 'what', 'when', 'where', 'whether', and 'how'. For example, ascriptions of agnosticism most naturally take a *whether*-clause; one may be agnostic about *whether* God exists, *whether* string theory is true, or *whether* Lee Harvey Oswald killed Kennedy. Moreover, while it is perfectly grammatical to employ agnosticism-ascriptions that do not include a *whether*-clause – for example, Thomas is agnostic towards the existence of God – such ascriptions seem stilted or overly academic and would rarely feature in conversational English. These observations about the syntax of agnosticism-ascriptions contrasts with the observation that belief-ascriptions most naturally take an indicative complement or *that*-clause; one may believe *that* God exists, *that* string theory is true, or *that* Lee Harvey Oswald killed Kennedy.

To be clear, the claim that an attitude is question-directed is different from the claim that ascriptions of that attitude take an interrogative complement. The first is a metaphysical thesis about the nature of a mental state and the second is a linguistic thesis about the ascription of a mental state to oneself or others. However, advocates of the question-directed attitude account hold that the truth of the linguistic thesis is at least partly explained by the truth of the metaphysical thesis. While I agree with the linguistic thesis that agnosticism-ascriptions take an interrogative complement, I take exception to the metaphysical thesis that it has interrogative content. My primary reason for rejecting the metaphysical thesis is that it fails to preserve the parity between judgement, belief, and disbelief, on the one hand, and agnosticism, on the other hand. Call this the *parity failure objection*.

Here, in brief, is my argument: It is common ground on both sides of the current debate that judgement, belief, and disbelief are all proposition-directed. Hence, according to advocates of the question-directed attitude account, agnosticism is the odd man out. Since questions are neither true nor false, they are not candidates for being judged true or false. And if

---

[6] Friedman (2013a: 145).

4.3 Agnosticism as Question-Directed

questions are not candidates for judgement, they cannot properly be considered candidates for withholding judgement. (Compare: insofar as human beings are not candidates for being prime [in the sense that a number may be], one cannot properly describe a human being as refraining from being prime.) The upshot is that if we hold that agnosticism is question-directed, then it is no longer true that a candidate for agnosticism is also a candidate for withholding judgement. Given that any proposition, **P**, that is a candidate for belief and disbelief is also a candidate for judgement and withholding judgement, it follows that the question-directed attitude account implies that the mental act of withholding judgement does not stand to the doxastic attitude of agnosticism as the mental act of judgement stands to the doxastic attitudes of belief and disbelief.

4.3.1 Agnosticism and Open-Ended Questions

In response to the parity failure objection, it may be argued that when one is agnostic about a question, one has a mental stance towards all of the possible answers to said question. This thesis is what Filippo Ferrari and Luca Incurvati describe as their 'minimal characterisation of agnosticism'(2022: 366). Ferrari's and Incurvati's minimal characterisation of agnosticism may be co-opted to defend a version of the question-directed attitude account.[7] On the present suggestion, saying that one is agnostic about **Q** is merely elliptical for saying that one is agnostic about some set of propositions, $P_1, P_2,\ldots,P_n$, where '$P_1, P_2,\ldots,P_n$' is the set of possible answers to **Q**. For example, if I am agnostic about who invented the telescope, the object of my agnosticism is a disjunction of all propositions of the form 'X is the inventor of the telescope' where X is a possible candidate for having invented the telescope. My being agnostic towards this question entails that for any such X, I am disposed to neither affirm nor deny the truth of the proposition in which X features. Furthermore, according to some formal theories of questions, the semantic content of a question just is the complete set of possible answers.[8] Hence, we may view the claim that agnosticism towards **Q** is actually agnosticism towards the

---

[7] To be clear, I am not here attributing the aim of defending the question-directed attitude account to Ferrari and Incurvati (2022). Taking my cue from an anonymous referee, I only claim that the defender of the question-directed attitude account may attempt to repurpose their arguments towards this end.

[8] A version of this semantic theory of questions is defended by Hamblin (1973), Karttunen (1977), Groenendijk & Stokhof (1984), and Ciardelli et al. (2018).

complete set of possible answers to **Q** as a version of the question-directed attitude account. The upshot is that we can endorse a version of the question-directed attitude account while also preserving the parity between withholding judgement, conceived of as a mental act directed at something truth-evaluable, and agnosticism, conceived of as a mental state directed at something truth-evaluable.[9]

Unfortunately, the above reply is insufficient to rescue the question-directed attitude account from the parity failure objection. This becomes clear when we consider open-ended questions for which we have no candidate answers. Consider the following questions:

(A) Where is the precise location of Cleopatra's tomb?
(B) How many stars are there in the Andromeda Galaxy?
(C) Who invented the telescope?

Questions (A), (B), and (C) are examples of what are standardly called 'open-ended questions'. These are questions that cannot be answered with a simple 'yes' or 'no' response. Open-ended questions contrast with yes-or-no questions. Examples of yes-or-no questions include:

(D) Does God exist?
(E) Did Lee Harvey Oswald kill John F. Kennedy?
(F) Is string theory true?

Yes-or-no questions ask if a certain proposition is true or false. Consequently, it is impossible to pose a yes-or-no question if one has no proposition in mind whose truth or falsity is in question. Open-ended questions, by contrast, are so named because they do not require the questioner to have a candidate answer in order to properly formulate the question. For example, I do not need to have any potential locations for Cleopatra's tomb in mind in order to meaningfully ask (A). In sum, one may pose an open-ended question even if one has no proposition in mind that could serve as a possible answer to it.

Notice that someone, let us call her Jane, may wonder, be curious about, or inquire into who invented the telescope even if not a single name comes to mind as a potential answer when she considers the question. If agnosticism is a question-directed attitude on par with wondering, curiosity, or inquiry, then Jane should also be able to be agnostic about who invented the telescope. However, since there is no proposition before her mind that could potentially be true or false, there is

---

[9] Special thanks to an anonymous referee for raising the present objection.

no proposition before her mind that could be a candidate for judgement or withholding judgement. The upshot is that Jane's agnosticism about who invented the telescope could not have been preceded by the mental act of withholding judgement with respect to some proposition. Consequently, the fundamental relationship between the mental state of agnosticism and the mental act of withholding judgement is undermined. Hence, according to the question-directed attitude account, there will be a wide range of cases in which what one is agnostic about is not a candidate for judgement or withholding judgement.

In order to avoid the above result, the advocate of the question-directed attitude account must hold that a proposition may be the object of an attitude even if the agent has never entertained the proposition. However, careful reflection on what it means to be the object of an attitude, in the sense relevant to the present discussion, reveals that this is implausible. In this regard, it is important to distinguish between the notion of the object of an attitude (which corresponds with the psychological description of a mental state's representational content) and the notion of the correctness-conditions of an attitude (which corresponds with the formal analysis of when a mental state is correct or incorrect). Consider the pre-schooler who believes there is a triangle on the blackboard. Given that the sum of the angles of a triangle is 180 degrees, it follows that the pre-schooler's belief is correct if and only if there is a closed figure whose angles sum to 180 degrees on the blackboard. Hence, if we are merely interested in whether the pre-schooler's belief is correct or incorrect, as opposed to offering an accurate psychological description of what is going on in the pre-schooler's head, then equating her thought about triangles with thoughts about closed figures whose angles sum to 180 degrees is unproblematic. However, suppose that the pre-schooler is unaware that the sum of the angles of a triangle is 180 degrees and that she has never entertained the proposition. In that case, it would be false that she believes or judges that there is a closed figure whose angles sum to 180 degrees on the blackboard. Moreover, insofar as she has never entertained the proposition that there is a closed figure whose angles sum to 180 degrees on the blackboard, it is false that she is withholding judgement with respect to the proposition. In short, the proposition, 'there is a closed figure whose angles sum to 180 degrees on the blackboard', cannot be the object of her belief, judgement, or withholding judgement. Notice that this remains the case despite the fact that her belief that there is a triangle on the blackboard is correct if and only if there is a closed figure whose angles sum to 180 degrees on the blackboard. This suggests that the salient notion, as far as the current debate is concerned, is not the notion of the correctness-conditions of an attitude. The takeaway is that on a proper understanding of the object of an attitude, it is implausible that a proposition, **P**, may be the object of an attitude of an agent even if said agent has never entertained **P**. In light of this, it would be a mistake to identify the object of agnosticism with a proposition (or set of propositions) that an agent has never entertained.

Furthermore, even if the proposal that the content of an open-ended question should be identified with its possible answers could be made to work, it would only 'rescue' the idea that the object of agnosticism is a question by essentially giving it up. Recall that the primary motivation for denying that the object of agnosticism is a question comes from the attempt to preserve the idea that the object of agnosticism – like the object of belief, disbelief, and judgement – is a proposition (i.e. something truth-evaluable). If one holds that open-ended questions merely stand proxy for their possible answers, then one is essentially agreeing that the object of agnosticism is a proposition or disjunction of propositions (i.e. something truth-evaluable). But this would imply that agnosticism is in fact proposition-directed. Hence, on the present suggestion, the claim that agnosticism is question-directed simply collapses into the claim that it is proposition-directed. While this would be a welcome result for those of us who hold that agnosticism is proposition-directed, it makes the claim that agnosticism is question-directed seem far less philosophically interesting than it initially purported to be. I conclude that insofar as we are committed to a philosophically interesting version of the claim that agnosticism is question-directed – that is, a version of the claim that does not, upon examination, simply collapse into the claim that agnosticism is proposition-directed – we are forced to give up on the idea that withholding judgement stands to agnosticism as judgement stands to belief or disbelief.

4.4 Agnosticism as Proposition-Directed

Holding that agnosticism is proposition-directed is an important first step to reinstating agnosticism in its rightful place as one of the three possible doxastic stances one may take towards a proposition. To this end, I claim that just as believing involves taking an affirming stance towards a proposition and disbelieving involves taking a denying stance towards a proposition, agnosticism involves taking a questioning stance towards a proposition. This not only allows for a univocal account of the content of the doxastic attitudes, but also preserves the *parity thesis*: the claim that the mental act of withholding judgement stands to the doxastic attitude of agnosticism as the mental act of judging stands to the doxastic attitudes of belief and disbelief.

4.4.1 Agnosticism as Questioning-Attitude

There are a number of things we could mean when we say that agnosticism involves taking a questioning stance towards a proposition. Often, the expression 'questioning' is employed roughly as a synonym for 'interrogating'; such as when we describe someone as being taken in for questioning by the FBI or when a lawyer questions a witness. Call this *forensic questioning*. It is also common to describe someone as questioning *X* when they are simply sceptical about *X*. For example, if Jane is sceptical about the reliability of Matt's testimony, we may describe her as questioning the reliability of Matt's testimony. Call this *sceptical questioning*. It is sceptical questioning (rather than forensic questioning) that I have in mind when I describe agnosticism towards **P** as questioning both the truth and falsity of **P**. The quasi-technical notion of sceptically questioning X that features in my analysis may be more colloquially described as having reservations about X. Hence, one sceptically questions both the truth and falsity of **P** just in case *one has reservations about **P** being true and one also has reservations about **P** being false.*

Unlike forensic questioning, sceptical questioning does not carry any implications of inquiry. For example, I may sceptically question the excuse offered by one of my students as to why she arrived late to class and yet (because I know that her being late on this particular occasion will not impact her overall performance) have no interest in finding out whether her excuse was indeed true. To be sceptical about her excuse simply entails that I have reservations about its truth, it does not entail that I wish, desire, or have the intention to determine whether it is true. Indeed, there may be cases in which one sceptically questions a proposition and actively desires or intends not to find out whether it is true or false. Consider the case of a politician who prefers to remain in the dark with respect to whether one of her staff members was engaged in wrongdoing so that she may maintain plausible deniability. So described, the politician would not only lack the aim of coming to know whether the staff member is guilty of wrongdoing, but has the explicit aim not to find out. This is consistent with the politician having reservations about the claim that her staff member is not guilty of wrongdoing. In sum, it is one thing to sceptically question both the truth and falsity of **P** and quite another to have the aim of coming to know whether **P** is true or false. Hence, the thesis that agnosticism involves sceptically questioning both the truth and falsity of **P** does not entail that the agnostic agent is inquiring into whether **P** is true or false.

Even if it is granted that sceptically questioning **P** at some time, t, does not entail that one is inquiring into whether **P** at t (or some time subsequent to t), it may be argued that it entails having previously inquired into whether **P**. On the present suggestion, while sceptical questioning need not entail present or future inquiry, one must have already inquired to get to the point of sceptically questioning **P**.[10] In response to the present objection, we may observe that it is possible for someone to have reservations about a proposition the very first time they encounter it. Consider the following exchange:

PAM : Do you think there are more H_2O molecules in a teaspoon of water than stars in the universe?
PAUL : I'm not saying that's not the case, but I have some reservations.
PAM : Have you previously looked into the matter?
PAUL : No. This is my first time encountering the question.

Paul's stance in the above exchange strikes me as both psychologically possible and intelligible. Indeed, the very first time I was asked if there were more H_2O molecules in a teaspoon of water than stars in the universe, I had reservations about a positive answer to the question as well. Admittedly, I was not prepared to regard the claim that there were more H_2O molecules in a teaspoon of water than stars in the universe as false. However, I would need to see the numbers provided by a reputable source before I would be prepared to believe it. (Spoiler: I later discovered that it is indeed true that there are more H_2O molecules in a teaspoon of water than stars in the universe.) Hence, having reservations about the truth of **P** need not be the result of previous inquiry into whether **P**. On the contrary, a proposition may strike us as more or less plausible the very first time we encounter it. If the initial plausibility of a claim is too low to facilitate belief, then it would be natural to have reservations about it, even if we have not previously engaged in inquiry into the matter. Moreover, we may further fill in the details of our example so that Paul also has reservations about the claim that there are more stars in the universe than H2O molecules in a teaspoon of water. Given that Paul has reservations about both claims, I maintain that he may be accurately described as being agnostic on the matter.

---

[10] I would like to thank an anonymous referee for raising this objection.

4.4 Agnosticism as Proposition-Directed

My diagnosis of why it may seem as though having reservations about **P** entails having previously inquired into whether **P** is that many (if not most) of the paradigm cases that come to mind when we think of ourselves as having reservations about **P** are also cases in which we have previously inquired into whether **P**. This is largely because we often describe ourselves as having reservations about a proposition when we feel we have some reason to believe it, but said reasons are ultimately less than convincing. Since having some reason to believe some proposition, **P**, typically requires having previously inquired into **P**, then it is often the case that having reservations about **P** entail having previously inquired into **P** (I take this point to be true of agnosticism as well; many instances in which we would describe ourselves as agnostic towards **P** are also instances in which we have previously engaged in inquiry with respect to **P**.) Acknowledging the above point is consistent with the observation that there are also instances in which one may be correctly described as having reservations about **P** despite not previously inquiring into whether **P**. This is what the conversation between Pam and Paul illustrates; even if prior inquiry is often our basis for having reservations about **P**, this need not always be the case. In sum, I am willing to grant that many (if not most) of the paradigm cases that come to mind in which a subject has reservations about **P** are also instances in which the subject has previously inquired into whether **P**. What I deny is that this is true of all instances in which a subject has reservations about **P**. The upshot is that insofar as agnosticism towards **P** entails having reservations about the truth of **P** and reservations about the falsity of **P**, agnosticism towards **P** at some time, t, does not entail inquiring into **P** at t, subsequent to t, or prior to t.

4.4.2 Agnosticism as Committed Neutrality

In Section 4.2, I proposed that we unpack the claim that believing **P** entails being committed to the truth of **P** in dispositional and normative terms. Similarly, I propose that we unpack the claim that agnosticism towards **P** entails being committed to neutrality with respect to the truth of **P** in dispositional or normative terms. Understood in dispositional terms, someone being committed to neutrality about whether **P** entails that, all things being equal, they are disposed to neither take it for granted that **P** is true nor take it for granted that **P** is false in their deliberation and action. Understood in normative terms, saying that someone who is agnostic about whether **P** is committed to being neutral about whether **P** entails that they are subject to rational criticism if they have sufficient evidence to establish either the truth or falsity of **P** or if they were to adopt an attitude that entailed affirming either the truth or falsity of **P**.

The dispositional and normative accounts of committed neutrality just sketched departs in significant ways from that offered by Whitney Lilly (2019). Building on the work of Pamela Hieronymi (2006), Lilly invokes the idea that agnosticism is a commitment-constituted attitude, which Lilly describes as follows:

> A commitment-constituted attitude is just an attitude that one forms by settling a question for oneself. To settle a question for oneself is to become committed to the truth of the content of one's answer to this question ... [S]ettling a question like 'whether **P**' results in forming a doxastic attitude. Settling positively the question 'whether it is raining' results in forming the belief that it is raining, and settling negatively the question 'whether I brought my umbrella' results in disbelieving that you brought your umbrella.[11]

Given the framework being sketched in the cited passage, it is not clear what neutrally settling a question would amount to, or even if there could be such a thing. By Lilly's lights, settling whether **P** positively would involve a commitment to the truth of **P** and settling whether **P** negatively would involve a commitment to the falsity of **P**. Consider the question: 'Is it raining?' Possible answers to this question include 'yes', 'no', 'I'm unsure', and 'I do not know'. However, while the former pair of answers are plausibly described as settling the question of whether it is it raining, it appears that the same cannot be said of the latter pair. Indeed, 'yes' or 'no' seem like the only two potential candidate answers that settle whether it is raining. However, of the responses offered above, only the latter pair could be sincerely uttered by someone who was agnostic about whether it is raining. Hence, we seem to have defined out of existence the possibility of agnosticism being a commitment-constituted attitude. The takeaway from the preceding observation seems to be that (pace Lilly) Hieronymi's notion of a commitment-constituted attitude – which identifies being committed with settling a question either positively or negatively – is poorly suited to capture what it means for agnosticism to be an attitude of committed neutrality. I conclude that the claim that agnosticism is an attitude of committed neutrality is better understood not in terms of positively or negatively settling whether **P**, but in the dispositional and normative terms sketched above.

---

[11] Lilly (2019: 217–218).

Pulling together all of the above points, I define agnosticism towards **P** as follows:

Agnosticism towards P =^{def} the dispositionally and normatively commitment-involving mental state of sceptically questioning both the truth and falsity of **P**.

4.5 Agnosticism Attitude-Ascriptions

The remainder of this chapter will aim to establish that the questioning-attitude account displays what I take to be the two most attractive features of Friedman's question-directed attitude account: namely (1) it provides an explanation of why agnosticism attitude-ascriptions take an interrogative complement and (2) it identifies what makes agnosticism a *sui generis* attitude. Given that it has already been shown that the question-directed attitude account is subject to the parity failure objection, the fact that the questioning-attitude account also satisfies (1) and (2) should be sufficient to establish that the latter is the superior account of agnosticism.

The question-directed attitude account offers a straightforward explanation of why agnosticism-ascriptions take an interrogative complement. Simply put, agnosticism-ascriptions take an interrogative complement because the attitude has a question as its object. However, the questioning-attitude account is equally well-placed to explain this feature of our agnosticism-ascriptions. Simply put, agnosticism attitude ascriptions take an interrogative complement because the attitude of agnosticism involves taking a sceptically questioning stance towards a proposition. Both the question-directed attitude account (defended by Friedman) and the questioning-attitude account (being defended here) favour describing the agnostic agent as being agnostic about *whether* **P**. However, whereas the question-directed attitude account locates the interrogative marker in the content of the attitude, yielding the interpretation: 'being agnostic about [whether **P**]', the questioning-attitude account locates the interrogative marker in the attitude itself, yielding the interpretation: 'being agnostic about whether [**P**]'.

The first step to appreciating the adequacy of the alternative explanation provided by the questioning-attitude account is to observe that the fact that an attitude-ascription may take an interrogative complement (i.e. the linguistic thesis) does not entail that the attitude being ascribed has a question as its object (i.e. the metaphysical thesis). Consider ascriptions of knowledge. While knowing is widely regarded as proposition-directed, ascriptions of knowledge often take an interrogative complement or whether-clause. For example, one can know *whether* God exists, know *whether* string theory is true, or know *whether* Lee Harvey Oswald killed Kennedy. Hence, the fact that ascriptions of an attitude may take an interrogative complement is not sufficient to establish that it has a question rather than a proposition as its object.

The explanation of why knowledge attitude-ascriptions may take an interrogative complement appears to share something in common with the explanation of why agnosticism attitude-ascriptions typically do the same. We often ascribe knowledge to others that we ourselves do not possess. For example, if I do not know whether Thomas will be at the party, but wish to ascribe such knowledge to Jane, I may say something along lines of (G):

(G) Jane knows *whether* Thomas will be at the party

Here, the use of the interrogative complement or whether-clause allows me to convey that Jane has a certain piece of knowledge – that is, whether the proposition 'Thomas will be at the party' is true or false – without my taking a stand one way or another, given that I do not share said piece of knowledge. We may also self-ascribe knowledge using an interrogative complement when we wish to convey that we have some piece of knowledge but do not wish to disclose to our audience what we know. For example, if I want to convey that I know whether Thomas will be at the party, but I do not wish to disclose said information, then I may say something along the lines of (H):

(H) I know *whether* Thomas will be at the party.

In sum, the use of the interrogative complement in an attitude-ascription involving a proposition-directed attitude seems tied to a speaker's unwillingness to go on record one way or the next with respect to the truth or falsity of the relevant proposition. This unwillingness may be due to the fact that the agent does not have an opinion either way or because the agent does not (for whatever reason) wish to disclose the content of said opinion. Both explanations may be operative in ascriptions of knowledge, with the first explanation tending to hold in third person knowledge-ascriptions and the second motivation tending to hold in first-person knowledge-ascriptions. Since the agnostic agent occupies a position of committed neutrality, it is the agnostic agent's failure to have an opinion either way that accounts for their unwillingness to go on record with respect to the truth or falsity of the relevant proposition. Hence, we can see that, when viewed from a sufficiently high level of abstraction, there is a shared explanation of why both agnosticism-ascriptions and knowledge-ascriptions may take interrogative complements, despite the

4.5 Agnosticism Attitude-Ascriptions

fact that the attitudes in question are proposition-directed. To wit, the person ascribing the attitude is unwilling to go on record with respect to the truth or falsity of the target proposition. I conclude that the fact that agnosticism-ascriptions take an interrogative complement poses no special challenge to the thesis that agnosticism is proposition-directed.

4.5.1 Agnosticism-Ascriptions and Open-Ended Questions

The linguistic practice of using interrogative complements in knowledge-ascriptions also sheds light on how we should conceive of agnosticism-ascriptions that involve open-ended questions. Consider the following knowledge-ascriptions:

(I)   Verena knows how many people will be attending the party.
(J)   Luca knows who took the last cookie.
(K)   Filippo knows when the caterer will arrive.

In each of the above cases, the knowledge-ascription takes an interrogative complement implicating an open-ended question. To wit, one could not answer the questions – how many people will be attending the party, who took the last cookie, or when will the caterer arrive – with a simple 'yes' or 'no'. Moreover, the following agnosticism-ascriptions also take interrogative complements implicating open-ended questions:

(L)   Verena is agnostic about how many people will be attending the party.
(M)   Luca is agnostic about who took the last cookie.
(N)   Filippo is agnostic about when the caterer will arrive.

At first pass, the fact that (L)-(N) appear to be felicitous agnosticism-ascriptions may seem at odds with my claim that open-ended questions pose a special problem for the thesis that the attitude of agnosticism is question-directed. However, as with knowledge-ascriptions, it is important to distinguish between the linguistic thesis that an attitude-ascription may take *complements* of a certain kind and the metaphysical thesis that an attitude has *content* of a certain kind. We may consistently hold that knowledge-ascriptions, like (I)-(K), are felicitous, while also denying that the attitude of knowledge has an open-ended question as its object. Likewise, we may consistently hold that agnosticism-ascriptions, like (L)-(N), are felicitous, while also denying that the attitude of agnosticism has an open-ended question as its object.

Open-ended questions pose a special problem for the thesis that the attitude of agnosticism is question-directed because there may be open-ended questions for which a subject has no candidate answers. In such cases, there are no candidate propositions for the subject to believe, disbelieve, judge, or refrain from judging. The upshot is that what a subject is agnostic about need not be a candidate for believing, disbelieving, judging, or withholding judgement. However, we do not run into the same problem if we endorse the linguistic thesis that agnosticism-ascriptions may take interrogative complements that implicate open-ended questions, so long as we do not infer from this that the attitude of agnosticism has an open-ended question as its object. There are at least two ways of making sense of agnosticism-ascriptions implicating open-ended questions that is consistent with the rejection of the metaphysical thesis. On the one hand, we may see the subjects described in (L), (M), and (N) – Verena, Luca, and Filippo, respectively – as having some specific proposition in mind that they are agnostic about. However, the speaker ascribing the attitude of agnosticism to Verena, Luca, and Filippo is either unaware of the identity of the proposition in question or wishes not to disclose said proposition to their audience. On this proposal, a speaker would resort to employing agnosticism-ascriptions like (L)-(N) for the same reason that a speaker would resort to employing a knowledge-ascription like (I)-(K); because while the targets of the attitude-ascriptions have a particular proposition in mind, the speaker who is ascribing the attitude is either not privy to the identity of the proposition or wishes not to disclose the proposition. On the other hand, we may see the subjects described in (L), (M), and (N) as having a disposition to be agnostic towards any of the candidate answers that may be offered in response to the open-ended question at issue. On this second proposal, the speaker is not ascribing some specific agnostic attitude to Verena, Luca, and Filippo, but is rather reporting a disposition to adopt an agnostic attitude towards a certain set of propositions – that is, the possible answers to (L), (M), and (N), respectively. In either case, granting the felicity of (L)-(N) does not require that we endorse the metaphysical thesis that the attitude of agnosticism has an open-ended question as its object.

4.6 Agnosticism as Sui Generis

A second attractive feature of Friedman's question-directed attitude account is that it offers one way of unpacking the claim that agnosticism is a sui generis attitude. Simply put, agnosticism cannot be reduced to or analysed in terms of belief and/or disbelief because agnosticism has a question as its content while belief and disbelief both have a proposition as their content. The questioning-attitude account also gives substance to

4.6 Agnosticism as Sui Generis

the claim that agnosticism is sui generis. Simply put, agnosticism cannot be reduced to or analysed in terms of belief and/or disbelief because while belief and disbelief entail an affirming and denying mental stance towards a proposition, respectively, agnosticism involves a sceptically questioning mental stance towards a proposition.

However, establishing the plausibility of the sui generis thesis requires more than merely advancing an account that it is at odds with the reduction of agnosticism to belief and disbelief. Raleigh offers two basic constraints that an account of agnosticism (or what he calls 'suspending judgement') should satisfy:

(I) Suspending whether **P** is an attitude that can be rendered more or less epistemically justified/rational, at least to some extent, according to one's evidence and one's cognitive relation to that evidence.

(II) Suspending whether **P** is different from simply having no opinion about whether **P**.

It is fairly easy to see that the questioning-attitude account satisfies constraint (II). The mental stance of sceptically questioning both the truth and falsity of **P** is clearly different from simply having no opinion about whether **P**. Questioning, being sceptical, or having reservations about **P** is an active cognitive phenomenon, and an agent who simply failed to consider **P** or who simply had no attitude towards **P** whatsoever could not be said to sceptically question both the truth and falsity of **P**. In this respect, the questioning-attitude account departs from what Raleigh, following Friedman, calls 'non-belief views', according to which agnosticism consists in simply neither believing that **P** nor disbelieving that **P**.[12]

However, it is less obvious that the questioning-attitude account satisfies constraint (I). Indeed, Raleigh maintains that any sui generis view would be unable to satisfy (I). He writes:

> According to [the sui generis view], suspending judgement does not constitutively involve any kind of belief, neither full belief nor partial belief (credence). So the alleged sui generis state would embody neither a commitment to, nor a degree of confidence about, the truth or falsity of anything – it would be an alethically uncommitted state. Whilst the sui generis attitude may have a propositional content, **P**, it does not involve any commitment or degree of confidence that **P** is actually the case, nor that anything else is or is not the case.[13]

---

[12] See and cf. Friedman (2013b: 178) and Raleigh (2021).   [13] Raleigh (2021: 2462).

Raleigh's point appears to be that insofar as agnosticism does not involve some kind of belief, it cannot involve an alethic commitment. However, holding that an attitude constitutively involves believing **P** is not the only way to arrive at the conclusion that it involves a commitment to the truth of **P**. We may also hold that an attitude involves a commitment to the truth of a proposition because said proposition is presupposed by the attitude. For example, suppose that I desire or intend to close my bedroom window. It is widely held that my desire and intention are distinct attitudes from the attitude of believing that my bedroom window is open. However, both my desire and intention to close my bedroom window can be said to involve an alethic commitment to the proposition, 'my bedroom window is open', in the sense that it would be irrational for me to continue to have the desire or intention if I were presented with conclusive evidence that my window was not open. Hence, evidence for or against the proposition, 'my bedroom window is open', may have some bearing on whether it is rational for me to have the desire or intention to close my bedroom window, despite the fact that these attitudes are distinct from the attitude of believing my bedroom window is open.

Admittedly, it is possible that my desire and intention to close my bedroom window constitutively involves the belief that my bedroom window is open and that it is this fact that explains why it would be irrational to have said desire or intention if my bedroom window were not open. However, this is not our only option. An alternative view would be to hold that the reason my desire and intention to close my bedroom window presupposes that my bedroom window is open has to do with the nature of the attitudes themselves – that is, with their direction of fit. For example, we may hold that my desire to close my bedroom window represents the proposition, 'my bedroom window is closed', as something to be made true. Since a proposition cannot be made true if it is already true, then conclusive evidence that my window is closed would imply that the representation of **P** as something to be made true is obsolete and this would constitute a reason not to have such a representation.

To be clear, the aim of the above line of argument is not to advocate for one conception of desire or intention over another. Such a project falls outside the scope of the present investigation. Rather, I merely wish to call attention to the fact that the logical space of possibilities vis-à-vis alethic commitments is broader than what is countenanced in Raleigh's objection. In sum, there are options for making sense of how an attitude may involve a commitment to the truth of a proposition, apart from holding that the attitude constitutively involves believing that proposition. If Raleigh's objection is going to be cogent, then he would need to establish that all competing strategies for making sense of how evidence for or against **P** may have some bearing on whether it is rational to have a certain attitude are moribund. Short of such a demonstration, Raleigh is yet to make his case.

In light of the preceding considerations, I maintain that we may make sense of the fact that agnosticism may be made more or less epistemically justified/rational based on the state of one's considered evidence without holding that agnosticism constitutively involves belief. Specifically, we may make sense of why the state of one's evidence has a bearing on whether agnosticism is epistemically justified/rational via a direct appeal to the nature of the attitude itself. In broad terms, believing **P** is epistemically justified/rational when one's evidence conclusively supports the truth of **P**, disbelieving **P** is epistemically justified/rational when one's evidence conclusively supports the falsity of **P**, and agnosticism towards **P** is epistemically justified/rational when one's evidence neither conclusively supports the truth or falsity of **P**. Here are some examples of cases in which one's evidence neither conclusively supports the truth or falsity of a proposition.

Case 1: Counterbalanced Positive Evidence

Three eyewitnesses, all of whom are widely regarded as reliable, report seeing the butler at the house between 8 pm and 10 pm on the night of the murder. However, three other eyewitnesses, all of whom are also widely viewed as reliable, report seeing the butler at a pub 50 miles away from the house between 8 pm and 10 pm on the night in question. Hence, the available positive evidence for and against the butler being at the house between 8 pm and 10 pm on the night of the murder is counterbalanced.

Case 2: Absent Positive Evidence

A political prisoner wakes up in a windowless room in an undisclosed location. The concrete walls insulate him from any sights or sounds from outside the room. The prisoner has no positive evidence that it is true that it is currently raining outside his room and no positive evidence that it is false that it is currently raining outside his room. Hence, his available evidence is counterbalanced, but whereas in Case 1, the agent's evidence is counterbalanced because his positive evidence in support of P is equally strong as his positive evidence against P, the evidence is counterbalanced in the present case because of a complete absence of positive evidence on both sides.

> **Case 3: Insufficient Positive Evidence**
>
> A physicist has some positive evidence – that is, in the form of single rigorous experiment that has not yet been replicated – that a heretofore unobserved subatomic particle exists. Since no other experiments have been conducted, he has no positive evidence that the subatomic particle does not exist. Hence, while he has some positive evidence that the particle exists, he has no positive evidence that it does not exist. Even so, given that the experiment is yet to be replicated, the positive evidence available is still insufficient to establish the existence of the hypothesised particle.

> **Case 4: Defeated Positive Evidence**
>
> Alvin is at a party and notices Whitney wearing what appears to be a light green shirt. This provides Alvin with some positive evidence that Whitney is wearing a light green shirt. However, Alvin is informed by the host of the party that the lights in the room are equipped with cyan filters that make white surfaces appear light green, but leaves the colour of light green objects unchanged. The host's revelation defeats the positive evidence provided by Alvin's perceptual experience.

> **Case 5: Positive Evidence of Equiprobability**
>
> When presented with a fair coin, one may lack any first-order evidence that the coin will land head-side-up on the next toss and also lack any first-order evidence that it will land tail-side-up on the next toss. Hence, one finds oneself in a situation akin to Case 2. However, given that one knows that the coin is fair, this knowledge constitutes positive higher-order evidence that it is equally probable that the coin will land head-side-up and tail-side-up on the next toss.

While not exhaustive, the above list of cases is representative of the kinds of cases in which it is widely agreed that one's available evidence makes it epistemically justified/rational to be agnostic. What all of the above cases have in common is that they represent instances in which an agent's available evidence is insufficient for establishing both the truth of **P** and the falsity of **P**. This lends credence to my claim that agnosticism is epistemically justified/rational just in case one's available evidence is insufficient to establish both the truth and falsity of **P**.

If it can be shown that the questioning-attitude account can explain why having insufficient evidential support for both the truth and falsity of **P** makes agnosticism epistemically justified/rational, then this should be sufficient to move the burden of proof from the shoulder of the defender of sui generis accounts and unto that of the critic who claims that such accounts are unable to satisfy constraint (I). This challenge is met by the questioning-attitude account. If one's evidence is insufficient to establish the truth of **P**, this justifies/rationalises sceptically questioning (i.e. having reservations about) the truth of **P**, and if one's evidence is insufficient for establishing the falsity of **P**, this justifies/rationalises sceptically questioning the falsity of **P**. Consequently, it follows from the questioning-attitude account that having insufficient evidence to establish the truth of **P** as well insufficient evidence to establish the falsity of **P** makes it epistemically justified/rational to be agnostic towards **P**. I conclude that Raleigh has failed to offer any compelling reasons to think that the questioning-attitude account is unable to satisfy constraint (I).

4.7 Applying the Seven Criteria

I conclude my discussion of the questioning-attitude account by demonstrating that it satisfies the four Friedman-inspired and three Wagner-inspired criteria for a satisfactory descriptive account of agnosticism adumbrated in Chapter 2. Here is a summary of how the questioning-attitude account satisfies each criterion.

4.7.1 The Friedman-Inspired Criteria

Cognitive Contact Criterion
According to the questioning-attitude account, agnosticism towards **P** entails sceptically questioning both the truth and falsity of **P**. Insofar as one may sceptically question both the truth and falsity of **P** only if one has considered **P**, the questioning attitude account precludes the possibility of someone being agnostic towards **P** if she has never considered or been in cognitive contact with **P**.

Inconsistency Criterion
Insofar as mental compartmentalisation makes it psychologically possible to have the doxastic attitudes of affirming the truth of **P** (i.e. believe **P**) at some time t and denying the truth of **P** (i.e. disbelieve **P**) at t, then parity of reasoning suggests that it should also be possible to have the attitudes of affirming the truth of **P** at t and sceptically question the truth of **P** (i.e. agnosticism towards **P**) at t. Hence, the questioning-attitude account is consistent with the possibility of agnosticism-involving doxastic inconsistency.

Spontaneity Criterion
One may sceptically question both the truth and falsity of **P** even if one has not previously deliberated about **P**. Consider the proposition: a chef's tall hat (officially known as a 'toque') has exactly 101 pleats, representing the 101 ways to cook an egg. You may sceptically question the truth and falsity of this proposition even if you never actively deliberated about it prior to my mentioning it here.[14]

Termination Criterion
Someone whose deliberation ends prior to them becoming dispositionally and normatively committed to sceptically questioning both the truth and falsity of **P** due to disinterest, distraction, or death does not qualify as agnostic, according to the questioning-attitude account. Hence, the questioning attitude account is able to explain the difference between someone who closes deliberation with the adoption of the attitude of agnosticism and someone who ends their deliberation prematurely.

4.7.2 The Wagner-Inspired Criteria

Neutrality Criterion
According to the questioning-attitude account, the attitude of agnosticism involves a questioning mental stance towards a proposition in the very same way that believing involves an affirming mental stance towards a proposition. In this view, sceptically questioning X entails having reservations about X. Insofar as having reservations about both the truth and falsity of **P** is neutral between affirming the truth of **P** and affirming the falsity of **P**, it follows that the questioning-attitude account includes a specification of which feature of agnosticism makes it a neutral doxastic attitude.

Commitment* Criterion
While the questioning-attitude account unpacks the neutrality implicated by agnosticism in terms of sceptically questioning both the truth and falsity of **P**, it unpacks a subject's commitment to said neutrality in terms of the disposition to neither take it for granted that **P** is true nor that **P** is false and in terms of the subject being open to criticism if they affirm the truth or falsity of **P**. Hence, the questioning-attitude account is able to

---

[14] Spoiler: a toque is traditionally made with exactly 100 pleats, so the claim that it has 101 pleats is actually false.

capture the difference between a subject's being neutral with respect to some proposition and a subject's commitment to said neutrality.

Appropriateness Criterion
In cases in which one's evidence for and against the truth of **P** is perfectly counterbalanced, it is rationally appropriate to sceptically question or have reservations about both the truth and falsity of **P**. It follows that the questioning-attitude account preserves the idea that agnosticism is rationally appropriate in cases in which one's evidence is perfectly counterbalanced.

4.8 Conclusion

The questioning-attitude account displays a number of theoretically attractive features. These include, but are not limited to, the following:

1. It offers an explanation of why agnosticism-ascriptions take an interrogative complement. Agnosticism-ascriptions take an interrogative complement because agnosticism involves taking a sceptically questioning stance towards a proposition analogous to how believing involves taking an affirming stance towards a proposition and disbelieving involves taking a denying stance towards a proposition.
2. It offers a univocal account of the content of agnosticism, on the one hand, and judging and withholding judgement, on the other. Consequently, it preserves the idea that what one is agnostic about is always a candidate for withholding judging. On this score, it contrasts with the question-directed attitude account defended by Friedman, which implies that the content of the mental acts of judging and withholding judgement is a proposition while the content of agnosticism is a question. Since open-ended questions do not include the specification of a proposition that can be judged true or false, allowing for the possibility of agnosticism about open-ended questions for which one has no candidate answers implies that what we are agnostic about is not always a candidate for judging or withholding judgement.
3. It fleshes out the claim that agnosticism is a sui generis attitude by offering a positive account of what makes agnosticism distinct from believing and disbelieving. Given that agnosticism involves a questioning mental stance towards a proposition, while believing and

disbelieving involve an affirming and denying mental stance, respectively, the questioning-attitude account implies that it is impossible to reduce the former to the latter. Moreover, the questioning-attitude account explains why agnosticism may be rendered more or less epistemically justified/rational based on one's available evidence.

4. It satisfies all seven of the criteria for a satisfactory descriptive account of agnosticism identified in Chapter 2. Of the six widely discussed attitudinal accounts of agnosticism found in the literature, only the questioning-attitude account has this honour.

In light of the preceding theoretically attractive features, I believe that the questioning-attitude account should be considered a serious contender for the preferred account of agnosticism.

CHAPTER 5

Agnosticism and the Inquiring State of Mind

5.1 Introduction

In Chapter 4, I argued that agnosticism is best conceived of not as a question-directed attitude, but as a proposition-directed attitude to which one has a questioning mental stance. However, even if one rejects the claim that agnosticism is question-directed, one may still think it has a special relationship to inquiry. This is the central contention of Jane Friedman's paper, 'Why Suspend Judging?' Her answer to her paper's titular question is that we suspend judgement to inquire. In this chapter, I will examine her paper's central contention: the thesis that agnosticism about some question is both necessary and sufficient for inquiring into that question.[1] I will restrict my attention to inquiry into yes-or-no questions – that is, cases in which a subject is inquiring about whether **P**. This will allow us to sidestep the difficulties associated with holding that one may be agnostic towards open-ended questions highlighted in Chapter 4.

By Friedman's lights, inquiring into whether **P** does not require engaging in investigative activities like asking questions, looking up information online, or conducting experiments in a laboratory. Rather, inquiring into whether **P** involves possessing an attitude of openness and sensitivity to information that is relevant to answering whether **P**.[2] In sum, inquiry, for Friedman, is a 'frame of mind' rather than an activity.[3] In order to keep this aspect of Friedman's view in sharp focus, I will henceforth forego talk of *inquiring* about whether **P** in favour of talk of having an *inquiring state of mind* about whether **P**. In sum, a putative case of inquiry is genuine just in case it involves an inquiring state of mind.

---

[1] Friedman (2017a: 302).
[2] I will have more to say about how we should conceive of the openness implicated by inquiry in Section 5.4.1.
[3] Friedman (2017: 307).

Hence, this chapter will be concerned with the thesis that Michele Palmira calls (BICON):

(**BICON**): Necessarily: One is in an inquiring state of mind about some matter if, and only if, one is agnostic about that matter.[4]

(BICON) conjoins the following two theses:

Inquiry-Entails-Agnosticism: One is in an inquiring state of mind about some matter only if, one is agnostic about that matter.
Agnosticism-Entails-Inquiry: One is agnostic about some matter only if one is in an inquiring state mind about that matter.

In the discussion that follows, I will seek to impugn both the inquiry-entails-agnosticism and agnosticism-entails-inquiry theses. In so doing, I hope to drive a wedge between agnosticism towards **P** and being in an inquiring state of mind with respect to **P**. To be clear, I do not deny that agnosticism often facilitates an inquiring state of mind or that most subjects who have an inquiring state of mind are also agnostic. Rather, I wish to affirm that it is not only metaphysically possible to be agnostic towards **P** while failing to possess an inquiring state of mind about whether **P**, but also that it is rationally permissible to do so. Hence, insofar as agnosticism and an inquiring state of mind often go together, I take this to be normative in a numerical rather than prescriptive sense.

5.2 Defining Inquiry

According to Friedman, one has an inquiring state of mind about whether **P** just in case the question of whether **P** is on one's 'research agenda'.[5] Moreover, having whether **P** on one's research agenda entails that one has the aim of resolving whether **P**. Friedman puts the point as follows:

> In general we can say that we are in this sort of inquiring frame of mind with respect to Q when (and only when) Q is on our research agenda. I take it that our research agendas record our epistemic goals by way of the questions we wish to answer...*[I]n inquiring into some question – we aim to resolve or answer the question*—we aim to (e.g.) know the answer to the question. (*Italics* mine)[6]

Having the aim of answering some question is the only explicitly stated necessary condition Friedman offers in the above passage for being in an

---

[4] Palmira (2020: 4950). [5] Friedman (2017: 308).
[6] Friedman (2017: 308). See and compare: Olsson and Westlund (2006).

5.2 Defining Inquiry

inquiry state of mind. I believe that this modesty bolsters the plausibility of Friedman's proposal since it does not saddle her with a conception of inquiry that involves engaging in the kinds of activities we typically associate with inquiry. One may have the aim of gaining tenure within the next two years at a certain moment – in time even if one happens to be watching cute cat videos online at that moment – that is, doing something that in no way contributes to one's gaining tenure within the next two years. In other words, one may count as having the aim of achieving a certain end even if one is not currently engaged in an activity that would facilitate the achievement of that end. Hence, saying that someone has an inquiring state of mind towards whether string theory is true does not entail that they are currently conducting experiments, gathering data, and the like. This is why Friedman often prefers to speak of 'an inquiring frame of mind'[7] or of being in 'an inquiring mode'.[8] What she has in mind is a certain mental attitude and not merely a certain set of behaviours.

Friedman's conception of inquiry is also meant to exclude cases in which an agent is merely engaged in the behaviours typically associated with inquiry, but in which the aim of answering a certain question is lacking. Friedman illustrates the point using a comparison between a detective and a trash collector:

> Picking up items at a crime scene does not make it that one is inquiring into who committed the crime. Whether those actions count as part of an inquiry into who committed the crime depends in part upon the state of mind of the relevant subject. When the detective does these things in the relevant sorts of cases they count as part of her inquiry because they are done with the aim of figuring out who committed the crime. The trash collector who has no such aim or goal, is not inquiring into who committed the crime, even if he picks up all of the same items as the detective.[9]

In sum, Friedman holds that a subject qualifies as engaged in genuine inquiry only if they are in a certain state of mind; performing the kinds of information-gathering activities we typically associate with inquiry is not enough.

I agree with Friedman's identification of inquiry with being in an inquiry state of mind as opposed to the kinds of information-gathering activities typically associated with inquiry. However, I believe her characterisation of being in an inquiry state of mind in terms of having the aim of resolving whether **P** to be too narrow. This is because there are cases of

---

[7] Friedman (2017: 308).   [8] Friedman (2017: 302).   [9] Friedman (2017: 307).

genuine inquiry about whether **P** in which a subject already (justifiably) believes or knows whether **P**, or at least so I shall argue below. Instead of identifying an inquiring state of mind about whether **P** with the aim of resolving whether **P**, I hold that it should be identified with the aim of improving one's epistemic standing with respect to whether **P**.[10] However, in order to avoid begging the question against Friedman at the outset, I will for the time being remain non-committal with respect to the precise definition of what it means to be in an inquiry state of mind. Hopefully, the virtues of my account of inquiry as compared to that of Friedman will become apparent once we begin to examine putative cases of genuine inquiry.

5.3 The Inquiry-Entails-Agnosticism Thesis

Palmira concurs with Friedman's endorsement of the inquiry-entails-agnosticism thesis: 'I agree with the right-to-left side of (BICON): being suspended about a question is a doxastic hallmark of open inquiry'(2020: 4951). Here, Palmira appeals to the intuition that if a subject already believes or takes themselves to know the answer to some question, then they cannot be sincerely described as inquiring into that question. However, several theorists have expressed reservations about the thesis. One widely discussed objection to the inquiry-entails-agnosticism thesis comes from putative cases of rational double-checking.[11] For example, Arianna Falbo presents the following case, adapted from Jessica Brown (2008):

> **EXPERT SURGEON**: Fatima, an expert surgeon, is scheduled to perform an operation this afternoon. She has spent the morning carefully studying the patient's file and knows that it is the left kidney that needs to be removed. A few hours later, before the surgery, she thinks to herself: 'Okay, now I know it's the left kidney, but I'm going to double-check the patient's file one last time – just to be sure. After all, imagine how horrible it would be if I removed the wrong kidney.'[12]

Not all cases of double-checking would be deemed rational (e.g. consider the obsessive-compulsive agent who constantly checks and re-checks

---

[10] See Archer (2021) for a detailed defence of this claim.
[11] I follow Friedman in conceiving of double-checking as cases in which 'you are trying to confirm an answer you already think is right'(2019a: 3). Theorists who appeal to the double-checking objection include Millson (2021) and Falbo (2021).
[12] Falbo (2021: 625).

5.3 The Inquiry-Entails-Agnosticism Thesis

whether he left the stove on). However, Falbo observes that if we were Fatima's patient, we would want her to double-check that it was indeed the left kidney that needed to be removed. This suggests that Fatima's double-checking is rationally permissible, if not praiseworthy. Moreover, preserving the idea that Fatima is rational when she double-checks requires that we deny that she both believes and is agnostic about whether the left kidney is to be removed. Hence, EXPERT SURGEON appears to represent a case in which a subject is inquiring into whether **P** and in which they are not agnostic towards **P**. Call this the *double-checking objection*. Errol Lord echoes the assessment of EXPERT SURGEON implicated by the double-checking objection:

> I agree that there are cases where one rationally believes **P** and is rationally disposed to gather more information (think of a surgeon who rationally believes she needs to take out your liver).[13]

Friedman (2019a) attempts to defend the inquiry-entails-agnosticism thesis from the double-checking objection by claiming that in cases of rational double-checking, the subject shifts from a state of belief to a state of agnosticism at the point at which they begin to inquire. One way to unpack this suggestion would be to hold that while Fatima initially knows that it is the left kidney that is to be removed, due to the high cost of error, she opts to instrumentally suspend her belief so that she can confirm that this is indeed the case. Given that knowing **P** requires believing **P**, Fatima also temporarily loses her knowledge that it is the left kidney that needs to be removed while engaged in double-checking.

Falbo objects to this line of argument on the grounds that Fatima's expertise as a surgeon, along with her careful consideration of the patient's charts, ensures that she preserves her knowledge of which kidney is to be removed. Falbo puts the point as follows:

> Does Fatima no longer know that it is the left kidney when she double-checks the patient's file? This seems highly unlikely, given that she is an expert surgeon and that she had carefully studied the patient's file just a few hours earlier. We can assume that her memory on this issue is fresh, and that in the meantime she has not encountered any defeating evidence or reason to think otherwise. So she is plausibly interpreted as maintaining her knowledge when she seeks confirmation before the surgery.[14]

It is not obvious that Falbo's argument in the above passage successfully mollifies the force of Friedman's reply to the double-checking objection.

---

[13] Lord (2020: 137). [14] Falbo (2021: 626).

Falbo observes that Fatima has good reason to believe that it is the left kidney that is to be removed and that this evidence is sufficient to ground her knowledge that it is the left kidney. However, this argument overlooks that Friedman's argument is most charitably interpreted as advancing a psychological rather than normative conclusion. To wit, Friedman does not deny that Fatima has sufficient evidence to ground knowledge that it is the left kidney. Rather, she is claiming that the process of double-checking is one that, as a psychological matter, requires the suspension of belief for it to be successfully executed. This is the natural upshot of Friedman's commitment to inquiry-entails-agnosticism as a metaphysical thesis. Hence, whether Fatima has sufficient evidence to ground knowledge is ultimately irrelevant. Fatima stops knowing that it is the left kidney because she (temporarily) stops believing that it is the left kidney.

Furthermore, the defender of the inquiry-entails-agnosticism thesis appears to have a principled basis for holding that, as a psychological matter, Fatima stops believing it is the left kidney that is to be removed. Let us say that one believes **P** only if one has a sufficiently high level of confidence that **P** is true. This gives rise to the question of how much confidence in **P** is necessary for one to count as believing **P**? One plausible suggestion is that one qualifies as believing **P** only if (barring cases of irrationality and mental compartmentalisation) one is prepared to take **P** for granted in one's deliberation and action. Given this necessary condition for belief, the defender of the inquiry-entails-agnosticism thesis has a non-ad hoc basis for denying that Fatima believes that the left kidney is to be removed; namely she is unwilling to take it for granted at the point at which she engages in the double-checking. Admittedly, her suspension of belief appears to be both temporary and purely instrumental. She suspends belief so that she may double-check. Nevertheless, insofar as Fatima is not prepared to take it for granted that it is the left kidney, the defender of the inquiry-entails-agnosticism thesis has a principled basis for claiming that she does not believe that it is the left kidney.[15]

Whatever its merits, the above response to EXPERT SURGEON is ineffective as a response to putative cases of inquiry aimed at achieving certainty about something already known. For example, consider the following case:

---

[15] My aim, here, is not to endorse the preceding response on behalf of the defender of the inquiry-entails-agnosticism thesis, but to illustrate that they have rhetorical manoeuvres at their disposal for responding to the double-counting objection.

5.3 The Inquiry-Entails-Agnosticism Thesis

CERTAINTY SEEKER: Jeanie, a third-year philosophy undergrad, knows that other people have mental states like pain, anger, or beliefs. However, while Descartes' cogito argument is enough to render the existence of her own mind beyond doubt, at least as far as she is concerned, she is unaware of any arguments that are sufficient to render the existence of other minds beyond doubt. Jeanie is not content with merely knowing that other minds exist; she wants to have the same indubitable confidence that she has with respect to the existence of her own mind. To this end, she checks out several philosophy books on the topic from her school library in the hope that she will find some argument that would allow her to ratchet up her knowledge that other people have minds to the status of Cartesian indubitability.

Unlike Fatima, Jeanie is prepared to take it for granted that other people have mental states in both her deliberation and action. Her desire to inquire stems not from practical considerations, but from the entirely theoretical impulse to achieve Cartesian-like certainty about a certain proposition.

In addition to inquiry aimed at moving a subject from knowledge to certainty, there are also putative cases of inquiry aimed at moving a subject from (justified) belief to knowledge. Consider the following example, borrowed from my paper, 'The Aim of Inquiry':

EXTRATERRESTRIAL ENTHUSIAST: Myles believes that there is extraterrestrial life based on the following considerations: the five elements necessary for life also happen to be the most common in the universe, the vastness of the universe offers numerous opportunities for life to evolve, and earth is unexceptional when compared to the billions of other earth-like planets. However, while Myles takes these considerations to be enough to make his belief justified, he does not take it to be enough to ground knowledge. In order to have knowledge that there is extraterrestrial life, Myles believes he would either need to see direct evidence of extraterrestrial life (like fossils or actual life forms) or receive reliable testimony from someone who has observed such direct evidence. Since Myles has not received any reliable testimony on this point, when he is offered the opportunity to join a scientific expedition in search of direct evidence of extraterrestrial life, he jumps at the opportunity to acquire the kind of evidence that would elevate his (justified) belief to the status of knowledge.[16]

Myle's scientific expedition to find direct evidence of extraterrestrial life would qualify as genuine inquiry as the term is ordinarily understood. This remains true even though Myles already believes in the existence of extraterrestrial life. Moreover, Myles appears to have good reason to believe

---

[16] Archer (2021: 110).

in extraterrestrial life. However, it also seems reasonable for Myles to hold that his belief in extraterrestrial life would amount to knowledge only if he is able to secure more tangible evidence that such life exists. Given this fact, it also seems reasonable for Myles to seek such evidence. If this is right, then it is not only true that one may inquire about whether **P** even if one (justifiably) believes **P**, but also that one may be rational in so doing.

Significantly, the inquiring state of mind exhibited by both Jeanie and Myles is on par with that often exhibited by professional philosophers. On a wide range of questions – for example, do we know other people have minds? Is induction a source of knowledge? Is murder morally wrong? – we philosophers often find ourselves engaged in inquiry into questions for which we already believe or take ourselves to know the answer. We have an inquiring state of mind towards these questions because we wish to improve our epistemic standing with respect to them, and not because we fail to already believe or know the relevant answers. Hence, to deny that Jeanie and Myles possess an inquiring state of mind (and are consequently not engaged in genuine inquiry) would be to impugn a great deal of the inquiry that takes place within academic philosophy.

Insofar as both CERTAINTY SEEKER and EXTRATERRESTRIAL ENTHUSIAST describe genuine cases of inquiry, we cannot identify an inquiring state of mind with having the aim of answering a question. For example, if one were to ask Jeanie if other people have minds, we can imagine her confidently responding in the affirmative. That other people have minds is not merely something Jeanie takes herself to justifiably believe, it is also something she takes herself to know. Moreover, unlike Fatima, who is not prepared to perform the operation until she has double-checked that it is the left kidney that is to be removed, Jeanie is psychologically disposed to take it for granted that other people have minds in her deliberation and action. As such, Jeanie is not someone that can be accurately described as not already having the answer to the question of do other people have minds. Jeanie is most naturally described, not as seeking to answer the question of whether other people have minds, but as improving her epistemic standing with respect to the answer she already has.

What both the CERTAINTY SEEKER and EXTRATERRESTRIAL ENTHUSIAST examples have in common is that the subjects described seek to improve their epistemic standing regarding some matter. Myles aims to rachet up his (justified) belief in extraterrestrial life to knowledge and Jeanie aims to rachet up her knowledge that other people have minds to certainty. Hence, one of the lessons of the preceding examples is that having an inquiring state of mind should be more broadly understood as involving the aim of improving one's epistemic standing in some way, rather than narrowly understood as having the aim of answering or resolving a question.[17]

The main takeaway from our analysis of CERTAINTY SEEKER and EXTRATERRESTRIAL ENTHUSIAST is that one may have an inquiring state of mind about whether **P** even though one is not agnostic about whether **P**. Hence, the inquiry-entails-agnosticism thesis is false. Furthermore, since neither Jeanie nor Myles are guilty of irrationality for engaging in their respective inquiries, it follows that normative prohibitions against having an inquiring state of mind about something one knows or (justifiably) believes are misguided.[18]

5.4 The Agnosticism-Entails-Inquiry Thesis

While I reject both directions of (BICON), I take the agnosticism-entails-inquiry thesis to be of particular interest for two reasons. First, it challenges what many self-described agnostics would say about themselves. For example, there are many individuals who would describe themselves as agnostics about whether a god exists who would flatly deny that they have an inquiring state of mind towards the question of whether a god exists. (Indeed, I would class myself among such individuals.) If the agnosticism-entails-inquiry thesis proved correct, then all such individuals would either be conceptually confused or suffer from a gross lack of self-knowledge. Second, the agnosticism-entails-inquiry thesis, if correct, would fundamentally undermine the conception of agnosticism defended in this book. Specifically, it would impugn the claim that having one's competently considered evidence be insufficient to establish both the truth and falsity of **P** is a sufficient condition for the rational appropriateness of agnosticism towards **P**. This follows from the fact that one's competently considered evidence may be insufficient to establish both the truth and falsity of **P** and yet one fail to possess an inquiring state of mind with respect to **P**. Hence, if the agnosticism-entails-inquiry thesis turned out to be true, then the conception of agnosticism as fundamentally a doxastic response to one's competently considered evidence would be false.

---

[17] See and cf. Falbo (2021: 628–629).
[18] Theorists who endorse some version of the prohibition against inquiring into a question if one already believes a particular answer to said question include: Friedman (2019a, 2019b) and Kelp (2020, 2021).

Friedman's main theoretical motivation for holding the agnosticism-entails-inquiry thesis appears to be her desire to preserve the idea that the function or primary purpose of agnosticism is to facilitate inquiry. Indeed, the answer to the titular question of her paper, 'Why Suspend Judging?', is so that one may inquire. It is worth noting that holding to the agnosticism-entails-inquiry thesis is not a prerequisite for either holding that facilitating inquiry is one of the many roles that agnosticism may play (as I do hold) or that it is the primary function of agnosticism (as Friedman holds). It is a truism that something may have a function and yet fail to perform said function on a given occasion. Hence, holding that facilitating an inquiring state of mind is the primary function of agnosticism, at most, requires that we hold that agnosticism is infelicitous or somehow defective in cases in which it does not facilitate an inquiring state of mind. It does not require that we subscribe to the metaphysical impossibility of being agnostic towards **P** at *t* and failing to possess an inquiring state of mind about whether **P** at *t*. Thus, Friedman appears to burden herself with a stronger position than necessary if she merely wishes to preserve the idea that the function of agnosticism is to facilitate an inquiring state of mind.

Let us call the metaphysical claim that one is agnostic towards **P** at *t* only if one is in an inquiring state of mind about whether **P** at *t* the *descriptive thesis*, and the claim normative claim that one should be agnostic towards **P** only if one is in an inquiring state of mind about whether P at the *prescriptive thesis*. The remainder of this chapter will be devoted to refuting both the descriptive and prescriptive theses. First, I will describe a case that I believe represents a counterexample to both. I will then offer detailed arguments applying my counterexample to each, followed by replies to potential objections to each argument.

5.5 The Unanswerable Questions Objection

I believe the strongest counterexample to the agnosticism-entails-inquiry thesis comes from cases in which one is agnostic towards **P** and one (justifiably) believes the question of whether **P** to be unanswerable. Sometimes, we may discover that only a certain kind of evidence relevant to whether **P** is unattainable. For example, Kurt Gödel's incompleteness theorem, which proves that within any mathematical framework there will be true statements that you cannot prove are true within that framework, is an example in which we know that a certain specific kind of evidence is unattainable. However, Gödel's theorem still leaves it open that other kinds of evidence (i.e. evidence from outside the mathematical framework

5.5 The Unanswerable Questions Objection

in question) are attainable. Hence, this is not yet an instance in which we know or believe that we will never acquire sufficient information to answer a certain question.

The kind of cases that interest us at present are ones in which investigation reveals that there could never be sufficient information to answer a question, *tout court*. Consider the following yes-or-no question:

Q1: *Is there a double-ringed galaxy containing exactly 129 thousand million stars located exactly 1.3 billion light years outside of our Hubble sphere?*

According to our currently leading cosmological theories, *Q1* is unanswerable. Firstly, *Q1* is a question about an astronomical object that exists outside of our Hubble sphere. A Hubble sphere is the spherical region surrounding an observer (with a radius of roughly 14.4 billion light years) beyond which objects recede from the observer at a rate greater than the speed of light due to the expansion of the universe. Because the speed of light constitutes the upper limit by which any information can be transmitted, no information leaving an object that exists outside of our Hubble sphere – that is, an object receding away from us at a rate greater than the speed of light – could, in principle, ever reach us. This means that any object or event occurring outside our Hubble sphere is unobservable. Second, the subject matter of *Q1* is so specific that the question could only be answered by observing the region of space that the question is about. By way of comparison, if the question were simply 'are there hydrogen atoms beyond our Hubble sphere?', then, given the assumption that the unobservable universe is similar to the observable universe (which I would regard as a perfectly reasonable assumption to make) and the fact that hydrogen is the most common element in the observable universe, it is arguable that we could reasonably give a positive answer to this question despite our inability to ever observe said hydrogen atoms. However, *Q1* is not a general question of this kind. A double-ringed galaxy is the rarest type of galaxy ever observed. Hence, even if we assume that the unobservable universe is similar to the observable universe, we would not be warranted in assuming that there is such a galaxy in a particular unobserved region of space in the way that we would be warranted in assuming that there are hydrogen atoms in a particular unobserved region of space. Moreover, there is a great deal of variation in how many stars a galaxy may contain. Hence, that there is a galaxy with exactly 129 thousand million stars in a particular region of space is too specific a claim to be adjudicated without observation of that region of space. Finally, while being exactly 1.3 billion light years outside of our Hubble sphere is a very specific region of space, it is also an expansive enough region of space that the existence of a double-ringed galaxy with exactly 129 thousand million stars could not be reasonably assumed not to exist sans observational confirmation. Given these facts, we can neither justifiably affirm nor deny that a double-ringed galaxy with exactly 129 thousand million stars exists exactly 1.3 billion light years beyond our Hubble sphere. With these points in mind, here is a description of the case that will form the focal point of my argument against both the descriptive and prescriptive theses:

> AGNOSTIC ASTRONOMER: At time t_1, a young amateur astronomer, Jocelyn, begins inquiring into $Q1$: Is there a double-ringed galaxy containing exactly 129 thousand million stars located exactly 1.3 billion light years beyond our Hubble sphere? At the beginning of her investigation, Jocelyn recognizes that she currently lacks sufficient information to answer $Q1$. This recognition prompts Jocelyn to adopt an attitude of committed neutrality towards $Q1$ at t_1. At t_2, following a brief period of research into the matter, Jocelyn forms the justified belief that it is impossible to acquire the kind of specific information necessary to answer $Q1$ given that doing so would require observing a region of space that it is, in principle, impossible to observe. In other words, Jocelyn comes to justifiably believe that $Q1$ is, in principle, unanswerable. Furthermore, this belief prompts Jocelyn to do two things at t_2: First, it prompts her to resign herself to an attitude of committed neutrality with respect to $Q1$. Given her belief that not only is her currently available information insufficient for answering $Q1$, but also that she will never acquire sufficient information to answer $Q1$, Jocelyn judges that it would be best to maintain an attitude of committed neutrality towards $Q1$ and chooses to do so. Second, it prompts her to intentionally give up the aim of answering $Q1$. Given that she now believes it would be pointless to try to answer $Q1$, Jocelyn judges that it would be best to give up her aim of answering $Q1$ and chooses to do so.

In AGNOSTIC ASTRONOMER, Jocelyn is described as choosing to refrain from having an inquiring state of mind towards $Q1$. It may be protested that having an inquiring state of mind towards a certain question is not something one chooses or intentionally adopts. For example, it is seldom the case that we decide to be curious about a certain question; we are either curious about whether **P** or we are not. It may therefore be argued that AGNOSTIC ASTRONOMER describes an implausible scenario since it describes a fundamentally non-intentional process – that is, adopting an inquiring state of mind towards whether **P** – **as** if it were intentional. While I am inclined to agree that in many instances the adoption of an inquiring state of mind towards some question is an unintentional process, I also believe it is a process that may be brought under a subject's intentional control should they choose to do so. For comparison, breathing is not ordinarily something we intentionally control. However, we still have the power to bring our breathing under our intentional control should we choose to do so. Likewise, while it may be true that adopting an inquiring state of mind towards a certain question is not something we typically do intentionally, it may still be true that we could either intentionally adopt an inquiring state of mind towards a question or intentionally refrain from doing so.

This is an important point to stress since it underscores a potential cost of the agnosticism-entails-inquiry thesis; namely it requires that we deny that epistemic agents are free to choose to refrain from adopting or maintaining the aim of answering a question that they have an attitude of committed neutrality toward. Not only does such a restriction on our agency seem ad hoc, but it is also at odds with what some of us are prepared to say about ourselves. For example, many strong agnostics about the existence of God see themselves as intentionally refraining from adopting or maintaining an inquiring state of mind towards whether God exists. Often, this decision is motivated by various ideological considerations. For example, a strong agnostic about whether there is a god may view a concern with the god-question as historically having had a net negative effect on human social and moral progress. This belief may make such an individual determined to refrain from adopting an inquiring state of mind towards it. Even if we regard such ideological motivations as misplaced, it seems like we should wish to make room for the psychological possibility, if not the rational permissibility, of such subjects. Hence, given that the agnosticism-entails-inquiry thesis imposes an ad hoc restriction on human agency by implying that it is impossible for a subject who is agnostic towards **P** to choose to refrain from adopting or maintaining an inquiring state of mind about whether **P**, the plausibility of the agnosticism-entails-inquiry thesis will partly hinge on whether we think human agency is restricted in this way.

5.6 My Argument against the Descriptive Thesis

With the example of the AGNOSTIC ASTRONOMER now on the table, here is my argument against the descriptive thesis:

P1. If it is plausible that Jocelyn does not have the aim of answering Q_I at t_2 and it is plausible that Jocelyn has an attitude of committed neutrality towards Q_I at t_2, then the agnosticism-entails-inquiry thesis is implausible.

P2. It is plausible that Jocelyn does not have the aim of answering Q_I at t_2.
P3. It is plausible that Jocelyn has an attitude of committed neutrality towards Q_I at t_2.
C. The agnosticism-entails-inquiry thesis is implausible.

Let us review each of the above premises in detail.

First, given that the agnosticism-entails-inquiry thesis precludes the existence of the sort of subject described in AGNOSTIC ASTRONOMER, then to the extent that it is plausible that agents like the one described in AGNOSTIC ASTRONOMER exist, to that very extent the agnosticism-entails-inquiry thesis is implausible. Recall, according to the agnosticism-entails-inquiry thesis, a subject is agnostic towards **P** at some time, t, only if they have an inquiring state of mind towards whether **P** at t. However, AGNOSTIC ASTRONOMER describes a subject, Jocelyn, who is agnostic (i.e. has an attitude of committed neutrality) towards Q_I at t_2, but who does not have an inquiring state of mind towards (i.e. the aim of answering) Q_I at t_2. Hence, we arrive at premise P1.

Second, there is no good reason to think that Jocelyn would be incapable of giving up her aim of answering Q_I once she comes to believe that it is unanswerable. On the contrary, given what we know about human nature, it is common for individuals to give up on endeavours they believe to be pointless. Moreover, we can easily imagine that having become convinced that Q_I is unanswerable, Jocelyn may come to see having the aim of answering Q_I as pointless and that this may prompt her to abandon said aim. To be clear, I do not wish to claim that a subject would necessarily view it as pointless to have the aim of answering a question they believe to be unanswerable. Nor do I deny that it is possible for a subject to continue to have the aim of answering a question after coming to believe that it is unanswerable. We often aspire to achieve aims we believe to be unattainable. I only claim that there are plausibly cases in which the opposite response obtains – that is, cases in which a subject's belief that a certain question is unanswerable is sufficient to motivate her to give up her aim of answering said question. Since, *ex hypothesi*, AGNOSTIC ASTRONOMER is just such a case, we arrive at premise P2.

Third, there is no good reason to think that Jocelyn would be incapable of having an attitude of committed neutrality towards Q_I at t_2. She is first moved (at time t_1) to adopt an attitude of committed neutrality towards Q_I because she believes that her currently available evidence is insufficient to settle the matter. Later (at time t_2) she acquires the belief that she will never gain sufficient information to answer *Q1*. But notice, at time t_2, Jocelyn's original motivation for adopting an attitude of committed neutrality remains the same – that is, it continues to be true that she believes that her available evidence is insufficient to answer *Q1*. Hence, if the belief was enough to move her to adopt the attitude of committed neutrality at t_1, then it should also be sufficient to move her to continue to do so at t_2. After all, the only change that has taken place between t_1 and t_2 is that, in addition to believing that her available evidence is insufficient for answering *Q1*, she also believes that she will never acquire sufficient information to answer *Q1* in the future. But I see no reason to assume that this additional belief would, of necessity, cause Jocelyn to give up her attitude of committed neutrality. On the contrary, we would expect that the belief that she will never have sufficient information to answer *Q1* would increase rather than decrease Jocelyn's overall motivation to maintain an attitude of committed neutrality towards *Q1*. If this is right, then we seem to be on firm ground in accepting P3. Hence, we may safely conclude that the agnosticism-entails-inquiry thesis is implausible.

5.6.1 An Objection and Reply

The defender of the descriptive thesis may attempt to forestall counterexamples like AGNOSTIC ASTRONOMER by claiming that being agnostic towards **P** requires a level of interest in whether **P** that is incompatible with not being in an inquiring state of mind about whether **P**. Friedman puts the point as follows:

> I think that the general difficulty is this: the sorts of cases in which it seems clearest that the subject is not in an inquiring mode with respect to [whether **P**] are ones in which the subject has absolutely no interest in [whether **P**] or resolving [whether **P**] at all. And the problem is that once we start to describe these sorts of circumstances we also start to describe circumstances in which it seems implausible that the subject has any sort of attitude towards [whether **P**]. We simply do not tend to have attitudes towards contents that we do not care about in the least.[19]

The above passage invokes the idea that a subject must be sufficiently interested in some question in order to have 'any sort of attitude towards' that question. However, it is important to distinguish between two senses of being interested in a question: the *answer-seeking sense* and the *attention-*

---

[19] Friedman (2017: 320).

holding sense. Being interested in a question in the answer-seeking sense entails being motivated to answer the question, having the question on one's research agenda, or being on the lookout for information that may bring one closer to answering the question. Being interested in a question in the attention-holding sense entails that the question holds one's attention in a manner that is sufficient for one to adopt various attitudes towards it. Significantly, it is possible to be interested in a question in the attention-holding sense without being interested in it in the answer-seeking sense. For example, suppose I am presented with the following question:

Q2:   *Was 'Xanthippe' the name of Socrates' wife?*

However, falsely believing that Socrates was unmarried, I erroneously assume that the question is infelicitous because it rests on a false presupposition. Insofar as I have the belief that Q2 is infelicitous, it follows that Q2 holds my attention in the way required for me to have some sort of attitude toward it. However, insofar as I believe Q2 to be infelicitous, I may be entirely unmotivated to have the aim of answering Q2. Of course, given that I believe Q2 is infelicitous, I would not be agnostic about Q2 either. Hence, I do not take the present case to be a counterexample to the agnosticism-entails-inquiry thesis. What the present case illustrates is that it is possible for a question to hold one's interest in the attention-holding sense without being interested in said question in the answer-seeking sense. This means that if we are concerned with which of the two kinds of interest in whether **P** is necessary for having 'any sort of attitude towards' whether **P**, then the relevant notion of interest in whether **P** should be the attention-holding rather than the answer-seeking sense. In sum, being interested in whether **P** in the answer-seeking sense is not necessary for having 'any sort of attitude towards' whether **P**.

If we understand the just-cited passage as referring to being interest in a question in the attention-holding sense, then we may see Friedman as claiming that for a subject to be agnostic towards **P**, whether **P** must hold that subject's attention (i.e. be of interest to the subject) in the manner required for that subject to have any sort of attitude towards whether **P** whatsoever. Moreover, it is plausible that if whether **P** holds a subject's attention in the manner necessary for being agnostic towards **P**, then the question also holds that subject's attention in the manner necessary for having an inquiring state of mind towards it. Being agnostic towards **P** and having an inquiring state of mind towards whether **P** seem to be equally demanding as far as a subject's level of interest in the question of whether

5.6 My Argument Against the Descriptive Thesis 99

P is concerned. On the present view, if whether **P** does not hold a subject's attention enough for them to have an inquiring state of mind towards it, then it does not hold that subject's attention enough for them to be agnostic towards **P**.

I am willing to grant all the immediately preceding points. However, saying that whether **P** holds a subject's attention in the manner necessary for having any attitude towards whether **P** falls short of saying that whether **P** holds a subject's attention in a way that is sufficient for them to have some specific attitude. This is because the attitudes a subject has at a given time is not merely a function of which attitudes they are in a position to have (i.e. given their level of interest in the attention-holding sense). It is also dependent on a subject's overall motivational state at the time. In sum, when attempting to ascertain what attitudes a subject is likely to have at a given time, we must consider that subject's motivational makeup at that time.

Consider the following analogy from the case of intention. Suppose that the question of whether I should eat some vegemite is one that has never occurred to me. Given this fact, it would be accurate to say that I do not have the intention to eat vegemite. However, by that very same token, it would also be accurate to say that I do not have the intention not to eat vegemite. The question of whether I should eat vegemite is simply not one that has held my attention in the way required for me to have either intention. But suppose I am offered some vegemite while visiting a friend in Melbourne. Now that the question sufficiently has my attention, I may decide to either eat some or refrain from doing so. Which of the two intentions I adopt will depend on certain facts about my motivational state at the time. Do I desire to try something novel? Am I especially disgusted by yeast-based foods? Am I afraid of offending my host by turning down their offer to try a local delicacy? But notice, whichever intention I adopt, it would have been true that the question of whether to eat vegemite holds my attention in a manner necessary for me to adopt some sort of attitude towards it, including the attitudes of intending to eat it or intending not to eat it. This follows from the fact that I am free to adopt either intention. It is in this sense that having a question hold one's attention in the manner required for having any sort of attitude towards it falls short of one having some specific attitude towards it. The practical question of whether to eat vegemite may hold my attention in the manner required for me to adopt the attitude of intending to eat it and yet I may choose not to eat any (based on my overall motivational state at the time). Likewise, a theoretical question, like Q_1, may hold my attention in the manner required for me to adopt the aim of answering it, and yet I may choose to refrain from adopting the aim of answering it (based on my overall motivational state at the time).

Ex hypothesi, this is the kind of situation Jocelyn is in. At time t_2, *Q1* does hold Jocelyn's attention in the manner required for her to have some sort of attitude towards it. Moreover, we may also assume that *Q1* holds her attention in the manner necessary for her to have an inquiring state of mind towards it. However, this does not settle the question of whether Jocelyn has an inquiring state of mind towards *Q1*. Whether she does will depend on facts about her overall motivational state at the time. Moreover, the facts about Jocelyn's overall motivational state at the time are these: (i) she believes that her evidence warrants agnosticism towards *Q1* and she is motivated to adopt the doxastic attitude that is warranted by her evidence and (ii) she believes that since *Q1* is unanswerable, it would be pointless to have the aim of answering *Q1*, and she is motivated to avoid having attitudes she deems to be pointless.[20] Notice that so characterised, it is false that Jocelyn has absolutely no interest in *Q1*. On the contrary, we may suppose that *Q1* continues to hold her attention in the manner necessary for her to both suspend *Q1* and have an inquiring state of mind towards *Q1*. However, once we register that which attitudes a subject adopts will largely depend on her overall motivational state at the time, it becomes clear how it might be possible for a subject to be agnostic towards **P** at some time, *t*, without having an inquiring state of mind towards whether **P** at *t*. If a subject is motivated to have an attitude of agnosticism towards whether **P** (e.g. she believes that doing so is warranted by her available evidence), but is also motivated to give up her aim of answering whether **P** (e.g. because she believes it would be pointless to have such an aim given that whether **P** is unanswerable), then her overall motivational state may be such that she is motivated to be agnostic towards **P** at *t* and to refrain from having an inquiring state of mind towards whether **P** at *t*.

To sum up, I agree with Friedman's observation that most of the cases in which a subject lacks an inquiring state of mind towards whether **P**, the subject may also be said to have no interest in whether **P**. The questions that interest us constitute only a small subset of all possible questions and the set of questions that are absolutely of no interest to us is primarily

---

[20] It is worth emphasising that it is not being claimed that Jocelyn must necessarily feel this way, or that any subject in Jocelyn's position would feel this way. Nor does this argument assume that Jocelyn is right to feel this way (though my secondary argument will explore this possibility). All that is being claimed is that it is plausibly possible for Jocelyn to feel this way.

(if not entirely) constituted by questions we neither have an inquiring state of mind towards nor are agnostic about. However, *Q1* is not such a question for Jocelyn. *Q1* does hold Jocelyn's attention in the manner necessary for her to adopt attitudes towards it. However, because of her overall motivational state, the attitude she chooses to have towards *Q1* is that of refraining from having the aim of answering it. Another way this point may be put is to say that having the aim of answering a question is not the sole manifestation of its holding one's attention. Insofar as deciding to give up the aim of answering a question is possible only if the question holds one's attention in the manner necessary for having any sort of attitude towards it, then deciding to give up the aim of answering a question may itself be a manifestation of the relevant kind of interest in it (i.e. interest in the attention-holding sense). On the present suggestion, deciding to refrain from inquiring into a question is as much a stance towards it as is deciding to inquire into it. Both decisions require that we be interested in the question enough to adopt some sort of attitude towards it.

5.7 My Argument against the Normative Thesis

As far as I can tell, Friedman never claims that it is rationally inappropriate for a subject to be agnostic towards **P** at *t* and not have an inquiring state of mind about whether **P** at *t*. Indeed, since the agnosticism-entails-inquiry thesis regards such cases as metaphysically impossible, the question of whether it is rationally appropriate arguably never arises on Friedman's account. Nevertheless, having dispensed with the descriptive thesis, it is worth considering whether the weaker prescriptive claim has any merit. Predictably, I shall argue that it does not. I take as my point of departure the intuition that it is always rationally permissible to be agnostic towards **P** if one knows or justifiably believes that one's available evidence is insufficient for answering whether **P**. Hence, I am committed to the following epistemic norm:

> **The Agnosticism Permissibility Norm**
> If at some time, *t*, one knows or justifiably believes that one's available evidence is insufficient for answering whether **P**, then it is rationally permissible to be agnostic towards **P** at *t*.

As we noted in Section 5.6, if we are to make room for the freedom of subjects to decide not to inquire into questions they deem unworthy of inquiry (as might be the case in at least some instances in which a subject believed a question to be unanswerable), then our account of agnosticism cannot preclude the possibility of an agnostic subject deciding to refrain from inquiring into what they are agnostic about. Taking this idea one step further, I hold that it is always our epistemic prerogative to refrain from having an inquiring state of mind towards a question we know or justifiably believe to be unanswerable. There is no need for us to first give up our attitude of committed neutrality towards the question. Hence, I am also committed to the following epistemic norm:

> **The Optional Inquiry Norm**
> If at some time, t, one knows or justifiably believes that whether **P** is unanswerable, then it is rationally permissible for one to refrain from adopting or maintaining an inquiring state of mind towards whether **P** at t.

It is worth emphasising that the Optional Inquiry Norm is consistent with the claim that it is rationally permissible to adopt an inquiring state of mind towards a question one deems to be unanswerable. The modest nature of the Optional Inquiry Norm reflects my wish to leave room for the rational permissibility of a subject being curious about whether **P** even if they regard whether **P** as unanswerable. I only claim that in the case of questions that are known or justifiably believed to be unanswerable, such curiosity (or any other inquiring state of mind) is not rationally required.

With the above pair of modest principles now on the table, here is my argument against the prescriptive thesis:

1. If at some time, t, one knows or justifiably believes that one's available evidence is insufficient for answering whether **P**, then it is rationally permissible to suspend whether **P** at t. (Suspension Permissibility Norm)
2. If at some time, t, one knows or justifiably believes that whether **P** is unanswerable, then it is rationally permissible for one to refrain from taking an inquiring state of mind towards whether **P** at t. (Optional Inquiry Norm)
3. At t_2, Jocelyn justifiably believes that her available evidence is insufficient for answering Q_1 and justifiably believes that Q_1 is unanswerable. (AGNOSTIC ASTRONOMER)
4. It is rationally permissible for Jocelyn to be agnostic about Q_1 at t_2. (from 1 and 3)
5. It is rationally permissible for Jocelyn not to take an inquiring state of mind towards Q_1 at t_2. (from 2 and 3)
6. It is rationally permissible for Jocelyn to be agnostic about Q_1 at t_2 and for her to refrain from taking an inquiring state of mind towards Q_1 at t_2. (from 4 and 5)

5.7 My Argument Against the Normative Thesis

Generalising from the case of Jocelyn, I conclude that there are cases in which it is rationally permissible for a subject to be agnostic towards **P** at t and for that subject to refrain from having an inquiring state of mind towards whether **P** at t. Embracing this conclusion allows us to preserve two desiderata that the agnosticism-entails-inquiry thesis calls into jeopardy: (i) the truthfulness of the self-reports of the strong agnostic about the existence of God who insists that she does not have the aim of answering the question 'Does God exist?', and (ii) the rational permissibility of her choice to refrain from having the aim of answering the question 'Does God exist?' given her agnostic stance.

5.7.1 An Objection and Reply

It may be objected that even if one justifiably believes that a certain question is unanswerable, being a rationally virtuous subject requires that one remain open to the possibility that one may be mistaken. On the present suggestion, even if Jocelyn justifiably believes that she will never gain sufficient evidence to answer Q_I, she should still be open to the possibility that she may be proven wrong by receiving evidence that decisively answers Q_I. Failing to remain open in this way would be a recipe for dogmatism since it would mean that once one has formed the opinion that a question is unanswerable, one would close oneself off to having one's mind changed, even in cases in which one happens to be mistaken. Moreover, if we assume that being open to the possibility of receiving additional information bearing on a certain question is sufficient for having an inquiring state of mind towards that question, then being a rationally virtuous subject may require Jocelyn to have an inquiring state of mind towards Q_I even if she justifiably believes it to be unanswerable. Call the preceding objection to my argument against the prescriptive thesis the *Epistemic Humility Objection*.

A potential problem with the Epistemic Humility Objection is that it appears to trade on an ambiguity in what it means to be open to the possibility of receiving additional information bearing on a certain question. Specifically, we may distinguish between what I shall call *humility-inspired openness* and *goal-inspired openness*. The notion of epistemic humility currently at play is one rooted in a recognition of our own fallibility. Given our knowledge of our own fallibility, we should generally be open to the possibility that a given belief of ours is false, and this includes the belief that a certain question is unanswerable. This is what I call humility-inspired openness. I maintain that humility-inspired openness should be displayed in relation to most (if not all) of our empirical beliefs. For example, suppose that I believe that all life on earth has a common ancestor. It follows that for me, the following yes-or-no question is settled:

Q3: *Does all life on earth have a common ancestor?*

However, insofar as I am displaying the virtue of epistemic humility, I should still be open to the possibility that I may encounter decisive evidence against a universal common ancestor. For example, if I were to come across a *New York Times* article with the headline: 'Discovery of New Marine Organism Disproves Theory of a Universal Common Ancestor', it would be inappropriate for me to simply disregard the article on the grounds that I already believed in a universal common ancestor and the article purports to supply evidence incompatible with what I believe. On the contrary, one would expect me to be quite keen to survey the evidence against a universal common ancestor so that I may update my beliefs if necessary.

On the present suggestion, even if a question is settled for me in the sense that I believe a particular answer to it, insofar as I display the virtue of epistemic humility, there is a sense in which I should be open to the possibility of acquiring evidence that is incompatible with what I believe. Being open in the sense at hand does not entail the expectation that one would acquire evidence that is incompatible with what one believes. On the contrary, if I already believe a certain answer to a question, then I should not expect to acquire decisive evidence that is incompatible with what I believe. Being open in the sense at hand entails that if I were presented with the opportunity to acquire such evidence (e.g. as when I encounter the *New York Times* article purporting to provide decisive evidence incompatible with what I believe) I would be disposed to examine rather than ignore or disregard such evidence.

I take the above point to be no less true of a subject who believes that a certain question is unanswerable. Given that Jocelyn believes $Q1$ to be unanswerable, she believes she will never receive sufficient information to answer $Q1$. However, insofar as Jocelyn displays the virtue of epistemic humility, she should also be open to receiving evidence that is incompatible with her belief that $Q1$ is unanswerable (i.e. evidence that decisively answers $Q1$). For example, if she were to encounter a *New York Times* article claiming that, contrary to the leading cosmological theories, it has newly been established that we can acquire information about galaxies existing billions of light years outside our Hubble Sphere, we would expect Jocelyn to be keen to read said article, and may be disappointed in her (from an epistemic point of view) if she was not so keen. There is therefore a sense in which I am willing to grant that a subject should always be open to receiving information bearing on a certain question.

The salient question is whether humility-inspired openness is sufficient for having an inquiring state of mind towards whether **P**? My response is that it had better not be. Why? Because if humility-inspired openness were sufficient for having an inquiring state of mind towards whether **P**, then it would follow that every subject who believed some particular answer to whether **P** with the requisite amount of epistemic humility would also have an inquiring state of mind towards whether **P**. It would follow that it is rationally appropriate (even required) to have an inquiring state of mind towards whether **P** even in cases in which the question is settled for one. However, this is something Friedman flatly denies. Hence, the kind of openness to evidence that is a sufficient condition for having an inquiring state of mind cannot, by Friedman's lights, be humility-inspired openness.

A second kind of openness to receiving new evidence bearing on a question is that which arises from the desire or intention to answer or improve one's epistemic standing with respect to that question. This is what I call goal-inspired openness. Goal-inspired openness to receiving evidence bearing on whether **P** is sufficient for having the aim of answering whether **P**. As such, it represents a kind of openness to receiving evidence that is sufficient for having an inquiring state of mind. The question that now confronts us is whether Jocelyn is rationally required to display goal-inspired openness with respect to $Q1$? Saying that she is would imply that a subject is rationally required to have the goal of answering a question they know or justifiably believe to be unanswerable. This strikes me as a rather bizarre epistemic requirement. Perhaps it may be rationally permissible to have the goal of answering a question one knows or justifiably believes to be unanswerable. But to hold that one is rationally obligated to do so seems like a step too far. If this is right, then Jocelyn is not required to display goal-inspired openness towards $Q1$. At best, she is required to display humility-inspired openness towards $Q1$. However, since displaying humility-inspired openness is not sufficient for having an inquiring state of mind, saying that Jocelyn is rationally required to display humility-inspired openness towards $Q1$ is consistent with my claim that it is rationally permissible for her to refrain from adopting or maintaining an inquiring state of mind towards $Q1$.

5.8 Conclusion

In this chapter, I have mounted a sustained argument against (BICON). The central takeaway from the preceding discussion is that we can only make room for cases like CERTAINTY SEEKER if we reject the inquiry-entails-agnosticism thesis and we can only make room for cases like AGNOSTIC ASTRONOMER if we reject the agnosticism-entails-inquiry thesis. My argument against the inquiry-entails-agnosticism thesis also impugns the claim that one is engage in genuine inquiry about whether **P** only if one has the aim of resolving whether **P**. Insofar as one may consistently inquire about something one already believes or knows, it follows that one may inquire about whether **P** even if one does not have the aim of resolving whether **P**. In lieu of having the aim of resolving whether **P**, I propose that what is necessary for genuine inquiry about whether **P** is the aim of improving one's epistemic standing regarding whether **P**.

My argument against the agnosticism-entails-inquiry thesis is consistent with the observation that in many (or even most) instances, agnosticism is a precursor to inquiry. However, it is my contention that agnosticism is fundamentally a *response* to our competently considered evidence. This point becomes clearest in the case of questions we justifiably believe to be unanswerable. In such cases, it is still possible and rationally permissible to adopt an attitude of committed neutrality towards the question at hand. However, given that one justifiably believes a question to be unanswerable, it is also rationally permissible to decide to refrain from having an inquiring state of mind towards that question. It should come as little surprise that I view the case of unanswerable questions as merely a way to get my foot in the door. Ultimately, I wish to extend my claim that one may be agnostic towards **P** even if one lacks an inquiring state of mind about whether **P** to cases in which one does not regard whether **P** to be unanswerable. Indeed, the considerations offered against the agnosticism-entails-inquiry thesis in Section 5.6.1 apply with equal force to instances when one is motivated to refrain from answering (or improving one's epistemic standing with respect to) a question one deems answerable. Merely finding the question of whether **P** boring may be enough to justify refraining from adopting an inquiring state of mind towards it, even if one's competently considered evidence makes agnosticism towards **P** rationally appropriate.

I conclude that facilitating inquiry is not the raison d'être of agnosticism. What all instances of agnosticism have in common is not their connection to inquiry but the fact that they are rationally appropriate just in case one's competently considered evidence is insufficient to establish both the truth and falsity of a proposition. Why be agnostic? Because our competently considered evidence rationally recommends doing so.

CHAPTER 6

The Act-Attitude Account of Doxastic Neutrality

6.1 Introduction

In this chapter, I will be defending a bipartite account of doxastic neutrality, which distinguishes between the mental act of withholding judgement and the doxastic attitude of agnosticism. Roughly, I hold that withholding judgement stands to agnosticism as judging stands to belief. This analogy is significant in at least three important respects. First, just as judging and believing are metaphysically distinct, because the former is a mental act while the latter is a mental attitude[1], I hold that withholding judgement and agnosticism are metaphysically distinct due to the fact that withholding judgement is a mental act while agnosticism is a mental attitude. Second, just as judging **P** is the mental act that (following a period of deliberation about whether **P**) typically puts one in the mental state of believing **P**, withholding judgement is the mental act that (following a period of deliberation about whether **P**) typically puts one in the mental state of agnosticism towards **P**. Third, just as one's competently considered evidence makes judging **P** rationally appropriate in the same circumstances that makes believing **P** rationally appropriate, one's competently considered evidence makes withholding judgement with respect to **P** rationally appropriate in exactly the same circumstances that makes agnosticism towards **P** rationally appropriate. In sum, I hold that withholding judgement and agnosticism share the same normative profile. Call the account of doxastic neutrality just sketched the *act-attitude account*. In this chapter, I offer a defence of the act-attitude account, using the analysis of neutrality offered by Matthew McGrath (2021) as a foil.

---

[1] See and cf. Shah and Velleman (2005: 503).

6.2 McGrath's Tripartite Account of Neutrality

The act-attitude account represents an alternative to the account of neutrality offered by McGrath, who has advanced the thesis that there are three distinct mental phenomenon that represent ways of being neutral: agnosticism, refraining from judgement, and suspension of judgement. Call McGrath's view the *tripartite account of neutrality* (henceforth, *TAN*). I shall argue that TAN should be rejected since suspension of judgement, as conceived of by McGrath, is not a distinct way of being neutral, on par with agnosticism and refraining from judgement. This turns out to be noteworthy since TAN features as an important step in McGrath's defence of his paper's second contention: namely that while only epistemic factors can be reasons to be agnostic, there may be non-epistemic (e.g. pragmatic) reasons to refrain or suspend judgement. This allows McGrath to preserve the traditional view that only epistemic considerations can be reasons in favour of the three doxastic attitudes of believing, disbelieving, and agnosticism, while leaving room for a limited anti-evidentialism with respect to two of the three ways of being neutral.

McGrath defines the three distinct ways of being neutral that feature in TAN as follows:

1. **Agnosticism** = ^{def} Having an intermediate state of confidence concerning whether **P** (i.e. not strong enough for belief that **P** nor low enough for disbelief that **P**).[2]
2. **Refraining from judgement** = ^{def} To intentionally omit belief-forming judgement on some question.
3. **Suspending judgement** = ^{def} To put off belief-forming judgement because one aims to have it later (and not before) or when and only when certain conditions obtain.

By McGrath's lights, both refraining from judgement (henceforth, *refraining*) and suspension of judgement (henceforth, *suspension*) are distinct mental phenomenon from the neutral doxastic attitude of agnosticism.

McGrath employs TAN to defend what he calls 'traditionalism'. Traditionalism combines the following two claims: (i) in addition to belief and disbelief, there is a third, neutral, doxastic attitude and (ii) the only thing relevant to determining which doxastic attitude one adopts are considerations that help 'fix the strength of your epistemic position with respect to whether **P**'.[3] However, his defence of traditionalism still allows

---

[2] McGrath (2021: 471). [3] McGrath (2021: 464).

6.2 McGrath's Tripartite Account of Neutrality

for a limited anti-evidentialism. This is because, by McGrath's lights, non-epistemic factors may determine whether one should be neutral. However, while McGrath is committed to there being non-epistemic reasons to refrain from judgement or suspend judgement, he denies that there may be non-epistemic reasons to be agnostic. Since, of the three ways of being neutral implicated by TAN, only agnosticism qualifies as a doxastic attitude, McGrath's limited anti-evidentialism remains consistent with traditionalism.

McGrath motivates his limited anti-evidentialism with a pair of examples. The first is one borrowed from Mark Schroeder (2012):

CLEARER AND BETTER EVIDENCE: On several occasions you have had skin discolorations that seemed suspicious for cancer. Each time the relevant tests came back negative. So, you have good but not definitive reason to think the latest round of spots, too, are benign. Nevertheless, when your doctor notes the spots, she orders a test (it's standard practice), which will come back in a few days. The results of this test, you know, will be definitive.[4]

McGrath notes that the fact that one will get better evidence in a few days provides one with a reason to suspend judgement. However, he observes that the fact that one will get better evidence in a few days is not a reason to have an intermediary state of confidence about whether the skin discolorations are cancerous. Hence, while the fact that one will get better evidence in the future is a reason to refrain from judgement, it is not a reason to be agnostic.

McGrath's second example is borrowed from Joseph Raz (1975):

TEMPORARY IMPAIRMENT: You know your abilities to make sound judgements on subtle matters, such as whether which of two insurance plans is a better deal overall, are mildly impaired. (Perhaps it's 12 am and you are tired, or you have had two drinks.) You also know that these impairments will be gone by tomorrow morning. There is no need to arrive at a conclusion until tomorrow evening, and you have time tomorrow to think it through.[5]

McGrath acknowledges that the fact that one will be a better assessor of one's evidence tomorrow is a reason to put off judgement until tomorrow. However, insofar as the fact that one will be a better assessor tomorrow fails to constitute a reason to hold an intermediary state of confidence about which of the two insurance plans is better than the other, this consideration fails to provide one with a reason to be agnostic. McGrath concludes that neither example offer a genuine non-epistemic reason to be agnostic. Given that, by McGrath's lights, agnosticism is a doxastic

---

[4] McGrath (2021: 465).   [5] McGrath (2021: 465).

attitude while suspension of judgement is not, it follows that the fact that one's evidence or one's ability to assess one's evidence will improve in the future fails to constitute a genuine problem for traditionalism.

6.2.1 An Initial Point of Disagreement

Before we get to my various criticisms of TAN, it is worth highlighting an important respect in which my conception of the normative profile of the attitude of agnosticism differs from that of McGrath. It is widely held that there at least two broad kinds of justification for being agnostic: *positive justification* and *negative justification*. The paradigm example of a positive justification for being agnostic is where a subject's considered evidence supports the conclusion that the likelihood of **P** is 0.5. In Chapter 4, I described such cases as ones in which a subject has 'positive evidence of equiprobability'. However, possessing positive evidence of the equiprobability of **P** and ¬**P** is not a necessary condition for agnosticism to be rationally appropriate. Agnosticism may also be negatively justified due to the absence of positive evidence in support of both **P** and ¬**P**. Consider the following case introduced in Chapter 4:

> ABSENT POSITIVE EVIDENCE: A political prisoner wakes up in a windowless room in an undisclosed location. The concrete walls insulate him from any sights or sounds from outside the room. The prisoner has no positive evidence that it is true that it is currently raining outside his room and no positive evidence that it is false that it is currently raining outside his room. Hence, his available evidence is counterbalanced, not because he has some, but equal amounts of positive evidence in support of both possibilities, but because of a complete absence of positive evidence for both.

Notice that the justification for the political prisoner's agnosticism does not depend on positive evidence showing that the likelihood of it raining outside is 0.5. Rather, it is the fact that he lacks sufficient evidential support to justify belief and lack sufficient evidential support to justify disbelief (or, if you like, his justified higher-order belief that this is so) that justifies his agnosticism. This is what I shall refer to as *negative justification* for agnosticism – that is, instances in which one's justification for being agnostic is not grounded in evidence showing that the proposition one is agnostic about has a likelihood of or close to 0.5.

Cases in which agnosticism is negatively justified includes instances in which one has some, but insufficient positive evidence – in support of P. Consider another case introduced in Chapter 4:

INSUFFICIENT POSITIVE EVIDENCE: A physicist has some positive evidence – that is, in the form of single rigorous experiment that has not yet been replicated – that a heretofore unobserved subatomic particle exists. Since no other experiments have been conducted, he has no positive evidence that the subatomic particle does not exist. Hence, while he has some positive evidence that the particle exists, he has no positive evidence that it does not exist. Even so, given that the experiment is yet to be replicated, the positive evidence available is still insufficient to establish the existence of the hypothesised particle.

The preceding example underscores that what makes negative justification for agnosticism qualify as such is not the absence of positive evidence per se, but rather the absence of positive evidence that **P** and ¬**P** are equiprobable.

The possibility of negative justification for agnosticism does not sit well with certain aspects of McGrath's account. For example, regarding a subject who knows close to nothing about a new subject, McGrath writes:

> Suppose a college freshman, flipping open the textbook on Day 1 of Intro to Neuroscience, reads a question about which neurotransmitters play certain roles in certain forms of depression. He does not know the relevant evidence, and he can see that the question is given a detailed chapter-length treatment. In situations like this, a person might feel rather silly in having any state of confidence at all. Suspension of opinion might seem to make more sense until you have a much better sense of the lay of the land in this field.[6]

Putting aside the idiosyncratic question of whether one would feel silly being agnostic about a matter one knows close to nothing about (personally, I would not feel the least bit silly doing so), I maintain that it is rationally appropriate to do so. As explained above, I maintain that being agnostic is rationally appropriate whenever one's considered evidence for and against **P** is perfectly counterbalanced. This includes cases in which one has no evidence bearing on the truth or falsity of **P**, which may be seen as a limiting case of one's evidence being perfectly counterbalanced. This means that being agnostic about whether **P** does not rationally require that one has already considered evidence bearing on the question. For example, one may justifiably be agnostic about something at the very outset of a piece of inquiry, even if one is yet to consider any of the evidence bearing on the subject into which one is inquiring. Hence, one need not have some evidence bearing on whether **P** for the attitude of agnosticism to be

---

[6] McGrath (2021: 473–474).

rationally appropriate, in the way that one would need to have some evidence bearing on whether **P** (or ¬**P**) for believing or disbelieving to be rationally appropriate.

By contrast, McGrath appears committed to the view that agnosticism is rationally appropriate only if one has considered some of the evidence bearing on whether **P**. Why else would we need to wait until after we have gained some sufficient level of familiarity with the evidence bearing on whether **P** before feeling entitled to be agnostic about whether **P**? My diagnosis of the source of the present disagreement between McGrath and I has to do with the disanalogy between agnosticism, on the one hand, and believing and disbelieving, on the other hand, to which I just alluded: namely that while believing and disbelieving **P** is only rationally appropriate if one's considered evidence provides some first-order support for **P** or ¬**P**, it may be rationally appropriate to be agnostic about whether **P** even if one lacks any first-order evidence bearing on whether **P**.

6.3 The Mongrel Concept Objection

When conceived of along the lines suggested by McGrath, suspension turns out to be a composite of two distinct mental acts: (i) omitting judgement now and (ii) adopting the aim to judge later. One may perform the mental act of omitting judgement now without performing the mental act of adopting the aim to judge later. For example, I may omit judgement with respect to the proposition that the Baltimore Ravens have won more than three Super Bowls (since I know close to nothing about American football) and fail to adopt the aim to judge later (because I have no interest American football). Furthermore, having the aim to judge later does not seem to entail that one is omitting judgement now. Consider the following case:

SUSPICIOUS SUSAN: Susan suspects that her wife may be having an affair and hires a private investigator to look into the matter over the course of the next 48 hours. Twelve hours into the investigation, the private investigator emails Susan photographs of her wife leaving a motel together with another woman. Based on this evidence, Susan judges that her wife is indeed having an affair. However, hoping beyond hope that the private investigator would acquire evidence in the remaining twelve hours that could change her mind, she also adopts the aim to form a judgement after she has been able to examine whatever additional evidence the private investigator uncovers.

The SUSPICIOUS SUSAN example describes a subject who adopts the aim to judge later despite failing to omit judgement now. Arguably, there may

6.3 *The Mongrel Concept Objection*

be something rationally problematic about adopting the aim to judge later if one has already judged now. On the one hand, if one thought that there was a strong possibility that forthcoming evidence may potentially change one's mind, then it is arguable that one should omit judgement now. On the other hand, if one did not think there was a strong possibility that the forthcoming evidence would change one's mind, then there seems to be little justification for adopting the aim to judge again later. Either way, it seems to be rationally inappropriate to adopt the aim to judge later insofar as one already judges now. Even if this is right, it is ultimately beside the point as far as the present argument is concerned. I am currently concerned with metaphysical possibility, not rational permissibility. Moreover, it is a truism that we do not always do what is most rationally appropriate.

The question before us is whether it is possible to adopt the aim to judge later even if one fails to omit judgement now. I maintain that the SUSPICIOUS SUSAN example illustrates just such a possibility. The cogency of my argument will depend on whether I have described a psychologically plausible case. I believe I have. As described, Susan's available evidence is already strong enough to warrant her believing that her wife is having an affair. However, the potentially far-reaching negative consequences of the belief makes it intelligible that Susan may have some difficulty coming to terms with said belief and may be highly motivated to revise it if given the opportunity to do so. Susan's adoption of the aim to judge later, despite the persuasiveness of the evidence already available, may reflect this desire. We may suppose that this reflects mere wishful thinking on Susan's part. While it is certainly within the logical space of possibilities that there is some perfectly innocent explanation of why her wife was leaving a hotel room with another woman, we may suppose that said possibility is so remote that it fails to warrant the adoption of the aim to judge later. And yet, Susan may find herself with the aim to judge (again) once the private investigator supplies her with additional evidence. Given that SUSPICIOUS SUSAN describes a real possibility, it follows that omitting judgement now is not a (metaphysical) precondition for adopting the aim to judge later.

Even if it is not, in general, a precondition for having the aim to judge later, omitting judgement now is a precondition for having the aim to judge later in cases of suspending judgement. While I do not dispute this fact, it should not lead us to hold that adopting the aim to judge later – is one and the same mental act as omitting judgement now. A mental act is distinct from the preconditions for performing it. In sum, even if we accept McGrath's characterisation of suspension as omitting judgement now because one aims to judge later, it is plausible that the mental act of omitting judgement now is distinct from the mental act of adopting the aim to judge later and that McGrath's conception of suspension therefore combines two distinct mental acts.

Once we register that omitting judgement now and adopting the aim to judge later are metaphysically distinct mental acts, the next step in my argument against McGrath's account is to observe that the latter – that is, the mental act of adopting the aim to judge later – is not itself a way of being neutral. I take this to be one of lessons of SUSPICIOUS SUSAN. Although Susan has the aim to judge later – that is, once the private investigator has completed his investigation – there is no sense in which she can be plausibly described as neutral. She both judges and believes that her wife is having an affair. Given that it is possible to consistently describe a subject as having the aim of judging later, despite the agent's lack of neutrality, implies that having the aim to judge later is not itself a way of being neutral. The upshot is that suspension, as conceived of by McGrath, combines a mental act that is a way of being neutral (i.e. the act of omitting judgement now) with a mental act that is not itself a way of being neutral (i.e. the act of adopting the aim to judge later). Hence, from the point of view of an analysis of the ways of being neutral, McGrath's notion of suspension is a mongrel concept. Call this the *mongrel concept objection*.

A couple points of clarification about what is presently being claimed seems to be in order. First, the present contention is not that there is only one way of being neutral. For all I have said thus far, it may still be true that refraining and agnosticism are distinct ways of being neutral. Indeed, in Section 5.6, I offer my own motivations for thinking that omitting judgement and agnosticism are metaphysically distinct phenomena. What is presently at issue is whether refraining and suspending are distinct ways of being neutral. My contention, then, is that suspending, as conceived of by McGrath, is most plausibly seen as an instance of refraining (i.e. a way of being neutral) that is accompanied by the aim to judge later (i.e. something that is not itself a way of being neutral). Hence, as characterised by McGrath, suspension is a mongrel concept.

Second, I am not claiming that suspension of judgement, as understood by McGrath, lacks theoretical value. There may be any number of motivations for paying special attention to those instances in which omitting judgement now is accompanied by the aim to judge later. For example, as I shall discuss in Section 5.5, there appear to be norms that apply to suspension that do not apply to refraining or agnosticism. This fact alone

6.3 The Mongrel Concept Objection

may make suspension a philosophically interesting notion that is worth discussing in its own right. However, acknowledging that those instances of omitting judgement that are accompanied by the aim to judge later hold some special theoretical significance does not entail that such instances represent a distinct way of being neutral on par with refraining or agnosticism. After all, a state's being a way of being neutral is not the only way for that state to be philosophically interesting; suspension may be of theoretical interest even if it does not constitute a distinct way of being neutral.

Compare: I may adopt the mental attitude of affirming the truth of **P** (i.e. believe **P**) without the intention to have my belief guide the implementation of a certain intention. For example, I may affirm the truth of the proposition that earth is not the only planet with life in the universe, without the intention of having said belief guide any foreseeable actions. I may also adopt the mental attitude of affirming the truth of **P** for the express purpose of having my belief guide the implementation of a certain intention. For example, I may affirm the truth of the proposition that I must turn right at the light to get to the nearest gas station with the aim of having my instrumental belief guide the implementation of my intention to get gas. However, it would be wrong to conclude from these observations that there are two distinct ways of affirming the truth of a proposition, one that simply entails affirming the proposition and another that entails affirming the proposition in order to have said affirmation guide one's actions. Moreover, a theory of 'instrumental beliefs', which conceived of them as a distinct way of being non-neutral or affirming the truth of a proposition, over and above non-instrumental beliefs, would be introducing a mongrel concept: one that combines the mental attitude of affirming a proposition and the practical attitude of intending to employ said affirmation to guide one's actions. This remains true even if it turns out that instrumental beliefs (like my belief about how to get to the gas station) have a special significance in our theorising that non-instrumental beliefs (like my belief that earth is not the only planet with life) do not have. With these points of clarification in mind, I now turn to my primary objection to McGrath's view, which builds on the mongrel concept objection.

The analysis of McGrath's conception of suspension implicated by the mongrel concept objection suggests a different take on cases like TEMPORARY IMPAIRMENT to that offered by McGrath. According to McGrath, the subject described in TEMPORARY IMPAIRMENT has a reason to suspend but no reason to be agnostic. Contra this view, I maintain that subjects in such cases have reasons to suspend (in McGrath's sense) and also have reasons to be agnostic. This point may be brought out more clearly by considering the following modified version of McGrath's TEMPORARY IMPAIRMENT case:

TEMPORARY VISUAL IMPAIRMENT: Matt is comparing two insurance plans, Plan A and Plan B, to determine which is better. Before him are two sheets of paper detailing the features of each plan. The breakdown contains all the information Matt needs to arrive at the right answer as to which of the two insurance plans is better. However, when he pats his pockets for his glasses, he discovers that they are empty. He then recalls that he left his glasses in his desk drawer at work. Without his glasses, the words and figures on the pages in front of him are nothing more than an unintelligible blur. Given his visual impairment, Matt decides to postpone any attempt to form a judgement about which policy is better until after he has retrieved his glasses from his office.

Given my contention in Section 5.2.1 that agnosticism is amendable to negative justification, the fact that Matt has insufficient positive evidence in support of Plan A being better and insufficient positive evidence in support of Plan A not being better is sufficient to make agnosticism towards Plan A being better rationally appropriate.

Significantly, Matt has all the information he needs right in front of him to determine if Plan A is better. However, this fact makes no difference given that his visual impairment precludes him from considering the information in the manner necessary to make a competent determination. Let us assume, for the sake of argument, that it is true that Plan A is better and that the information on the sheets of paper in Matt's possession conclusively establishes that this is so. One of the lessons of TEMPORARY VISUAL IMPAIRMENT is that having sufficient evidence to establish **P** in front of you is not enough to make belief rationally appropriate. One must consider the relevant evidence in the manner necessary to appreciate that the available evidence establishes **P**. This observation reminds us that possessing evidence, in the epistemically salient sense, is not simply a matter of having the requisite evidence before one. One must consider the evidence in question.

TEMPORARY IMPAIRMENT differs from TEMPORARY VISUAL IMPAIRMENT in that the subject described in the former is presumed to be able to visually make out what is written on the page regarding the competing insurance policies. Nevertheless, what both cases share is that there is some temporary physical (or physiological) impairment that precludes the competent consideration of the evidence at hand. One of the lessons of TEMPORARY IMPAIRMENT is that what one is justified in believing is a function of one's *competently* considered evidence. If one's

6.3 The Mongrel Concept Objection 117

level of intoxication or exhaustion is sufficient to preclude one's appreciation of the fact that the available evidence establishes that Plan A is better, then one fails to possess (in the epistemically salient sense) positive evidence that Plan A is better. Given that one also has insufficient positive evidence in support of its being false that Plan A is better, it follows that agnosticism is the rationally appropriate attitude. Hence, I submit that McGrath's claim that the subject described in TEMPORARY IMPAIRMENT does not have any reason to be agnostic is based on the problematic assumption that agnosticism is only amenable to positive justification. Once we dispense with this problematic assumption, the path is cleared for us to hold that agnosticism is rationally appropriate in both TEMPORARY VISUAL IMPAIRMENT and TEMPORARY IMPAIRMENT.

In addition to having reason to be agnostic, I hold that the subject in TEMPORARY VISUAL IMPAIRMENT has a reason to suspend (in McGrath's sense). This reason is supplied by the fact that the subject knows that his impairment is temporary and that he would be in a better position to make a judgement on the matter later. Given that Matt will be able to read the documents with the requisite information once he has recovered his glasses from his office drawer, he has good reason to adopt the aim to form a judgement on the matter after he has retrieved his glasses and is able to read and competently consider what is written. Hence, one point on which McGrath and I agree is that the fact that one will be in a better position to assess one's evidence later is a reason to put off judgement until that time. This comports with analysis of suspension offered by the mongrel concept objection. On the one hand, the fact that Matt's competently considered evidence is neither sufficient to establish the proposition that Plan A is better nor sufficient to establish its negation (i.e. it is not the case that Plan A is better) entails that he has negative justification for being agnostic about whether Plan A is better. On the other hand, the fact that there is a future point at which his visual impairment will no longer preclude the competent consideration of his evidence entails that he has positive justification for putting off judging until that future point in time.

In summation, I submit that McGrath's failure to appreciate that the subject in TEMPORARY IMPAIRMENT has reasons to be agnostic illustrates the danger of failing to register that suspension (as he conceives of it) consists in two distinct mental acts. If we assume that suspension, like refraining, is a single mental act, and that suspension essentially involves putting off judgement, then it makes sense to assume that once one has considered the reasons relevant to whether one has put off judgement, one has considered all the reasons relevant to suspension. Given that one may have reasons to put off judgement that are not also reasons to have an intermediate state of confidence, one is naturally led to conclude that there are cases in which one has a reason to suspend but no reason to be agnostic. However, once we register that suspension is a composite of two distinct mental acts, we are not so easily lulled into thinking that once we have considered the reasons a subject has to put off judgement, we have considered all the reasons relevant to suspension. Registering that suspension is a composite of both omitting judgement now and adopting the aim to judge later invites us to inquire into not only a subject's reasons for adopting the aim to judge later but also their reasons for omitting judgement now. Once the latter question is posed, it becomes evident that the subject in cases like TEMPORARY IMPAIRMENT does in fact have a reason to omit judgement now – namely the fact that their competently considered evidence fails to establish either the truth or falsity of **P**.

6.4 Negative versus Positive Neutrality

Another noteworthy feature of McGrath's account is that he distinguishes between refraining from judgement and suspension of judgement, on the one hand, and refraining from belief and suspension of belief, on the other. The need to draw this distinction arises from the fact that McGrath regards 'refraining' and 'suspension as 'success notions: if you suspend X, you do not X, and similarly for refraining'.[7] This means that refraining from judging **P** at t is sufficient for not judging **P** at t and refraining from believing **P** at t is sufficient for not believing **P** at t. However, McGrath wishes to allow that in cases of irrationality or fragmentation,[8] it is possible to believe **P** at t and refrain from judgement at t.[9] This implies that it is possible for a subject to refrain from judgement at t and not refrain from belief at t. Here is the point in McGrath's own words:

> Given that we have the general notion of suspension as putting off and the general notion of refraining as intentionally omitting, we can apply them directly to belief itself. Whereas we must be careful in stating how belief excludes suspending and refraining from judgment, by noting qualifications about irrationality and fragmentation, we can say without qualification that belief excludes suspending and refraining from belief. (As noted above,

---

[7] McGrath (2021: 470).
[8] 'Fragmentation' appears to be McGrath's term for what I have been calling mental compartmentalisation.
[9] McGrath (469ff. 470).

6.4 Negative versus Positive Neutrality

these are success notions: if you suspend **X**, you do not **X**, and similarly for refraining.)[10]

One implication (perhaps unanticipated) of McGrath regarding suspension and refraining as success notions is that there are two distinct notions of neutrality at work in his account. First, there is the neutrality constituted by having an intermediate state of confidence in a proposition. This is the kind of neutrality implicated in McGrath's conception of agnosticism. Since this notion of neutrality involves having a stance towards a proposition, I will refer to it as **positive neutrality**. Second, there is the neutrality constituted by the absence of belief and disbelief. This is the kind of neutrality implicated in McGrath's conception of *refraining from belief* and *suspension of belief*. Since this notion of neutrality does not require any kind of stance towards a proposition, I will refer to it as *negative neutrality*.

A careful examination of McGrath's account reveals that he is committed (whether wittingly or unwittingly) to the possibility of someone being negatively neutral without them being positively neutral. Two aspects of McGrath's view suggests that this is so. First, McGrath holds that there are cases in 'which someone intentionally fails not only to judge but to have any opinion', where an opinion includes 'belief, disbelief, as well as states of confidence'.[11] Since being positively neutral requires having some kind of stance towards a proposition, cases in which a subject refrains from having an opinion cannot be instances of positive neutrality.[12] Moreover, every instance of refraining from an opinion is ipso facto an instance of refraining from both belief and disbelief. Hence, insofar as instances of refraining from an opinion are cases of neutrality (a thesis to which McGrath appears committed), they can only be instances of negative neutrality.

Second, McGrath maintains that in cases like TEMPORARY IMPAIRMENT, a subject has a reason to suspend but no reason to be agnostic (i.e. have an intermediate level of confidence). This only makes sense if suspension of judgement does not itself involve having an intermediate state to confidence. Moreover, McGrath holds that suspension of judgement entails refraining from judgement.[13] It follows that refraining from judgement

---

[10] McGrath (2021: 470).   [11] McGrath (2021: 473).
[12] McGrath considers refraining from an opinion to be among the ways of being neutral. Indeed, every instance of refraining from an opinion is ipso facto an instance of refraining from belief. This follows from the fact that refraining from 'belief, disbelief, as well as states of confidence' entails refraining from belief and disbelief. This means that McGrath cannot deny that refraining from an opinion is a way of being neutral without also denying that refraining from belief is a way of being neutral.
[13] McGrath (2021: 467).

also fails to involve having an intermediate state of confidence. Hence, by McGrath's lights, neither refraining from judgement nor suspension of judgement entail positive neutrality. It follows that insofar as suspending and refraining are cases of neutrality (a thesis to which McGrath is most certainly committed), they can only be instances of negative neutrality. I conclude that McGrath is committed (whether wittingly or unwittingly) to two distinct kinds of neutrality.

To be clear, the present claim is not that negative neutrality is incompatible with positive neutrality, such that one cannot be both negatively and positively neutral at the same time. Since negative neutrality only requires the absence of belief and disbelief, then (barring cases of irrationality or fragmentation) a subject who is agnostic (i.e. positively neutral) will also refrain from belief and disbelief (i.e. be negatively neutral). My point is only that the two kinds of neutrality can come apart on McGrath's account and that he is therefore committed to them being metaphysically distinct.

Having distinguished between positive and negative neutrality, it is worth taking stock of what kind of neutrality (if any) is entailed by each of the various ways of being neutral that McGrath has identified. To this end, it is clear that agnosticism involves positive neutrality (i.e. having an intermediate state of confidence). Indeed, McGrath defines agnosticism as having just such a stance towards a proposition. Since McGrath regards 'refraining' and 'suspending' as success notions, it follows that refraining from belief and suspension of belief both involve negative neutrality (i.e. the absence of both belief and disbelief). However, matters are less straightforward when it comes to refraining from judgement and suspension of judgement. While refraining from judgement typically results in refraining from belief (assuming all goes well), we noted that McGrath holds that there may be cases in which (due to irrationality or fragmentation) a subject refrains from judging **P** at t but also believes **P** at t. Presumably, McGrath would also wish to allow that there are cases in which (due to irrationality or fragmentation) a subject suspends judging **P** at t but also believes **P** at t. This means that (in cases of irrationality or fragmentation) neither refraining from judgement nor suspension of judgement entail being negatively neutral. Furthermore, we already noted that McGrath is committed to denying that refraining from judgement and suspension of judgement involve positive neutrality. The upshot is that, as McGrath conceives of them, refraining from judgement and suspension of judgement are, at best, conditional forms of (negative) neutrality. We may represent the preceding observations in Table 6.1.

6.4 Negative versus Positive Neutrality

Table 6.1 *McGrath's Account of Neutrality*

	Overview of McGrath's Account of Neutrality	
Positive Neutrality	Negative Neutrality	Conditional Negative Neutrality
Agnosticism (Entails intermediate level of confidence; compossible with believing and disbelieving in cases of irrationality and fragmentation)	**Refraining from Belief** (Entails omitting belief and disbelief) **Suspension of Belief** (Entails putting off belief and disbelief)	**Refraining from Judgement** (Entails omitting judgement; compossible with believing and disbelieving in cases of irrationality and fragmentation) **Suspension of Judgement** (Entails putting off judgement; compossible with believing and disbelieving in cases of irrationality and fragmentation)

One takeaway from the preceding discussion is that a subject who refrains or suspends judgement only counts as being neutral if they also refrain or suspend belief, respectively. This means that refraining from judgement and suspension of judgement are not ways of being neutral per se. At best, they facilitate the negative neutrality implicated by refraining from belief and suspension of belief. Moreover, since someone only qualifies as being negatively neutral when their refraining and suspension of judgement yields a refraining and suspension of belief, it seems like it is the refraining and suspension of belief that is doing the real work as far as being (negatively) neutral is concerned. This means that we lose nothing, as far as the project of offering a taxonomy of neutrality is concerned, if we simply dispense with the refraining and suspension of judgement and concern ourselves only with the refraining and suspension of belief. The upshot is that whatever their theoretical value, as far as the project of offering a taxonomy of neutrality is concerned, McGrath's notions of refraining from judgement and suspension of judgement are both superfluous.

The present analysis of McGrath's views suggest that his account of neutrality is not as advertised. McGrath purports to offer an account of neutrality in which the main players are refraining from judgement, suspension of judgement, and agnosticism. However, upon closer examination, it turns out that only McGrath's notion of agnosticism may unproblematically be described as a way of being neutral. The mental act of omitting belief-forming judgement with respect to **P** only results in being (negatively) neutral in those cases in which one does not already believe **P**. However, since McGrath allows that it is possible (in cases of irrationality and fragmentation) for such a state of affairs to arise, the fact that one omits belief-forming judgement with respect to **P** does not guarantee that one neither believes nor disbelieves (i.e. is negatively neutral with respect to) **P**. This is not a problem that afflicts the positive notion of neutrality. Positive neutrality does not require the absence of belief and disbelief. It only requires the presence of an intermediate state of confidence. This means that even in those cases in which (due to irrationality or fragmentation) one is agnostic towards **P** at t and believe **P** at t, agnosticism still qualifies as a form of neutrality.

Unlike McGrath, who tasks himself with offering an account of neutrality, *simpliciter*, I am only concerned with the kind of neutrality that implicates a doxastic attitude or act. Let us call this more restricted notion of neutrality 'doxastic neutrality'. Table 6.2 summarises the alternative act-attitude account advocated in this chapter.

It should be evident that doxastic neutrality is a species of positive rather than negative neutrality. After all, the mere absence of certain attitudes is not sufficient for performing a mental act or having a mental attitude. The fact that I am only concerned with offering an account of doxastic neutrality means that my target explanans in this chapter is narrower than that of McGrath. Nevertheless, it should also be clear that the difference between our accounts is not simply one of explanatory scope. Specifically, while I am committed to a univocal normative characterisation of withholding judgement and agnosticism, McGrath is committed to a multivocal normative characterisation of refraining from judgement and agnosticism.

To briefly recap, I hold that the normative relationship between withholding judgement and agnosticism is analogous to the normative

Table 6.2. *The Act-Attitude Account*

Overview of Act-Attitude Account of Doxastic Neutrality	
Mental Act	Mental Attitude
Withholding Judgement (Entails intermediate level of confidence; amenable to positive and negative justification; compossible with believing and disbelieving in cases of irrationality and mental compartmentalisation)	**Agnosticism** (Entails intermediate level of confidence; amenable to positive and negative justification; compossible with believing and disbelieving in cases of irrationality and mental compartmentalisation)

6.4 Negative versus Positive Neutrality

relationship between judging and believing. Although judging and believing are metaphysically distinct (owing to the fact that the former is a mental act while the latter is an attitude), both are subject to the same sort of normative considerations; to wit, judging is rationally (in)appropriate under exactly the same circumstances that believing is rationally (in)appropriate and vice versa. In the present view, if my considered evidence sufficiently supports **P** to make believing **P** justified, then it also sufficiently supports **P** to make judging **P** justified. And if my considered evidence does not sufficiently support **P** to make believing **P** justified, then it also fails to sufficiently support **P** to make judging **P** justified. This normative parity between belief and judgement makes sense given that judging that **P** is the standard means by which we reflectively arrive at the belief that **P**. Likewise, according to my proposed account, withholding judgement is rationally (in)appropriate under the same circumstances that agnosticism is and vice versa. To wit, if one's considered evidence justifies withholding judging **P** then it also justifies being agnostic towards **P**. This normative parity between withholding judgement and agnosticism makes sense given that, just as judging is the standard means of reflectively arriving at belief, withholding judgement is the standard means of reflectively arriving at the attitude of agnosticism.

By contrast, McGrath is explicit about his defence of a multivocal normative account of neutrality:

> I will argue that there are both normative and non-normative differences between suspension of judgment and agnosticism, understood as having an intermediate state of confidence. These are two distinct phenomena. In fact, they come apart in numerous ways that it is useful to chart. I'll make similar arguments afterward for refraining from judgement.[14]

As we noted above, McGrath's commitment to a multivocal account of neutrality is rooted in his failure to recognise that agnosticism is amendable to negative justification and his commitment to holding that suspension of judgement (understood as putting off judgement) is a distinct way of being neutral over and above refraining from judgement and agnosticism. Once we dispense with these assumptions, we are free to embrace the more parsimonious univocal account of doxastic neutrality defended in this chapter.

One upshot of the univocal account of doxastic neutrality is that the evidentialist credentials of agnosticism and withholding judgement stand

---

[14] McGrath (2021: 472).

or fall together. As already alluded to, McGrath employs a bifurcated account of neutrality to argue that while there may be non-epistemic reasons to refrain from or suspend judgement, there can only be epistemic reasons to be agnostic. By contrast, I maintain that if there may be non-epistemic reasons to refrain from judgement, then there may be non-epistemic reasons to be agnostic as well; the two ways of being neutral share the same evidentialist fate. Moreover, it is worth noting that the primary motivation for holding that there may be non-epistemic reasons to be agnostic come not from cases like TEMPORARY IMPAIRMENT – that is, ones in which one will be in a better position to assess one's evidence at some future time – but from cases in which pragmatic factors appear to influence how much evidence is necessary for a belief to be justified. In this context, examples like the following are typically discussed:

CAUTIOUS CARL: Carl has the option of depositing a check either today, Friday, or tomorrow, Saturday. As he approaches the bank, he notices through the bank window that there are very long lines inside. Not wanting to wait in line, he thinks it would be best to make the bank deposit the following day. He recalls that he was at the bank two weeks ago on a Saturday and he is unaware of any special holidays coming up. (Let us assume that under normal circumstances, this would be sufficient evidence to justify believing that the bank is open on Saturdays.) However, Carl is also aware that it is not unheard of for banks to change their hours. Moreover, he has just written a very large cheque, and should it turn out that he is mistaken about the bank being open tomorrow, the cheque will bounce. Hence, there are very high stakes attached to Carl being correct about the bank hours. (Let us assume that Carl has no means currently at his disposal to check if the bank is open on Saturdays.) Given the high cost attached to being mistaken, Carl decides to adopt an attitude of agnosticism towards the bank being open tomorrow and decides to brave the long lines in order to be on the safe side.

CAUTIOUS CARL describes a case in which a subject is motivated to adopt an attitude of agnosticism because of the high cost of getting things wrong. However, the fact that there is a high cost to being mistaken about whether the bank is open on Saturdays is not evidence bearing on whether the bank is open on Saturdays. Hence, insofar as the high cost of falsely believing the bank is open on Saturdays is a reason to be agnostic about whether it is open on Saturdays, it is a non-epistemic reason for being agnostic. Furthermore, there is some reason to think that agnosticism is indeed the rationally appropriate attitude for Carl to adopt. First, it seems like it would be irrational for Carl to simply drive home with the intention to make the deposit the following day, given the high cost attached to getting things wrong and his inability to double-check if he's mistaken.

Second, if it is rationally permissible to believe **P** at *t*, then it should be rationally permissible to take **P** for granted in one's planning at *t*. The combination of the preceding two points suggests that it would be rationally impermissible for Carl to continue to believe that the bank is open on Saturdays after he recalls the high cost of getting things wrong. If this is right, then adopting an attitude of agnosticism appears to be the rationally appropriate course. The upshot is that the high cost of getting things wrong appears to constitute non-epistemic reasons for adopting an attitude of agnosticism towards the bank being open on Saturdays.

Whether one agrees with the above argument, it should be clear that the putative reasons Carl has for being agnostic do not include the fact that he will have better evidence or be in a better position to weigh his evidence later. In short, future comparative factors are not the only candidate non-epistemic reasons for being agnostic. Hence, even if McGrath were correct about future comparative factors being reasons to suspend judgement but not reason to be agnostic, this would not go very far towards establishing that there are no non-epistemic reasons to be agnostic. This suggests that McGrath's strategy for preserving traditionalism may be ill-motivated. Even if successful in handling cases like TEMPORARY IMPAIRMENT, it would still fail to address the standard sort of cases that theorists take to support the claim that there may be non-epistemic reasons to be agnostic. When this fact is combined with the other problems confronting McGrath's proposal – that is, the fact that his notion of suspension is a mongrel concept, the fact refraining from judgement and suspension of judgement turn out to only be conditional forms of neutrality on his account, and the fact that his account omits all mention of a mental act by which we may reflectively arrive at the mental state of agnosticism – it furnishes us with compelling reason to hold out for a better account of neutrality. I submit that the act-attitude account is just such an account.

6.4.1 A Minor Terminological Quibble

While unpacking the implications of the mongrel concept objection, I noted that my contention that suspension of judgement (as characterised by McGrath) is not a distinct way of being neutral does not entail that the notion is without theoretical value. Given that omitting judgement for the purpose of judging later is a very common phenomenon and given that it has a different normative profile to merely omitting judgement, it may be deserving of special attention. However, I am reluctant to follow McGrath in using the term 'suspension of judgement' to refer to the act of omitting judgement for the purpose of judging later. Instead, I think it would be better to use the expression 'postponing judgement' to pick out the act of omitting judgement for the purpose of judging later. There are at least two reasons to prefer the expression 'postponing judgement' over 'suspension of judgement' in the present context. First, the terms 'suspension', 'suspending', and 'suspension of judgement' are already widely used in the literature as a synonym for the attitude of agnosticism. Hence, employing a different term seems prudent to avoid potential confusion. Second, there can be little confusion about what is meant by the expression 'postponing judgement'. Admittedly, this would also be true of the expression 'suspension of judgement' if it were understood in its most literal sense. However, the long history of the term 'suspension of judgement' being employed as a synonym for agnosticism underscores that it has not typically been used literally. As such, it seems prudent to defer to actual usage over literal meaning. In light of the above considerations, I believe it would be best to use an entirely new term, like 'postposing judgement', to describe the mental act of omitting judgement now in order to judge later.

6.5 Interrogative and Anti-interrogative Attitudes

In my clarificatory remarks regarding the mongrel concept objection, I noted that my rejection of the claim that suspension (as conceived of by McGrath) does not represent a distinct way of being neutral is consistent with there being other ways of being neutral apart from the attitude of agnosticism. Hence, nothing I have said thus far requires that we reject the thesis, defended by Errol Lord (2020), that interrogative and anti-interrogative attitudes should be included among the ways of being neutral. The notion of an interrogative attitude was introduced and popularised by Friedman, who describes them as follows:

> In this paper I want to argue that there is a class of attitudes that have questions as contents. These attitudes are a class of inquiry-related states and processes... In virtue of their relations to questions, I will call these focal attitudes, *Interrogative Attitudes (IAs)*...They are the sorts of attitudes we typically have as we move ourselves from ignorance to knowledge. They are the sorts of attitudes we have when we try to figure something out, or work to acquire new information, or when we are searching for new knowledge.[15]

---

[15] Friedman (2013a: 145).

6.5 Interrogative and Anti-Interrogative Attitudes

Lord attempts to round off Friedman's analysis by introducing the notion of an anti-interrogative attitude. The following passage offers a preliminary gloss of anti-interrogative attitudes:

> I'll call attitudes that are directed towards questions that *bury* those questions anti-interrogative attitudes. So, while adopting an interrogative attitude keeps **P** in your outlook in a way that orients you towards settling the question, adopting an anti-interrogative attitude puts whether **P** in the outlook by, in effect, taking whether **P** to be a bad question.[16] (*Italics*, mine)

Elaborating on what it means to 'bury' a question, Lord writes:

> Rather than merely dropping the issue, you can bury the issue, which is to say you can adopt an attitude towards whether **P** that disposes you to ignore the question. This attitude makes you insensitive to information relevant to the question.[17]

While Friedman's notion of an interrogative attitude seems fairly straightforward, Lord's account of anti-interrogative attitudes stands in need of some clarification. Take, for example, the notion of a 'bad question'. I may adopt an attitude towards a question that disposes me to ignore it on the grounds that it is a 'bad question' without being neutral with respect to that question. For example, suppose I decided to ignore the question 'What colour is Thomas Jefferson's Ferrari?' on the grounds that it rests on a faulty presupposition. It does not follow that I am neutral with respect to the question. Given that presupposition failure is among the reasons we may regard a question as a 'bad question', it follows that not every instance in which we bury a question because we view it as a 'bad question' qualifies as a case of neutrality with respect to that question. Hence, if Lord wishes to preserve the idea that having an anti-interrogative attitude with respect to whether **P** ipso facto makes one neutral with respect to whether **P**, then he must deny that in cases in which we bury a question because of presupposition failure we qualify as having an anti-interrogative attitude. Below, I consider and reject one possible strategy Lord may employ to accomplish this task.

Even if we build in the requirement that one can only take an anti-interrogative attitude towards a question if it does not suffer from presupposition failure, there remains a potentially more troubling set of objections to the claim that having an anti-interrogative attitude – is a way of being neutral. This is because it is not obvious that being disposed to

---

[16] Lord (2020: 131). [17] Lord (2020: 131).

ignore or bury a question entails that one is neutral with respect to that question. For example, suppose I was raised in a religious tradition and my religious indoctrination has led me to accept by faith that God exists, where faith is here understood as being committed to the truth of a proposition in the absence of evidence in favour of that proposition. Suppose further that my religious tradition has taught me that it is sinful to question, doubt, or inquire into whether God exists, and this prompts me to ignore or bury the question. In such a case, I may exhibit both characteristics Lord specifies for having an anti-interrogative attitude; that is, it may both be true that I am disposed to ignore the question and that I am insensitive to information relevant to the question. However, it seems implausible to suggest that this ipso facto makes me neutral on the question of whether God exists. On the contrary, my unwillingness to consider the question may be due to my dogmatic commitment to a certain answer to that question as opposed to my being neutral with respect to that question.

Lord anticipates and responds to a similar objection to the one just sketched. He acknowledges that there are cases where one rationally believes **P** and is rationally disposed to gather more information (e.g. the surgeon who rationally believes she needs to remove a patient's liver but double-checks her medical chart to make sure), and cases where one rationally believes **P** and is rationally disposed to ignore **P**-related information (e.g. the pathological over checker who has already checked seventeen times adopts an anti-interrogative attitude in order to preclude further double-checking). However, Lord notes that these cases are not enough to establish that there are cases where it is rational to believe **P** and rational to have an interrogative or anti-interrogative attitude. He writes:

> Remember, interrogative and anti-interrogative attitudes are essentially not worldly determining. That means they are partly individuated by a functional lack – the lack of dispositions to move around as if it is a **P** or ¬**P** world.[18]

The above passage introduces a distinction between an (anti-)interrogative *attitude* and an (anti-)interrogative *disposition*. Building on this distinction, Lord posits that a subject has an interrogative attitude only if they possess an interrogative disposition 'in virtue of having a questioning attitude' and a subject has an anti-interrogative attitude only if they have an anti-interrogative disposition 'in virtue of having an agnostic attitude'.[19]

---

[18] Lord (2020: 139).   [19] Lord (2020: 139).

If this suggestion can be plausibly maintained, then it appears to offer an effective reply to both of the objections just adumbrated. In response to the worry about 'bad questions', it may be argued that someone who is motivated to bury a question due to presupposition failure does not have an interrogative disposition in virtue of having an agnostic attitude towards that question. This seems like a potentially effective response given that it is difficult to conceive of someone being agnostic about what colour is Thomas Jefferson's Ferrari if they believed that Jefferson did not own a Ferrari. Similarly, it may be argued that the religious dogmatist does not have an anti-interrogative disposition in virtue of being agnostic about whether God exists. Furthermore, the religious dogmatist does not lack the disposition to move around as if he occupies a world in which God exists. Consequently, the religious dogmatist arguably fails to satisfy the requirement that her attitude towards God's existence not be worldly determining. The upshot is that in both cases, the agent in question may be said to have an anti-interrogative disposition but not an anti-interrogative attitude.

Unfortunately, the above strategy proves too much since it implies that agents who we would ordinarily conceive of as engaged in genuine inquiry (and hence, as possessing an interrogative attitude) have no such attitude. Consider, for example, the agent described in CERTAINTY SEEKER:

> CERTAINTY SEEKER: Jeanie, a third-year philosophy undergrad, knows that other people have mental states like pain, anger, or beliefs and that solipsism is therefore false. However, while Descartes' cogito argument is enough to render the existence of her own mind beyond doubt, as far as she's concerned, she is unaware of any arguments that are sufficient to render the existence of other minds beyond doubt. Jeanie is not content with merely knowing that other minds exist; she wants to know that other minds exist with the same indubitable confidence that she knows that her own mind exists. To this end, she checks out several philosophy books on the topic from her school library in the hope that she will find some argument that would allow her to ratchet up her knowledge that other people have minds to the status of Cartesian indubitability.

Ordinarily, we would regard Jeanie's library research as an instance of genuine inquiry.[20] However, since she knows that other minds exist, her interrogative disposition – like that of the surgeon who double-checks her patient's charts – does not arise out of a questioning attitude. Hence, by Lord's lights, her interrogative disposition fails to constitute an interrogative attitude. This presents Lord with a dilemma. On the one hand, he

[20] See Archer (2021: 103ff) for an in-depth discussion of this example.

may maintain that being a genuine inquirer requires the possession of an interrogative attitude, but deny that Jeanie is engaged in genuine inquiry. However, in so doing, Lord's account would be revisionary of our ordinary linguistic practice that would regard the subject described in CERTAINTY SEEKER as engaged in genuine inquiry. On the other hand, he may grant that Jeanie is engaged in genuine inquiry but maintain that genuine inquiry does not require the possession of an interrogative attitude. However, in so doing, he would be stripping the term of one of its most defining features that motivated its positing by Friedman. Recall, Friedman introduced the notion of an interrogative attitude as part of an attempt to provide necessary and sufficient conditions for genuine inquiry. If we dispense with this role for the concept, its theoretical value is called into question. Either way, attempting to restrict the notion of an (anti-)interrogative attitude in the way Lord proposes seems like an unattractive strategy for responding to the objections limned in this chapter.

A second, and more pressing, worry is that the stipulation that (anti-)interrogative dispositions be had in virtue of having a questioning attitude or being agnostic threatens to undermine their status as a distinct and independent way of being neutral. The problem is that both possessing a questioning attitude (if it is going to do the theoretical work required) and agnosticism are already agreed-upon ways of being neutral. (Recall my earlier point that the surgeon can only be said to lack a questioning attitude if we assume that possessing such an attitude requires that she be doxastically neutral.) If an (anti-)interrogative disposition qualifies as an (anti-)interrogative attitude only if it is accompanied by and arises out of a neutral state, then it seems that all the heavy lifting, as far as the neutrality of (anti-)interrogative attitudes is concerned, is being done by the accompanying neutral state. After all, the only thing that stands between an (anti-)interrogative disposition qualifying as a neutral state (which an (anti-)interrogative attitude is supposed to be) is that a subject possesses the (anti-)interrogative disposition in virtue of a neutral state. But if that is the case, then the neutrality is not located in the (anti-)interrogative disposition per se but rather in the accompanying neutral state. In short, (anti-)interrogative attitudes are not a distinct way of being neutral over and above the already recognised ways of being neutral.

In light of the above considerations, I am inclined to treat the notion of an (anti-)interrogative attitude in a manner similar to my treatment of McGrath's notion of suspension. Instead of a distinct way of being neutral, (anti-)interrogative attitudes, as described by Lord, seem best conceived of as attitudes that accompany being neutral but that are not themselves a way of being neutral. This is consistent with saying that having reason to believe a question is unanswerable may constitute reasons for both being neutral and for adopting an anti-interrogative attitude. Hence, my claim that anti-interrogative attitudes merely accompany rather than constitute being neutral does not necessarily require a rejection of Lord's characterisation of the normative profile of anti-interrogative attitudes. It merely calls into question whether those attitudes represent a genuine and distinct way of being neutral. In sum, while the mongrel concept objection is consistent with the thesis that the (anti-)interrogative attitudes represent a distinct way of being neutral, there are independent reasons for being sceptical about the claim that they are.

6.6 Conclusion

This chapter has gone some distance towards establishing that a bipartite act-attitude account provides an adequate analysis of doxastic neutrality. In this respect, it resists two recent attempts to expand the number of ways of being neutral – that of McGrath and Lord. I have argued that the accounts of neutrality of McGrath and Lord share a common flaw; they assume that because a certain mental state entails being neutral, it should be added to our taxonomy of neutral attitudes or acts. The result is an ever-growing list of alleged ways being neutral that includes refraining from judgement, suspension of judgement, refraining from belief, suspension of belief, and (anti-)interrogative attitudes. However, I have argued that the putative neutral states these theorists have identified count as such (insofar as they do at all) only because they implicate either withholding judgement or agnosticism. To this end, I maintain that postponing judgement (or what McGrath calls 'suspension') is a way of being neutral because it involves withholding judgement. Likewise, insofar as (anti-)interrogative attitudes are a way of being neutral, it is only because they involve either withholding judgement or agnosticism. If this is right, then the act-attitude account appears to be more parsimonious and attractive alternative.

CHAPTER 7

On the Non-existence of Practical Agnosticism

7.1 Introduction

If intending to do **X** (where **X** picks out some action) is the practical analogue of believing **P** (where **P** picks out some proposition), and intending not to do **X** is the practical analogue of disbelieving **P**, then what is the practical analogue of agnosticism towards **P**? In this chapter, I shall argue that there is no such attitude. To this end, I claim that there is no practical attitude that stands in the same relationship to intending to do **X** and intending not to do **X** as agnosticism towards **P** stands to believing **P** and disbelieving **P**. Call this the *non-existence thesis*.

One reason the non-existence thesis is significant is because it represents a heretofore unrecognised challenge to **strong cognitivism**, the thesis that intention is identical to belief.[1] Strong cognitivists identify the intention to do **X** with the belief that one will (or will probably) do **X**. However, according to the non-existence thesis, belief has a relational property that intentions lack: namely that while belief is a member of a multi-attitudinal complex that includes believing, disbelieving, and agnosticism, intention is a member of a multi-attitudinal complex that includes intending to do **X** and intending not to do **X**, but that does not include a third practical attitude that is analogous to agnosticism. Since beliefs have a property that intentions lack, intention cannot be identical to or a species of belief. Or at least so the argument goes. My aim in this chapter is not to assess or defend the efficacy of the preceding argument. Instead, and more modestly, my focus will be restricted to an articulation and defence of the

---

[1] The thesis that intention is identical to belief is defended in Velleman (1985) and more recently in Marušić and Schwenkler (2018). For a critical discussion of strong cognitivism, see Velleman (1989/2007, esp. ch. 4). A weaker version of cognitivism, according to which intention involves (but need not be identical with) belief, is advanced by Grice (1971), Harman (1976; 1986, ch.8), Davis (1984), Setiya (2003; 2007; 2008), and Ross (2009).

argument's first (and perhaps most controversial) premise – that is, the claim that there is no practical analogue to agnosticism.[2]

7.2 The Appropriateness Norms for Belief

Let us say that one of the three doxastic attitudes is **rationally appropriate** under some circumstance, C, just in case it is rationally permissible in C and the other two doxastic attitudes are rationally prohibited in C. For example, if a subject's competently considered evidence conclusively supports **P**, then the only doxastic attitude the subject is rationally permitted to take towards **P** is one of belief. As such, we may say that believing **P** is the rationally appropriate attitude in cases in which one's competently considered evidence conclusively supports **P**. Some work will need to be done to specify what it means for a subject's competently considered evidence to *conclusively support* **P**. If one's considered evidence is sparse or ambiguous, then it will plausibly fail to provide conclusive support for **P**. If there are defeaters in the vicinity this may also be enough to prevent one's available evidence from providing conclusive support for **P**. Hence, a complete account of what it means for a subject's competently considered evidence to provide conclusive support for **P** will need to exclude such cases. Moreover, it is plausible that such an account will need to appeal to a subject's evidential standards, and these may vary across time and from subject to subject. However, these are not details we need settle here. It is sufficient for our present purposes to note that there are instances when the level of support for **P** provided by one's competently considered evidence is so great that one would be irrational if one were agnostic about whether **P** or disbelieved **P**. Indeed, to deny this would be to leave us without the resources necessary for holding that subjects who stubbornly ignore their evidence are rationally criticisable for so doing. Hence, I take belief to be subject to something along the lines of the following *Appropriateness Norm*:

Appropriateness Norm for Believing P = ^{def} If one's competently considered evidence conclusively supports **P**, then one is rationally permitted to believe **P** and rationally prohibited from disbelieving **P** or agnosticism towards **P**.

I take being subject to appropriateness norms to be a definitive feature of doxastic attitudes. There may be some disagreement about the precise

---

[2] In addition to its possible implications for strong cognitivism, the non-existence thesis is of independent interest to action theorists like myself, who are interested in the nature of belief and intention, especially the ways in which the two attitudes are similar and different.

formulation of the appropriateness norm for believing **P**. However, it is more important for my argument that something like the above appropriateness norm exists, than that I have identified the exact formulation that the norm should take. The preceding disclaimer notwithstanding, I believe the above formulation of the appropriateness norm for belief has a lot going for it. For example, the above appropriateness norm does not entail that if a subject has conclusive evidential support for **P**, the subject must believe that **P**. Perhaps the subject is indifferent towards **P**, and therefore cannot be bothered to form the belief that **P**, even though the subject has conclusive evidence that **P**. It is not obvious that such a subject would be rationally criticisable. (Perhaps **P** is some piece of idle gossip about the royal family that the subject cannot be bothered to think about, though conclusive evidence for **P** is already at hand if the subject took the time to reflect on it.) What the above appropriateness norm for believing **P** claims is that if one's evidence conclusively supports **P**, then one must believe **P**, insofar as one adopts any doxastic attitude towards **P** at all. Hence, while it is not crucial that the reader buys into my exact formulation of the appropriateness norm for believing **P**, I have still attempted to come up with the most plausible formulation of the norm that I could.

We may represent the corresponding appropriateness norms for disbelieving and agnosticism as follows:

Appropriateness Norm for Disbelieving P $=^{def}$ If one's competently considered evidence conclusively supports ¬**P**, then one is rationally permitted to disbelieve **P** and rationally prohibited from believing **P** or agnosticism towards **P**.

Appropriateness Norm for Agnosticism towards P $=^{def}$ If one's competently considered evidence equally supports **P** and ¬**P**, then one is rationally permitted to be agnostic about whether **P** and rationally prohibited from believing **P** or disbelieving **P**.

If there were such a thing as an attitude of practical agnosticism, it too should be governed by something along the lines of the above appropriateness norm for agnosticism. However, in Section 7.3, I shall argue that there is no practical attitude that satisfies this specification.

7.3 The Appropriateness Norms for Intention

As we noted in Chapter 1, the expression 'doxastic attitude' is sometimes used to pick out a wide range of belief-like attitudes, including accepting (e.g. Weintraub [1990: 165]), presuming (e.g. Kapitan [1986: 235]), hypothesising (e.g. Williams [1989: 124]), and having a degree of confidence in (e.g. Kaplan [1981: 310]). However, it is often more narrowly used to refer to any member of the multi-attitudinal complex consisting in believing, disbelieving, and withholding.[3] It is in its narrow sense that the term has been employed in this monograph. Since my arguments in this chapter will involve a comparison between believing **P**, disbelieving **P**, and agnosticism towards **P**, on the one hand, and intending to do **X**, intending not to do **X**, and practical agnosticism towards doing **X**, on the other hand, it would be handy to have a catchall term that can stand proxy for the latter three attitudes, one that corresponds with the narrow usage of 'doxastic attitude'. Exploiting the contrast between the Greek terms *doxa* and *praxis* (the etymological progenitors of 'doctrine' and 'practice', respectively), I will use the term *praxistic attitude* for this purpose.

Like belief, intention is governed by appropriateness norms. For example, let us suppose that my recognition of the fact that my friend is severely intoxicated and about to drive herself home provides me with conclusive evidence that I should take her car keys. (One may fill in the details of the case however one pleases to make this plausible, such as specifying that my friend and I have the shared goal of keeping her safe, and so on.) It would be irrational, given my goal of keeping her safe, for me to intend not to take her car keys. Hence, intention appears to be governed by something along the lines of the following appropriateness norm:

Appropriateness Norm for Intending to do X =^{def} If one's competently considered evidence conclusively supports doing **X**, then one is rationally permitted to intend to do X and rationally prohibited from intending not to do **X** (or from practical agnosticism towards doing **X**).

The above appropriateness norm for intending to do **X** assumes that reasons for action take the form of evidence that supports doing **X**. This is merely for the sake of convenience. The arguments in this paper may be revised, mutatis mutandis, in order to accommodate most of the standard theories of practical reasons found in the literature. For example, instead of evidence in support of doing **X**, we may substitute evidence that one will do **X** (Velleman, 1989/2007). Moreover, if one prefers to conceive of reasons for action as explanations of why the action is worthwhile rather than evidence that the action is worthwhile, then one may restate the

---

[3] Examples of the narrow usage of the term 'doxastic attitude' include Conee and Feldman (1985), Steup (1988), Chisholm (1989), Sosa (1991), Feldman (2003), and Steup (2008). For an argument that the attitudes of believing, disbelieving, and withholding (or suspending judgement) are not reducible to degrees of belief, see Friedman (2013b).

appropriateness norm in terms of explanations (Kearns and Star 2008: 37; 2009: 216–217). Moreover, one may also hold that a reason for action only counts as such for an agent if the agent already has certain desires in place or would have certain desires if they were rational and sufficiently informed. The arguments in this paper will tolerate all such reformulations so long as the following condition is met: it should be possible to have conclusive reasons for performing an action such that one would be irrational for failing to act in light of those reasons. What the preceding appropriateness norm claims is that given that one possesses such conclusive reasons, it would be irrational to adopt any praxistic attitude other than intending that which one has conclusive reasons for. Hence, while in the discussion that follows I will generally speak of one's competently considered evidence supporting doing **X**, buying into some particular conception of practical reasons is not a requirement of my argument.

The counterpart to the above appropriateness norm for intending to do **X** is the following appropriateness norm for intending not to do **X**:

Appropriateness Norm for Intending not to do X = ^{def} If one's competently considered evidence conclusively supports not doing **X**, then one is rationally permitted to intend not to do **X** and rationally prohibited from intending to do **X** (or practical agnosticism towards doing **X**).

For example, suppose that I am at the train station and the train conductor tells me that the D train will be out of service for the next two hours and that this constitutes conclusive evidence in support of not taking the D train. According to the above appropriateness norm for intending not do **X**, it would be irrational for me to intend to take the D train.

I have included 'practical agnosticism towards doing **X**' (in parentheses) in my statement of the appropriateness norms for intending to do **X** and intending not to do **X** in order to avoid begging the question against those who affirm the existence of practical agnosticism. Of course, given the aims of this chapter, I ultimately wish to deny that there is any such thing. Even so, the inclusion of 'practical agnosticism towards doing **X**' in appropriateness norms for intending to do **X** and intending not to do **X** underscores a very important point. If there were such a thing as an attitude of practical agnosticism, then it would feature in the appropriateness norms for intending to do **X** and intending not do **X,** just as agnosticism features in the appropriateness norms for believing **P** and disbelieving **P**. Furthermore, practical agnosticism, if there were such a thing, would be governed by an appropriateness norm analogous to the appropriateness norm that governs agnosticism:

7.3 The Appropriateness Norms for Intention

Appropriateness Norm for Practical Agnosticism towards doing X = ^{def}
If one's competently considered evidence equally supports doing **X** and not doing **X**, then one is rationally permitted to be agnostic towards doing **X** and rationally prohibited from intending to do **X** or intending not to do **X**.

However, as I shall argue at present, no such appropriateness norm exists. Suppose I am trying to decide whether to stop by the bookstore on my way home from work. Let us stipulate that the evidence I have in favour of stopping by the bookstore (e.g. I will be able to purchase a novel I have been meaning to read) is equal to the evidence in favour of not stopping by the bookstore (e.g. I will run into an unsavoury associate I have been actively trying to avoid), with the upshot being that my total evidence equally supports going to the bookstore and not going to the bookstore.[4] According to the appropriateness norm for practical agnosticism just offered, I am not rationally permitted to intend to go to the bookstore or intend not to go to the bookstore. But this is clearly false. When confronted with such choice situations, I am free (rationally speaking) to simply pick one of the options. It follows that the rational requirement described by the appropriateness norm for practical agnosticism is false.

Often, when we find ourselves in situations in which we have equal reasons for and against some course of action, we resort to things like flipping a coin or reciting eeny-meeny-miny-moe. It may be claimed that in such situations, it is fact that we decided to flip a coin, and that the coin flip landed in favour of a particular option that gives us a reason to intend that option. However, there are at least two problems with this suggestion. First, even if we often resort to using things like coin-flips when our reasons equally favour two options, it is not obvious that we are rationally required to do so. It seems as though we are free to simply pick, and that such picking would be rationally permissible. Second, the suggestion that flipping a coin provides the agent with a reason generates a bootstrapping worry. If simply flipping a coin is enough to provide me with a reason I did not previously have, then I can always potentially give myself a reason to do something by flipping a coin. However, this seems to do violence to the very concept of a reason. After all, reasons, at their core, are supposed to be non-arbitrary considerations that count in favour of a particular belief or

---

[4] To keep my example simple (and relevant to the present discussion), I have stipulated that the considerations in favour of going to the bookstore and the considerations in favour of not going to the bookstore are commensurable. I do not deny that there may be cases of incommensurability, nor do I deny that one may resort to picking in such situations as well. However, decisions involving incommensurable reasons introduce complications and controversies we need not enter into at present given the aims of this paper.

intention. Moreover, flipping a coin or reciting eeny-meeny-miny-moe appears to introduce the very kind of arbitrariness into our decision-making that reasons are supposed to exclude. Consider an analogy from the case of belief. If I have equal evidence for and against **P**, I am not (rationally speaking) free to flip a coin or recite eeny-meeny-miny-moe to determine whether I should believe or disbelieve **P**. Hence, unless we are willing to give up on the conception of a reason as a non-arbitrary consideration in favour of a belief or intention, we should not hold that flipping a coin provides us with a reason in cases like the bookstore example.

The mistake that the above suggestion seems to make is that it assumes that the significance of flipping a coin or reciting eeny-meeny-miny-moe is normative, when it is in fact psychological. When we have equal reasons for and against a course of action, we are (rationally speaking) free to pick. However, in such cases, it may be psychologically difficult to decide to do one or the other. Consequently, we resort to things like coin flips, reciting eeny-meeny-miny-moe, or some other arbitrary selection procedure. These arbitrary selection procedures do not perform a normative function. They do not, by fiat, generate new reasons we did not previously possess. Rather their role is psychological, providing us with the motivational push we need in cases when our reasons are insufficient for settling the question of whether we should act or refrain from acting.

To briefly recap, the lesson of the bookstore example is that picking is rationally permissible when confronted with the choice between intending to do **X** and intending not to do **X**. This means that rationality does not require in cases in which one's competently considered evidence equally supports doing **X** and not doing **X** that one refrain from intending to do **X** or intending not to do **X**. One is instead free to pick. It follows that the aforementioned appropriateness norm for practical agnosticism does not exist and there is therefore no practical attitude that is normatively analogous to agnosticism towards **P**.

7.4 Agnosticism, Picking, and Buridan's Ass

My argument in favour of the claim that there is no practical analogue to agnosticism relies on an example in which an agent is rationally permitted to engage in picking. The standard examples of picking discussed in the literature involve cases in which an agent is confronted with the choice between two or more qualitatively indistinguishable alternatives. Such cases are what Edna Ullmann-Margalit and Sidney Morgenbesser refer to

7.4 Agnosticism, Picking, and Buridan's Ass

as 'picking situations proper'.[5] The classic example of a picking situation proper involves an agent selecting from two or more qualitatively indistinguishable cans of Campbell's tomato soup on a supermarket shelf.[6] It may be thought that my bookstore example is simply another example of a picking situation proper, and that my argument can therefore hardly be said to break any new ground. In short, all the observations made above have already been made (at least implicitly), and I have therefore done little more than reinvent a now all too familiar wheel. To defend the novelty of the argument presented above, I will demonstrate that there is an important respect in which my bookstore example differs from the standard examples of picking described in the literature, and that the bookstore example supports my conclusion in a way that the standard examples of picking do not.

Let us begin by observing that in picking situations proper, an agent's reasons or evidence is indifferent between two or more options because each consideration in favour of one option equally favours the other options as well. For example, suppose that my reason for buying Campbell's tomato soup, instead of Heinz, is that Campbell's tomato soup is cheaper than Heinz. This consideration is indifferent to whether I take the can of Campbell's tomato soup just to the right of me or the one next to it. This means that, insofar as I am in a picking situation proper, whatever consideration favours one option equally favours the alternative option(s) as well.

My bookstore example differs from a picking situation proper in two noteworthy respects. First, in the bookstore example, the considerations in favour of going to the bookstore are distinct from those that favour not going. This means that the explanation of why I have equal reasons for both options in the bookstore example differs from the explanation of why I have equal reasons for both options in the Campbell-soup-cans example. In the bookstore example, it is stipulated that the consideration in favour of going to the bookstore (i.e. being able to purchase a textbook) is equal in strength to the consideration in favour of not going to the bookstore (i.e. being able to avoid an unsavoury associate). In the Campbell-soup-cans example, it is stipulated that the cans of soup are qualitatively indistinguishable, which entails that any consideration that favours taking one can equally favours taking an alternative can.

---

[5] Ullman-Margalit and Morgenbesser (1977: 763). In addition to 'picking situations proper', Ullman-Margalit and Morgenbesser also briefly discuss 'picking situations by default' (763) and 'deeper-level picking' (783).
[6] I borrow this example from Ullman-Margalit and Morgenbesser (1977).

Second, in the bookstore example, my options are going to the bookstore or not going to the bookstore. This means that my choice is between doing **X** and not doing **X** (where **X** picks out one and the same course of action). By contrast, in the Campbell-soup-cans example, the competing courses of action are taking soup can A and taking soup can B. This means that my choice is not between doing **X** and not doing **X**, but rather between doing **X** and doing **Y** (where **X** and **Y** are entirely different courses of action). We may give a similar analysis of the other example of picking widely discussed in the literature: that of Buridan's ass. In the fictional scenario described by the French philosopher, Jean Buridan, we are invited to imagine a donkey that is presented with the choice between two qualitatively indistinguishable bales of hay. The donkey is unable to decide which of the two bales of hay to eat and eventually starves to death. The choice between eating bale of hay A and bale of hay B is akin to the choice between taking soup can A and taking soup can B, and not like the choice between going to the bookstore and not going to the bookstore. Most significantly, the act of eating bale of hay A is a different action from eating bale of hay B. Hence, like the Campbell-soup-cans case, Buridan's ass represents a case in which an agent is presented with the choice between two entirely different courses of action.

I will refer to cases in which an agent's evidence equally supports doing **X** and not doing **X**, and in which the agent selects one of the options based on extra-rational factors (like flipping a coin or reciting eeny-meeny-miny-moe) as *basic picking*. I call it 'basic picking' because unlike proper picking, which involves selecting between two or more independent actions, basic picking involves selecting between intending to and intending not to perform a single course of action. Hence, basic picking is the most basic case of picking. For ease of comparison, here are succinct definitions of the two kinds of picking just distinguished:

Proper Picking $=^{\text{def}}$ Cases in which one's competently considered evidence equally supports doing **X** and doing **Y**, and in which one decides to either intend to do **X** or intend to do **Y** based on extra-rational factors.

Basic Picking $=^{\text{def}}$ Cases in which one's competently considered evidence equally supports doing **X** and not doing **X**, and in which one decides to either intend to do **X** or intend not to do **X** based on extra-rational factors.

The Campbell-soup-cans example is a case of proper picking in which the competing options are taking soup can A and taking soup can B. The bookstore example is a case of basic picking in which the competing options are going to the bookstore and not going to the bookstore.

Once we observe the aforementioned differences between my bookstore example and picking situations proper, it quickly becomes evident that picking situations proper could not be used to establish that there is no practical analogue to agnosticism. Recall that the appropriateness norm for practical agnosticism (introduced in Section 6.3) takes the form of the following conditional:

Appropriateness Norm for Practical Agnosticism towards doing X = ^{def}
  If one's competently considered evidence equally supports doing **X** and not doing **X**, then one is rationally permitted to practically withhold doing **X** and rationally prohibited from intending to do **X** or intending not to do **X**.

My bookstore example presents a case in which the antecedent of the conditional is satisfied – that is, a case in which an agent's competently considered evidence equally supports doing **X** and not doing **X** – but the consequent of the conditional turns out to be false – that is, one is not rationally prohibited from intending to do **X** or intending not to do **X**. The upshot, I maintain, is that the appropriateness norm for practical agnosticism does not exist and there is therefore no practical attitude that has the normative significance of agnosticism.

The question we now need to ask is if a picking situation proper is also a case in which the antecedent of the aforementioned conditional is true and the consequent is false. The answer is no. In the Campbell-soup-cans example, the agent must choose between two courses of action: (i) taking soup can A and (ii) taking soup can B. In the Buridan's ass example, the ass must also choose between two courses of action: (i) eat from bale A and (ii) eat from bale B. However, the appropriateness norm for practical agnosticism is silent on what to do when one's competently considered evidence equally supports doing **X** and doing **Y** (where **X** and **Y** pick out different courses of action). The norm only tells us what to do when one's competently considered evidence equally supports doing **X** and not doing **X**. This means that neither the Campbell-soup-cans nor the Buridan's ass examples can be used to establish that the conditional instantiated in the appropriateness norm for practical agnosticism is false.

Another way the preceding point may be put is to note that an agent's evidence may equally support doing **X** and doing **Y** even though it does not equally support doing **X** and not doing **X**. This may be true in one of two ways. First, one's competently considered evidence may equally support doing **X** and doing **Y**, while favouring doing **X** over not doing **X**. For example, Buridan's ass may have no more reason to eat from bale A than from bale B, while also having more reason to eat from bale A than it does for not eating from bale A and more reason to eat from bale B than it does for not eating from bale B. This would be true if the ass would be better off eating from at least one of the bales of hay as opposed to eating from neither. Second, one's competently considered evidence may equally support doing **X** and doing **Y**, while favouring not doing **X** over doing **X**. For example, supposed I am presented with the choice between eating two mushrooms, mushroom A and mushroom B, both of which I know to be equally poisonous. In such a case, my competently considered evidence offers no more reason to eat mushroom A than it does to eat mushroom B. On the contrary, since both mushrooms are known to be poisonous, it is stipulated that my total evidence counts equally against eating either mushroom. This means that my competently considered evidence supports not eating mushroom A over eating mushroom A. Given that my evidence also supports not eating mushroom B over eating mushroom B (and to the very same extent), it may also be true that my competently considered evidence equally supports not eating mushroom A and not eating mushroom B. Hence, we cannot conclude from the fact that an agent's evidence equally supports **X** and **Y** that it equally supports doing **X** and not doing **X**. The upshot is that picking situations proper fail to satisfy the antecedent of the conditional described by the appropriateness norm for practical agnosticism and, therefore, cannot be used to establish that it is false.[7]

7.5 Is Indifference Practical Agnosticism?

There may be a temptation to see indifference to whether one does **X** or does not do **X** as a possible candidate for practical agnosticism. However, I shall argue at present that this temptation should be resisted. There are at least two conceptions of indifference that seem relevant to the present discussion: (i) the evidential conception and (ii) the motivational conception. According to the *evidential conception*, an agent is indifferent towards doing **X** just in case her total evidence equally supports doing **X** and not doing **X**. For example, if my total evidence equally favours going to the bookstore and not going to the bookstore, then I am indifferent towards going to the bookstore. On this first proposal, someone is practically

---

[7] Notice that the present point remains true whether we assume that X and Y are mutually exclusive. After all, I can intend not to perform two actions even if they happen to be mutually exclusive. For example, I can both intend not to take the A train and intend not to take the B train, even if taking the A train precludes taking the B train, and vice versa.

7.5 Is Indifference Practical Agnosticism? 143

agnostic towards doing **X** just in case she is evidentially indifferent towards doing **X**.

According to the *motivational conception*, an agent is indifferent towards doing **X** just in case she is equally motivated to do **X** and to not do **X**. (This includes cases in which an agent simply lacks any motivation whatsoever for or against doing **X**, with such instances being merely a limiting case of having equal motivation for and against doing **X**.) Sometimes, being motivationally indifferent about doing **X** is accompanied by a certain phenomenology; there is often something it feels like to be motivationally indifferent. However, it is not obvious that motivational indifference is always accompanied by a certain phenomenology. As such, I wish to remain neutral on the question of whether the feeling of indifference is necessary for being motivationally indifferent. According to this second proposal, someone is practically agnostic towards doing **X** just in case she is motivationally indifferent towards doing **X**.

Unsurprisingly, I do not think either conception of indifference should be identified with practical agnosticism. Let us begin by considering the evidential conception. The main problem with this suggestion is that it conflates the circumstances that give rise to a certain choice situation with a response to that choice situation. Practical agnosticism, were it to exist, would be an instance of the latter rather than former. However, close inspection reveals that evidential indifference is an instance of the former rather than the latter. This becomes clear when we consider the analogy from theoretical agnosticism. Having equal evidence in favour of **P** and ¬**P** is not itself an instance of agnosticism towards P. Rather, it is a description of the kind of situation in which one is rationally required to theoretically withhold **P**. However, we often fail to do what we are rationally required to do. An agent whose total evidence equally supports **P** and ¬**P** may nevertheless believe **P**. For example, an agent who has equal evidence for and against the existence of an all-powerful benevolent creator may nevertheless believe that such a being exists. This illustrates that an agent's total evidence may equally support **P** and ¬**P** and yet the agent fails to be agnostic towards **P**. Hence, agnosticism towards P cannot be identified with being in the situation of having equal evidential support for **P** and ¬**P**. Similarly, if one's competently considered evidence equally supports doing **X** and not doing **X**, this is not an instance of practical agnosticism towards doing **X**. Rather, it is the kind of situation in which it would be rationally appropriate to be practically agnostic towards doing **X**, were there such a thing. In sum, we can no more identify practical agnosticism with being evidentially indifferent than we can identify agnosticism with having equal evidential support for **P** and ¬**P**.

We turn now to the motivational conception of indifference. The problem with this proposal is that it fails to embody the kind of normatively governed attitude that practical agnosticism is supposed to embody. Recall that one feature of theoretical agnosticism is that it is the only doxastic attitude one is rationally permitted to adopt towards **P** when one's evidence equally supports **P** and ¬**P**. This means that if being motivationally indifferent is the normative analogue to agnosticism towards P, then it should be the only rationally permitted praxistic attitude towards doing **X** in cases in which one's evidence equally supports doing **X** and not doing **X**. However, this does not seem to be the case. Other practical attitudes, apart from being motivational indifferent, are rationally permissible in cases in which one's competently considered evidence equally supports doing **X** and not doing **X**. This is because there is no rational prohibition against being most motivated to do **X** when one's competently considered evidence equally supports doing **X** and not doing **X**.

To be clear, I am not here referring to cases of weakness of will, instances in which one is most motivated to perform the less rationally supported course of action. What I have in mind are cases in which one has equally strong reasons in support of doing **X** and not doing **X**, but in which one is more motivated to either do **X** or not do **X**. Consider the following slightly revised version of an example due to Ruth Chang.[8] Suppose that I am walking down the street and the thought of doing a cartwheel suddenly pops into my head. There are reasons for doing a cartwheel – it would be fun, no harm will befall me or anyone else if I did it, etc.—and reasons against doing a cartwheel – it would be a needless exertion of energy, it would make me feel silly, etc. Let us stipulate that my total evidence equally supports doing a cartwheel and not doing a cartwheel.[9] I may still find myself feeling most motivated to do a cartwheel. Or, alternatively, I may find myself most motivated not to do a cartwheel. In either case, it is implausible that I am being irrational because I am not equally motivated to do and not to do a cartwheel. To be clear, I do not wish to deny that often when our evidence equally supports two courses of

---

[8] Chang (2006: 62).
[9] If one holds that a motivational state, like the desire to do a cartwheel, may provide one with a reason, then (for the purpose of the present example) we can assume that whatever rational force the motivational state possesses has already been tallied in the aforementioned weighing of reasons for and against the course of action. This does not preclude the possibility that one may still be more motivated to pursue one of the options. Hence, the case I have described should be entirely

action, we feel no more motivated to do one than the other. I only claim that there is no rational requirement that we do. If this is right, then motivational indifference is not the practical analogue to agnosticism.

7.6 Agnosticism, Acceptance, and the Truth-Aim

In addition to illuminating some of the differences between belief and intention, the non-existence thesis also sheds light on the ways in which an attitude may be said to aim at the truth. To this end, we may distinguish between two ways in which an attitude may aim at truth: a negative sense and a positive sense. To say that an attitude towards **P** aims at truth in a **negative sense** means that acquiring evidence that **P** is false exerts rational pressure on one to give up or refrain from adopting that attitude. For example, to say that believing **P** aims at truth in a negative sense means that acquiring evidence that ¬**P** would exert rational pressure on one to give up the belief (if one already had it) or refrain from adopting the belief. To be clear, saying that some evidence exerts rational pressure on one to give up or refrain from adopting the belief that **P** does not mean that that evidence rationally requires that one give up or refrain from adopting said belief. The evidence in question may be outweighed by some other bit of evidence in favour of **P**. Alternatively, the evidence may be too weak or tentative to warrant giving up or refraining from adopting the belief that **P** all on its own. Hence, to say that acquiring evidence that ¬**P** exerts rational pressure on one to give up or refrain from adopting the belief that **P** means that the evidence is a pro tanto reason to give up or refrain from adopting the belief that **P**.

It will be helpful to have a label for the feature of an attitude in virtue of which it aims at truth in a negative sense. I will use the term 'acceptance' for this purpose.[10] In short, to say that an attitude involves **acceptance** means that the attitude aims at truth in a negative sense. More precisely, *an attitude towards **P** involves accepting **P** just in case acquiring evidence that **P** is false exerts rational pressure on one to give up or refrain from adopting that attitude.* It should be clear from the above definition that believing **P** entails accepting **P**. For example, if I believe that it is sunny, but visually perceive it to be overcast (i.e. I gain evidence that it is not sunny), my perceptual experience exerts rational pressure on me to give up my belief.

---

conceivable, even if one thinks (as does Chang) that the desire to do a cartwheel provides one with a reason to do a cartwheel.

[10] The present notion of acceptance differs from that which features in Bratman's (1992) paper, 'Practical Reasoning and Acceptance Within a Context', since I claim that there is an important sense in which acceptance aims at truth, while Bratman does not.

Hence, it follows from our definition of acceptance that believing **P** entails accepting **P**.

There are at least two ways in which we may conceive of the relationship between acceptance, as I have defined it, and the attitude that implicates it. We may hold that acceptance is a feature or property of an attitude. This is the conception being advocated here. Specifically, I claim that acceptance is the feature of an attitude in virtue of which it aims at truth in the negative sense. However, one may also hold that acceptance is its own distinct attitude, which merely accompanies the attitude of belief. Whatever the merits of this second conception, it is not the one I wish to defend here. For one thing, it seems wrong to say that the belief itself does not aim at truth in a negative sense, it is merely accompanied by an attitude that does. Furthermore, conceiving of acceptance as a feature of an attitude allows me to sidestep the kinds of problems that would arise if we assumed that acceptance was its own distinct attitude. Once it is granted that two distinct attitudes are being invoked, there arises the need for an explanation of why the two attitudes always go together. However, by conceiving of acceptance as a feature of an attitude, we forestall such questions.

To say that an attitude towards **P** aims at truth in a **positive sense** means that adopting or maintaining that attitude is rationally permissible only if one has a surplus of evidence for **P**. By surplus of evidence for **P** I simply mean that one has more evidence in favour of **P** than ¬**P**.[11] For example, suppose that my evidence equally supported the proposition 'It will rain today' and its negation. It would not be rationally permissible for me to either believe or disbelieve that it will rain today. The only rationally permissible attitude I may adopt towards its raining today is that of agnosticism. This means that it is not enough for one to have no evidence against **P** for it to be rationally permissible for one to believe **P**. In cases in which one lacks a surplus of evidence against **P**, but also lacks a surplus of evidence for **P**, agnosticism towards **P** is the rationally appropriate attitude. This is what it means to say that belief aims at truth in a positive sense.

7.6.1 *Acceptance Sans Belief*

Not every instance of accepting **P** is a case of believing **P**. Put differently, there are attitudes that aim at truth in a negative sense, but which do not

---

[11] Since this is merely meant to be a necessary condition for the rational adoption or maintenance of a belief, and not a sufficient condition, I will leave it open how much more evidence one should have in favour of **P** than ¬**P** for a belief to be rationally permissible.

7.6 Agnosticism, Acceptance, and the Truth-Aim

aim at truth in a positive sense. A paradigm example of such an attitude is the legal presumption of innocence in a criminal trial. According to Article 11 of the *United Nation's Universal Declaration of Human Rights*, the legal burden of proof in a criminal trial is always on the prosecution.[12] Within this legal context, it is deemed appropriate for a judge or members of a jury to take a defendant to be innocent, despite the fact that the judge or jury lacks a surplus of evidence in favour of the defendant's innocence. Indeed, since at the beginning of the trial, the defendant may be a complete stranger, the judge or jury may lack any evidence bearing on whether they are innocent. Of course, if during the course of the trial, the judge or jury were to be presented with evidence that the defendant was guilty, this evidence would exert pressure on the judge or jury to give up the legal presumption of innocence. Hence, the legal presumption of innocence may be said to aim at truth in the negative sense. However, since no evidence is needed to establish that a defendant is innocent at the outset for it to be legally permissible to presume that they are innocent, the legal presumption of innocence fails to aim at the truth in a positive sense.

Another case that appears to display the negative truth-aim of acceptance sans the positive truth-aim characteristic of belief is the acceptance that often features in scientific theorising. A scientist may accept a hypothesis for the purpose of conducting an experiment, despite the fact that she lacks a surplus of evidence in favour of the hypothesis. However, if during the course of the experiment, the scientist was to come across evidence that the hypothesis is false, this evidence would exert rational pressure on the scientist to give up the hypothesis. Hence, the acceptance displayed by our imagined scientist may be said to aim at truth in the negative sense. However, given that when the scientist first sets out to conduct the experiment, she need not have a surplus of evidence in favour of the hypothesis for its acceptance to be appropriate, her acceptance of the hypothesis fails to aim at truth in a positive sense.

A third potential example of acceptance sans belief is an argumentative premise that is assumed for reductio. It may be permissible to assume that such a premise is true even if one lacks a surplus of evidence in favour of its truth. However, if one can generate a contradiction, this may exert rational pressure on one to give up the assumed premise. If so, then one's assuming may be said to aim at truth in a negative sense. Hence, one's assuming would involve accepting a certain premise. However, insofar as one did not

---

[12] Brown (2016).

need a surplus of evidence to make the assumption permissible, one's assuming does not aim at truth in a positive sense.

Finally, it may be plausibly argued that intention involves acceptance. Specifically, intending to do **X** entails accepting that one will do **X**. Given our definition of acceptance, this means that evidence that it is false that you will do **X** exerts rational pressure on you to give up your intention. For example, let us suppose that I intend to catch the 11 am train to Toledo and that I learn from the train conductor that the 11 am train to Toledo has been cancelled. Insofar as the conductor's testimony constitutes evidence that it is false that I will be catching the 11 am train to Toledo, it exerts rational pressure on me to give up my intention to catch the 11 am train to Toledo. If follows that intending to catch the 11 am train to Toledo entails accepting that I will catch the 11 am train to Toledo. However, intending to do **X** does not seem to require a surplus of evidence that one would do **X**. This comports with Anscombe's observation that one knows what one is intentionally doing 'without observation'.[13] Contemporary theorists tend to view Anscombe's declaration as an invitation to figure out what positive evidence a subject has for believing that they are performing the action they are intentionally performing. However, if we held that the kind of knowledge to which Anscombe refers involves acceptance rather than belief, then it becomes possible that no positive evidence is required at all. All that is required is the absence of evidence establishing that one is not performing the action in question. While it is unlikely that this is what Anscombe had in mind, I think her intuition that knowledge of one's intentional actions is non-observational lends credence to the idea that intention does not require a surplus of evidence that one would perform the intended action. In short, I believe that Anscombe's claim that intentional action involves a kind of non-observational knowledge tracks something true about intention and that what underlies this truth is that intention fails to aim at truth in a positive sense.

7.6.2 Agnosticism and the Positive Truth-Aim

Significantly, the fact that belief aims at truth in a positive sense is closely tied to the fact that it is part of a tri-attitudinal complex that includes agnosticism. Recall that in cases in which one's evidence for and against **P** is perfectly counterbalanced, it is rationally appropriate for one to be

---

[13] Anscombe (1963: 13, 54).

agnostic towards **P**. One immediate implication of this fact is that believing **P** and disbelieving **P** are rationally appropriate only if one has a surplus of evidence for **P** or against **P**, respectively. This point will necessarily generalise to any attitude that is part of a tri-attitudinal complex that includes a normative analogue to agnosticism. One immediate implication of the present observation is that neither the legal presumption of innocence nor the acceptance of a hypothesis within a scientific framework displays a tri-attitudinal structure akin to believing, disbelieving, and agnosticism. In the case of the legal presumption of innocence, a subject is presumed innocent up until they are shown to be guilty beyond a reasonable doubt. There is no middle ground on the matter. Admittedly, members of a jury may be personally agnostic about whether a defendant is innocent. However, their agnosticism is legally moot. If one is agnostic about the defendant being innocent, one is still legally required to presume that they are innocent. One is only allowed to withdraw one's legal acceptance of their innocence when there is overwhelming evidence against said innocence. Hence, from a legal point of view, there are only two options, to presume that the defendant is innocent, or to pronounce the defendant guilty.

It is likely no accident that the examples of acceptance sans belief listed above are all instrumental or practical in nature. It is because the pronouncements of a jury are practical in their import that there seems to be no allowance for legal agnosticism. Juries deliberate to arrive at a verdict that will guide the court's actions. If the defendant is innocent, they are to be set free, and if they are pronounced guilty, they are subject to punishment. Within this practical framework, there is no instrumental value for an attitude of legal agnosticism. A similar point may be made regarding the acceptance of a hypothesis within an experimental context. One accepts a hypothesis to subject it to experimental confirmation or falsification. Once sufficient evidence has been gathered to establish that a hypothesis is false, it is rejected. Until then, the hypothesis is accepted so that it may perform its instrumental function. The same is plausibly true of the acceptance implicated by an intention. When one intends to do **X**, one accepts that one will do **X**, as a practical matter. As such, one's acceptance that one will do **X** is not subject to the same evidential demands implicated by the belief that one will do **X**.

7.7 Conclusion

In this chapter, I have argued that there is no practical attitude that is the normative analogue of agnosticism. This leaves untouched the idea that there are other praxistic attitudes, apart from intending to do **X** and intending not to do **X**. What does follow from my argument is that if there were some third, fourth, or fifth praxistic attitude, it would not be the practical analogue of agnosticism. The preceding point is one worth making because it not only sheds light on the nature of belief itself, but also highlights an important respect in which belief differs from related attitudes, such as presuming, hypothesising, and assuming. To this end, we have observed that the fact that belief is part of a multi-attitudinal complex that includes agnosticism is sufficient for belief to aim at truth in a positive sense. This follows from the fact that when one lacks a surplus of evidence for or against **P**, agnosticism towards **P** is the rationally appropriate attitude. By contrast, attitudes like the legal presumption of innocence, the acceptance of a hypothesis, or assuming a premise for the purpose of a reductio argument do not aim at truth in a positive sense. It follows that none of the aforementioned of attitudes belongs to a tri-attitudinal complex that includes a normative analogue to the attitude of agnosticism. Hence, the fact that belief belongs to such a tri-attitudinal complex turns out to be one of its most distinguishing features. Furthermore, I have argued that the non-existence of practical agnosticism represents a potential obstacle to the claim that intentions are a kind of belief since unlike belief, and like other attitudes that merely involve accepting, intention only appears to aim at truth in a negative sense but not in a positive sense. If this is right, then a strong cognitivist who identifies intention with belief may be better served claiming, instead, that intention involves acceptance.

CHAPTER 8

Agnosticism and Pragmatic Reasons

8.1 Introduction

The debate between evidentialists and pragmatists is often characterised as a dispute about what kinds of considerations may be reasons for belief. However, I shall argue that this way of characterising the debate is too narrow. Specifically, it leaves out the attitude of agnosticism. Reinstating agnosticism in its proper place in the debate between evidentialists and pragmatists reveals that matters are much more complicated than both sides have typically recognised and necessitates a more nuanced analysis than is standardly countenanced. In this chapter, I hope to go some distance towards supplying such an analysis by advancing a view I shall call **agnosticism-directed pragmatism**. Unlike the traditional formulation of pragmatism, agnosticism-directed pragmatism is consistent with a weak version of evidentialism according to which only a consideration that bears on the question of whether **P** is true can constitute a reason to believe **P**. However, it still constitutes a type of pragmatism in virtue of the fact that it holds that pragmatic factors may constitute a reason to remain agnostic. Hence, when we expand our concern from what kind of considerations may constitute reasons to believe to the question of what kind of considerations may determine which doxastic attitude we adopt, we find that even if pragmatic factors are not included among the former, they nevertheless may be included among the latter.

8.2 Agnosticism and Transparency

Doxastic deliberation is the deliberative process by which we decide whether to believe **P**. Moreover, there are two doxastic attitudes that fall under the umbrella of not believing **P**: disbelieving **P** and agnosticism towards **P**. This means that the process of deciding whether to believe **P** is best conceived of as the process of deciding between three possible doxastic attitudes – believing **P**, disbelieving **P**, or agnosticism towards **P**. This should all be familiar and uncontroversial. However, the implications of the preceding characterisation of doxastic deliberation for the debate between evidentialists and pragmatists is often overlooked. Specifically, while there has been intense and ongoing debate about what kinds of considerations can be reasons to believe **P**, comparatively little has been said about what kinds of considerations can be reasons to be agnostic towards **P**.[1] Hence, while evidentialists have long argued that only evidence – that is, considerations that bear on the truth of **P** – can be a reason for believing **P**, they have been silent on whether only evidence can be reasons for agnosticism towards **P**. However, this second question is also relevant to determining what kinds of considerations may feature in doxastic deliberation.

To illustrate the above point, consider the argument for evidentialism advanced by Nishi Shah (2006). Shah claims that a certain widely accepted feature of doxastic deliberation known as *transparency* entails that only evidence can be reasons for belief.[2] Shah and Velleman (2005) characterise the notion of transparency as follows:

> The deliberative question *whether to believe that **P*** inevitably gives way to the factual question of *whether **P***, because the answer to the latter question will determine the answer to the former. That is, the only way to answer the question *whether to believe that **P*** is to answer *whether **P***. (499)

Transparency is presumed to be an 'unalterable psychological fact' about human beings.[3] The defender of transparency does not deny that pragmatic considerations can and often do influence our beliefs. For example, the fact that I want **P** to be true may make me more inclined to believe **P**. However, according to transparency, pragmatic factors cannot feature as an explicit premise in my deliberation about whether to believe **P**. For example, one could not deliberatively arrive at the belief that **P** based on an inference from the fact that one finds it desirable that **P**. Hence, while the desirability of **P** may (non-deliberatively) influence or cause one to believe

---

[1] A notable exception to this omission is Schroeder (2012).
[2] Shah's argument, which I will not attempt to reconstruct in detail here, begins by arguing that transparency entails a principle which he calls the deliberative constraint (given that the truth of the former can only be satisfactorily explained by the truth of the latter), and that the combination of both transparency and the deliberative constraint entails evidentialism. The upshot of Shah's argument is that any theorist who accepts transparency – a set that includes many pragmatists – must also accept evidentialism. For criticisms of Shah's argument, see: Steglich-Petersen (2008), Yamada (2010), and Howard (2016).
[3] Shah (2006: 484).

8.2 Agnosticism and Transparency

P, it cannot do so by featuring as an explicit premise in one's reasoning about whether to believe **P**. Furthermore, Shah insists that only a consideration that could feature in a piece of reasoning about whether to believe **P** could be accurately described as a reason to believe **P**, a thesis Shah refers to as the 'deliberative constraint' on reasons.[4] When transparency is combined with the deliberative constraint, we arrive at evidentialism, the claim that pragmatic considerations cannot be reasons to believe **P**. Hence, transparency is an essential premise of Shah's argument for evidentialism.

However, there is an important limitation on the scope of transparency that Shah appears to overlook. While transparency imposes a clear restriction on the kinds of considerations that can be reasons to believe **P**, it is silent on the kinds of considerations that may be reasons to be agnostic towards **P**. To see this point clearly, we may distinguish between two versions of transparency, one relating to belief and another to agnosticism.

Belief Transparency: It is an unalterable psychological fact about us that we can deliberatively come to believe **P** only based on considerations that bear on the truth of **P**.

Agnosticism Transparency: It is an unalterable psychological fact about us that we can deliberatively come to be agnostic towards **P** only based on considerations that bear on the truth of **P**.

While Belief Transparency is highly plausible, the same cannot be said of Agnosticism Transparency. This is illustrated by the following example:

SUSPICIOUS SAMANTHA: Samantha is worried that her wife, Emily, may be having an affair and hires a private investigator to observe Emily over the next two weeks. One week into the investigation, the private investigator submits his preliminary findings, which includes photographs and email communication of an incriminating nature. After reviewing the evidence, Samantha concludes that it would be reasonable (i.e. rationally permissible) for her to believe that Emily is cheating on her, given the evidence already available. However, she also recognises that if she were to believe that Emily was being unfaithful, it would probably mean the end of their ten-year marriage. She also reminds herself that the private investigator was paid to conduct a two-week investigation and that it would therefore cost her no additional money to have him continue to gather evidence before she arrived at a final opinion. In light of these considerations, Samantha decides to remain agnostic about whether Emily is being unfaithful until the two-week investigation comes to a close.

Two sets of considerations ultimately dispose Samantha to remain agnostic: the negative consequences to her marriage of her coming to believe that

---

[4] A similar claim has been defended by Jonathan Way (2017).

Emily is cheating (i.e. the high costs of believing), and the fact that it would cost her no additional money to have the private investigator gather evidence for another week (i.e. the low cost of further inquiry). Neither the high cost of believing **P** nor the low cost of further inquiry into **P** bear on the truth of **P**. And yet, these appear to be just the sort of considerations that (for good or for ill) often dispose us to remain agnostic. Moreover, insofar as the high cost of belief and low cost of further inquiry constitute the basis of Samantha's decision to remain agnostic, the SUSPICIOUS SAMANTHA case represents a counterexample to Agnosticism Transparency.

It is worth emphasising that the efficacy of the immediately preceding argument does not require us to hold that it is rationally permissible for Samantha to remain agnostic. This is because transparency is supposed to be a purely descriptive claim about doxastic deliberation, not a normative one. In other words, transparency does not claim that we should settle the deliberative question of whether to believe **P** by answering the question whether **P**. Rather, it claims that it is an 'unalterable psychological fact' that we *do* settle the deliberative question of whether to believe **P** by answering the question whether **P**. Hence, Agnosticism Transparency implies that it would be psychologically impossible for Samantha to deliberatively decide to remain agnostic based on the high cost of belief and the low cost of further inquiry. Since this is false, I conclude that Agnosticism Transparency should be rejected.

The upshot is that the SUSPICIOUS SAMANTHA example reveals the account of transparency advanced by Shah and Velleman to be false. Recall, according to Shah and Velleman (2005, p. 499), 'the only way to answer the question whether to believe that **P** is to answer whether **P**'. What this characterisation of transparency overlooks is that there are at least three different ways in which a consideration may answer the question whether to believe that **P**: (1) it may do this by constituting a reason to believe **P**, (2) it may do this by constituting a reason to disbelieve **P** and thereby constitute a reason not to believe **P**, or (3) it may do this by constituting a reason not to believe **P** without constituting a reason to disbelieve **P**. Given that the high cost of belief or the low cost of further inquiry (i.e. pragmatic considerations) may be an agent's deliberative basis for agnosticism, and given that deciding to remain agnostic is an instance of deciding not to believe, it follows that we may answer the question whether to believe **P** without answering the question whether **P**.

The above observations significantly restrict the scope of the argument for evidentialism limned in Shah (2006). Recall, Shah argues that if we accept transparency, then we must also accept evidentialism. However, if

I am right that we should reject Shah and Velleman's characterisation of transparency in favour of the more restrictive notion of Belief Transparency, then the scope of Shah's argument for evidentialism must be similarly restricted. Even if we hold that only evidence can be a reason to believe (owing to the fact that only evidence can deliberatively dispose us to believe), it remains an open question whether pragmatic considerations may be reasons to remain agnostic (given that pragmatic considerations may deliberatively dispose us towards agnosticism). In sum, the more restrictive notion of Belief Transparency can, at best, only be used to support a more restrictive notion of evidentialism; namely one that is consistent with the thesis that pragmatic considerations may be reasons to be agnostic.

8.3 Agnosticism and Pragmatic Considerations

The aim of the SUSPICIOUS SAMANTHA example is to show that it is possible for pragmatic considerations to deliberatively dispose someone to be agnostic. However, I now wish to defend an even stronger thesis; namely that it is not only possible to be deliberatively disposed to be agnostic based on pragmatic considerations, but also that there are cases in which it is rationally permissible to be agnostic based on pragmatic considerations. Call this stronger, normative claim the *Agnosticism Permissibility Thesis*. Moreover, I hold that agnosticism towards **P** based on some consideration, R, is rationally permissible only if R is a reason in favour of agnosticism towards **P**. Call this the *Rational Agnosticism Constraint*. When the claim that it is rationally permissible to remain agnostic based on pragmatic considerations (Agnosticism Permissibility Thesis) is combined with the claim that a consideration can be a rationally permissible basis for agnosticism only if it is a reason (Rational Agnosticism Constraint), we arrive at the conclusion that pragmatic considerations may be reasons for agnosticism (agnosticism-directed pragmatism).[5]

8.3.1 *The Agnosticism Permissibility Thesis*

Let us begin with a defence of the Agnosticism Permissibility Thesis. Consider the following case:

---

[5] Let 'E(x)' stand for 'x is evidence', 'B(x)' stand for 'x is a rationally permissible basis for agnosticism' and 'R(x)' stand for 'x is a reason for agnosticism'. We may formally represent my argument for agnosticism-directed pragmatism as follows:
1. $\exists x(\neg E(x) \land B(x))$ (Agnosticism Permissibility Thesis)
2. $\forall x(B(x) \rightarrow R(x))$ (Rational Agnosticism Constraint)
3. $\exists x(\neg E(x) \land R(x))$ (Agnosticism-Directed Pragmatism, from 1 and 2).

CAUTIOUS CARL: Carl has the option of depositing a check either today, Friday, or tomorrow, Saturday. As he approaches the bank, he notices through the bank window that there are very long lines inside. Not wanting to wait in line, he thinks it would be best to make the bank deposit the following day. He recalls that he was at the bank two weeks ago on a Saturday and he is unaware of any special holidays coming up. (Let us assume that under normal circumstances, Carl would deem this sufficient evidence to justify believing that bank is open on Saturdays.) However, Carl is also aware that it is not unheard of for banks to change their hours. Moreover, he has just written a very large cheque, and should it turn out that he is mistaken about the bank being open tomorrow, the cheque will bounce. Hence, there are very high stakes attached to Carl being correct about the bank hours. (Let us assume that Carl has no means currently at his disposal to check if the bank is open on Saturdays.) Given the high cost attached to being mistaken, Carl decides to adopt an attitude of agnosticism towards the bank being open tomorrow and decides to brave the long lines in order to be on the safe side.

The process by which Carl arrives at the attitude of agnosticism may be unpacked as follows: Carl begins by considering the evidence for the bank being open next Saturday. He thinks the evidence available is strong enough to make his belief that the bank is open justified. However, his doxastic deliberation does not end there. He then begins to consider pragmatic factors like the high cost of getting things wrong and the ease with which he may acquire further evidence via a Google search. His consideration of these pragmatic factors leads Carl to adopt an attitude of agnosticism.[6] We may suppose that if Carl had not stopped to consider these additional factors he would not have been disposed to adopt an agnostic attitude. In short, Carl's deliberative decision to remain agnostic is based on pragmatic considerations. Moreover, it intuitively seems as though Carl is not guilty of irrationality for agnosticism based on the aforementioned pragmatic considerations.[7]

---

[6] The present characterisation of the CAUTIOUS CARL case comports with Jennifer Nagel's (2008: 291) observation that differences in stakes typically lead to differences in our level of confidence. However, the lessons I draw from this observation differ slightly from those of Nagel.

[7] Examples similar to the CAUTIOUS CARL case have been used to argue for contextualist accounts of knowledge (see, e.g., DeRose (1992: 913–916). However, while contextualists have used these examples to motivate a certain conception of knowledge, the CAUTIOUS CARL case is being marshalled in support of a claim about rationally permissible agnosticism. Fantl and McGrath (2002) also use a pair of similar examples to illustrate how the justificatory standing of a belief may vary based on pragmatic factors. However, they too draw conclusions about knowledge from their example. Unlike both sets of theorists, I am only concerned with rationally permissible belief, not knowledge. See and cf. Cohen (1999). For a similar argument in support of the conclusion that non-evidential reasons may make a difference to epistemic rationality, see: Lord (2020: 140–141).

8.3 Agnosticism and Pragmatic Considerations

There are at least two ways of making sense of the CAUTIOUS CARL case. On the one hand, we may hold that there is only one doxastic attitude Carl is rationally permitted to have at a given time, though what this attitude happens to be may shift across time based solely on pragmatic considerations. Let us begin with the assumption that the evidence Carl has available is strong enough to make his belief justified in most everyday situations. Suppose that at time t_1, Carl has considered the evidence that the bank is open on Saturdays, but has not yet considered the high cost attached to getting things wrong nor the low cost of further inquiry. Thus characterised, we may suppose that Carl is justified in believing at t_1 that the bank is open next Saturday. Moments later, at time t_2, Carl remembers that there is a high cost attached to getting things wrong and a very low cost attached to further inquiry. In the current interpretation of CAUTIOUS CARL, Carl is no longer justified at t_2 in believing that the bank is open. The only doxastic attitude Carl is rationally permitted to adopt at T_2 is one of agnosticism. (Recall, we are assuming that Carl has no positive reason to believe that the bank will be closed next Saturday, which means that disbelief would be rationally impermissible.) Hence, on the current interpretation of CAUTIOUS CARL, Carl is justified in believing that the bank is open next Saturday at t_1 and justified in adopting an attitude of agnosticism towards (but not believing) the bank is open next Saturday at T_2. Furthermore, Carl's evidence has not changed between t_1 and t_2. The only change that has taken place is Carl's consideration at T_2 of a pair of pragmatic factors – that is, the high cost of getting things wrong and low cost of further inquiry.

On the other hand, we may make sense of CAUTIOUS CARL by holding that Carl is rationally permitted at t_2 to either believe or suspend that the bank is open next Saturday (where the 'or' in question is the exclusive 'or'). According to this alternative interpretation, it would be rationally permissible for Carl to believe the bank is open next Saturday at both t_1 and t_2. Hence, were Carl to continue to believe at t_2, instead of switching to an attitude of agnosticism, he would be within his rational prerogative to do so. However, it is also rationally permissible for Carl to remain agnostic at t_2. Hence, Carl is rationally permitted to either believe or suspend at t_2, but not both. The main difference between these two ways of making sense of CAUTIOUS CARL is that the first is consistent with the thesis that there is a single, specific, doxastic attitude an agent is permitted to have, given their competently considered evidence, while the second is not. While this difference between the two interpretations is interesting, it does not bear on efficacy of the present argument. Whether we hold that Carl is justified in believing at t_1 but only justified in being agnostic at t_2 or we hold that Carl is justified in believing at t_1 and justified in either believing or being agnostic (but not both) at t_2, what remains constant is that the considerations that justify agnosticism at t_2 are pragmatic considerations. Hence, on either interpretation, it remains true that there are cases in which it is rationally permissible for an agent to remain agnostic based on pragmatic considerations. Hence, on either interpretation of CAUTIOUS CARL, we arrive at the Agnosticism Permissibility Thesis.

8.4 Schroeder's Belief Sufficiency Principle

In Chapter 6, I argued that the non-existence of a practical analogue to agnosticism accounts for an important difference between practical and theoretical rationality: namely that while picking[8] is rationally permissible in the practical sphere, the same is not true in the theoretical sphere. This difference between practical and theoretical rationality is captured in Harman's (2002) observation that the principle of 'Sufficiency' (below) is true of practical reasoning but false with respect to theoretical reasoning:

Sufficiency: It is rationally permissible for one to do **X** just in case one has at least as much reason to do **X** as to not do **X**.[9]

However, Mark Schroeder (2012) has argued that Harman's claim that Sufficiency governs practical reasoning but not theoretical reasoning rests on the mistaken assumption that practical considerations cannot be reasons for agnosticism. Once we dispense with this assumption, Schroeder insists, it becomes clear that the following more general version of Sufficiency is true of both practical and theoretical reasoning:

General Sufficiency: It is rationally permissible for one to do **X** just in case one has at least as much reason to do **X** as in favour of any of the alternatives to doing **X**.[10]

By Schroeder's lights, General Sufficiency applies as much to belief as it does to intention. In the present context, the relevant alternatives to believing **P** are disbelieving **P** and agnosticism towards **P**. This leads Schroeder to propose the following belief-specific version of General Sufficiency:

---

[8] Picking refers to cases in which two options enjoy equal rational support and one selects one of the two options based solely on extra-rational factors.
[9] Schroeder (2012: 273).   [10] See: Schroeder (2012: 274).

8.4 Schroeder's Belief Sufficiency Principle

Belief Sufficiency: It is rationally permissible for one to believe **P** just in case one has at least as much reason to believe **P** as to disbelieve **P** and one has at least as much reason to believe **P** as to be agnostic towards **P**.[11]

If we assume that only evidence may constitute epistemic reasons, then Belief Sufficiency would be a principle that an evidentialist could consistently accept. What pushes Schroeder's advocacy of Belief Sufficiency into pragmatist territory is the fact that he thinks that certain kinds of pragmatic considerations may constitute a reason to be agnostic. Specifically, Schroeder claims that two kinds of pragmatic considerations may be reasons to be agnostic:

(i) **Type 1 Error**: The costs related to having a false belief.
(ii) **Type 2 Error**: The costs related to not having a true belief.

Given that the costs related to having a false belief or not having a true belief is a pragmatic rather than evidential consideration, it follows that pragmatic considerations may constitute reasons for agnosticism.

The claim that pragmatic factors may constitute a reason to be agnostic is one on which both Schroeder and I agree. However, there are at least two respects in which my defence of agnosticism-directed pragmatism differs from that of Schroeder. First, Schroeder appeals to the existence of pragmatic reasons for agnosticism in an effort to defend Belief Sufficiency and Belief Consistency is a thesis I reject. Second, Schroeder claims that reasons to be agnostic cannot be evidence and this is something I also deny. Let us consider each of these points of disagreement between Schroeder and I in turn.

8.4.1 A Counterexample to Belief Sufficiency

We may arrive at a counterexample to Belief Sufficiency by considering a case in which a subject's evidence for and against **P** is perfectly counterbalanced and in which there are no reasons, as Schroeder conceives of them, for being agnostic towards **P**.

Consider ASTRONOMICAL BODY, the example introduced in Section 3.4 of this monograph in which an agent, Maria, is trying to determine whether there is an astronomical body located exactly 10^{90} cubic meters away from earth. As we previously noted, since 10^{90} cubic meters is outside earth's Hubble Sphere, light leaving that region of space could, in

---

[11] See: Schroeder (2012: 274).

principle, never reach earth. Hence, there is no possible observation that could either confirm or disconfirm the existence of an object in that region of space. Moreover, since the speed of light is actually the speed of causality, an object outside our Hubble Sphere could never causally influence us in any way. This means that, as a matter of fact, whether there is an astronomical body located exactly 10^{90} cubic meters away from earth can have no practical consequences for us earth-bound humans. It follows that there could be no cost attached to falsely believing or failing to truly believe that there is an astronomical body exactly 10^{90} cubic meters away from earth. Admittedly, were Maria inebriated, mentally exhausted, or otherwise cognitively compromised, this would constitute a reason for her to adopt an attitude of agnosticism until her cognitive faculties were back in order. However, since it is not always true that someone's cognitive faculties are compromised in one of the aforementioned ways, we may safely stipulate that Maria's mental faculties are in optimal condition on the occasion in question. This still leaves the scenario in which an assailant threatens someone with harm unless they form the belief that there is an astronomical body exactly 10^{90} cubic meters away from earth. However, Schroeder explicitly states that this would not be the kind of pragmatic factor that could constitute a reason to be agnostic.[12] The upshot is that all of the potential reasons to be agnostic – identified by Schroeder are absent in ASTRONOMICAL BODY.

Given the absence of reasons to be agnostic (at least, by Schroeder's lights), we are only left with the reasons for and against the existence of an astronomical body exactly 10^{90} cubic meters away from earth. Given that Maria has no observational evidence either for or against the existence of such an astronomical body – that is, she has at least as much reason to believe such an object exists as she does for disbelieving such an object exists – and given that Maria has no reason, as Schroeder conceives of them, to be agnostic – that is, her reasons for believing are at least as good as her reasons for agnosticism – it follows, according to Belief Sufficiency, that it is rationally permissible for Maria to believe that there is an astronomical object in a region of space that is, in principle, beyond all possible observation. This, it goes without saying, is the wrong result.

Significantly, the present objection to Belief Sufficiency does not presuppose that pragmatic reasons for agnosticism do not exist. Indeed, I am committed to the existence of such pragmatic reasons. Hence, the present objection to Belief Sufficiency differs from that due to Stewart Cohen

---

[12] See especially: Schroeder (2012: 277–278).

(2016). Cohen's argument relies on the general rejection of the idea of there are pragmatic reasons to be agnostic. By contrast, the present objection relies on the existence of a single case in which such pragmatic reasons are not operative in order to create a counterexample to Belief Sufficiency. Since one may consistently hold that pragmatic reasons for agnosticism exist and that such pragmatic reasons may be missing in a particular case, the argument against Belief Sufficiency presently on offer is one that the defender of agnosticism-directed pragmatism may accept.

My diagnosis of why Belief Sufficiency fails is that it offers a standard for rationally permissible belief that may be satisfied when we have no reasons for all three doxastic attitudes, as these are conceived of by Schroeder. This is because having no reasons for all three doxastic attitudes is one way for the reasons for believing **P** to be at least as much as our reasons for believing ¬**P** and at least as much as our reasons for agnosticism towards **P**. The problem with Belief Sufficiency is not, contra Cohen, that it implies that it is always rationally permissible to believe **P** when one's evidence for and against **P** is perfectly counterbalanced, but that it allows for this possibility in those cases in which all the pragmatic factors that could potentially provide one with reasons to be agnostic are absent. That such a situation may arise is what ASTRONOMICAL BODY illustrates. I conclude that Belief Sufficiency is false.

8.4.1 *Evidential Reasons for Agnosticism*

Schroeder summarises his argument in support of the claim that reasons to be agnostic cannot be evidence as follows:

> Why is it that reasons to withhold cannot be evidence? It is because the evidence is exhausted by evidence which supports **P** and evidence which supports ¬**P**. But the evidence which supports **P** is reason to believe **P**, and the evidence which supports ¬**P** is reason to believe ¬**P**. Consequently the reasons to withhold must come from somewhere else. So they cannot be evidence.[13]

Significantly, Schroeder's argument relies on a conception of evidence that is at odds with the one we have been presupposing in our discussion thus far. Recall, we defined evidence with respect to **P** as a consideration bearing on whether **P**. However, supporting **P** or ¬**P** is not the only way a consideration may bear on whether **P**. This point is illustrated by the following example:

---

[13] Schroeder (2012: 276).

RADIOACTIVE ISOTOPE: Margaret is considering whether a certain radioactive isotope will emit a single alpha particle within the next 60 seconds. The available data indicates (i) that since reality is fundamentally probabilistic at the level of physical process in question, the best she could hope for is a specification of the likelihood of a particle emission within a given time frame and (ii) that the likelihood of an alpha particle emission within the next 60 seconds by the isotope in question is exactly 0.5. This data prompts Margaret to adopt an attitude of agnosticism towards the proposition that the radioactive isotope will emit a single alpha particle within the next 60 seconds.[14]

Notice that Margaret lacks any data suggesting that there will be an alpha particle emission within the next 60 seconds. Hence, it seems correct to say that she has no evidence in favour of the proposition. She also lacks any data suggesting that there will not be an alpha particle emission within the next 60 seconds. Hence, it seems correct to say that she has no evidence against the proposition. Nevertheless, it is false that she lacks any data bearing on whether there will be an alpha particle emission within the next 60 seconds.

Margaret's epistemic situation after learning that the likelihood of an alpha particle emission seems quite different from the one she was in prior to considering the data. Before considering the data, Margaret was entirely in the dark with respect to the question. For example, if one of her colleagues invited her to make a bet about whether there would be such an emission, she would have no idea what level of risk would be involved in making such a wager and would therefore be unable to determine if it would be a wager she would be willing to undertake. However, after considering the data, Margaret is well-positioned to evaluate the level of risk and thereby ascertain whether it is a gamble she would be willing to make.

Furthermore, the information provided by the data Margaret considers appears to fall on a continuum that includes data for and against the proposition. It is uncontroversial that if the data revealed that there were a

---

[14] I assume that the days in which it was hotly debated, at least among theoretical physicists, whether god played dice with the universe are now behind us and that the current consensus is that physical reality, at its most fundamental level, is genuinely non-deterministic and irreducibly probabilistic. However, it will not matter, as far as the efficacy of any of the arguments to follow is concerned, whether the presumed consensus is correct. The question with which we will be concerned is what Margaret is rationally permitted to believe, as opposed to what Margaret knows. Given that a belief may be justified based on the available evidence even if false, we may safely suppose that the data Margaret has available indicates (i) and (ii), irrespective of what our personal metaphysical commitments on the matter happen to be.

8.4 Schroeder's Belief Sufficiency Principle

0.4 likelihood of an alpha particle emission within the next 60 seconds, this would have some bearing on whether there would be such an emission. Likewise, if the data had revealed that the likelihood of such an emission was 0.6. It therefore seems odd to suggest that because the data revealed the likelihood of an alpha particle emission to be 0.5 rather than 0.4 or 0.6, the data has no bearing on the question. In all three cases, Margaret learns something about the likelihood of an alpha particle emission. Moreover, in all three cases the information Margaret acquires may serve as a basis for various inferences; for example, she learns something about the state of the radioactive isotope an hour from now or about the likelihood of an emission if she were observing 60 as opposed to just one of the radioactive isotopes during the time in question. This would not be possible if the data indicating the 0.5 likelihood had no bearing on the matter. I take these considerations to show that her discovery that the likelihood of an alpha particle emission is 0.5 to have some bearing on the question of whether there will be such an emission.

It should be emphasised that it is not here being claimed that Margaret's discovery of the 0.5 likelihood of an alpha particle emission within the next 60 seconds is either evidence for or against said emission. Rather, what is here being claimed is that evidence for and against **P** are not the only kinds of evidence bearing on whether **P**. In short, I reject Schroeder's narrow conception of evidence along with the implication that reasons for agnosticism could not include evidence. Moreover, I am not alone in questioning the narrow conception of evidence presupposed by Schroeder's analysis. For example, Blake Roeber (2016) tentatively endorses the following account of non-evidential reasons to withhold judgement:

> **Non-Evidential Reasons**: R is a non-evidential reason for one to withhold judgement with respect to **P** just in case R is a reason for one to withhold with respect to **P** that is neither evidence for **P**, nor evidence for ¬**P**, nor some fact about one's evidence for and against **P**.[15]

Notice that the immediately preceding account of non-evidential reasons explicitly excludes facts about a subject's evidence. Roeber describes facts about a subject's evidence as follows:

> Let **P** be some proposition that I cannot rationally believe without evidence (e.g., that it will rain tomorrow), suppose that I do have some evidence for **P**, but suppose that my evidence for **P** is perfectly counterbalanced by equal evidence for ¬**P**, so that my credence in **P** should be exactly 0.5. This fact

---
[15] Roeber (2016: 442).

about my evidence (call it 'f') is a paradigm reason for me to withhold with respect to **P**.[16]

Two points about Roeber's account of non-evidential reasons for withholding are worth noting. First, insofar as a non-evidential reason for agnosticism excludes facts about one's evidence for and against **P**, then we may safely assume that such facts constitute an evidential reason to be agnostic by Roeber's lights.[17] Hence, Non-Evidential Reasons is at odds with the narrow conception of evidence found in Schroeder. The upshot is that I am not alone in endorsing a broader conception of evidence than that presupposed by Schroeder – that is, one that is not limited to evidence for and against a proposition.

While Roeber is open to a broader conception of evidence than that found in Schroeder, the specific example of evidence offered by Roeber differs in important ways from my own. Specifically, the putative example of evidence – implicated in RADIOACTIVE ISOTOPE is not a fact about Margaret's evidence. Margaret's situation is not that of a subject who has some evidence for **P** and some evidence for ¬**P**, and who, upon weighing both sets of evidence against each other, concludes that they are equally strong. Margaret does not have two competing sets of evidence – that is, evidence for and evidence against there being an alpha particle emission within the next 60 seconds. Rather, she has a single piece of putative evidence: namely evidence that there is a 0.5 likelihood of an alpha particle emission within the next 60 seconds. Hence, the consideration that leads Margaret to adopt an attitude of agnosticism is not a higher-order fact about her evidence for and against **P**, but rather a fact that bears directly on **P** – that is, on the likelihood of **P** being true. This means that the fact that features in Radioactive Isotope is an even better candidate for being a reason bearing on whether **P** than the fact that features in Roeber's analysis. If we are open to the possibility of facts about someone's evidence for and against **P** constituting evidence bearing on whether **P**, then a fortiori, we should be open to a consideration that directly shows that the likelihood of **P** is 0.5 constitutes evidence bearing on whether **P**.

8.5 Agnosticism and Evidentialism

I wish to conclude by highlighting a few of the implications of the preceding discussion for the debate between evidentialism and pragmatism.

---

[16] Roeber (2016: 441).
[17] See and cf: Feldman (2005), Kelly (2005, 2010), Christensen (2010a), and Lasonen-Aarnio (2014).

8.5 Agnosticism and Evidentialism

Evidentialism is sometimes equated with the claim that, as Anthony Booth puts it, 'only evidentialist considerations determine the rationality of belief (or of doxastic attitudes in general)' (Booth 2007, p. 405). However, the account defended in this paper suggests that the inclusion of the parenthetical 'or of doxastic attitudes in general' in Booth's definition of evidentialism is far from benign. This is because there is an important difference between the claim that only evidentialist considerations determine the rationality of belief and the claim that only evidentialist considerations determine the rationality of doxastic attitudes in general. Hence, it is important to distinguish between the following two versions of evidentialism.

Weak Evidentialism: R is a reason for one to believe **P** only if R is a consideration that is relevant to answering the question of whether **P** is true.

Strong Evidentialism: R is a reason for one to believe **P**, disbelieve **P**, or be agnostic towards **P** only if R is a consideration that is relevant to answering the question of whether **P** is true.

Weak Evidentialism is consistent with agnosticism-directed pragmatism. This is because Weak Evidentialism is a claim about what kinds of considerations can be a reason for belief while agnosticism-directed pragmatism is a claim about what kinds of considerations can be a reason for agnosticism. By contrast, Strong Evidentialism – which involves a claim about what kinds of considerations can determine the rationality of doxastic attitudes in general – is not consistent with agnosticism-directed pragmatism.

This leaves the evidentialist with a dilemma when confronted with the plausibility of agnosticism-directed pragmatism. On the one hand, the evidentialist may embrace Weak Evidentialism in lieu of Strong Evidentialism, thereby avoiding the challenge posed by agnosticism-directed pragmatism to the latter. However, the cost of doing this is that the evidentialist is forced to give up on the idea that only evidence can feature in doxastic deliberation. This is because doxastic deliberation involves more than deliberation that happens to lead to the belief that **P**. It also includes deliberation leading to disbelieving **P** and agnosticism towards **P**. Given the formal (if not psychological) equivalence of disbelieving **P** and believing ¬**P**, it is arguable that any satisfactory account of what may constitute a reason to believe may also serve as a satisfactory account of what may constitute a reason to disbelieve. But this still leaves the doxastic attitude of agnosticism towards **P** unaddressed. This means that establishing the truth of Weak Evidentialism is not sufficient to establish that only evidence qualifies as reasons in doxastic deliberation. On the other hand, the evidentialist may embrace Strong Evidentialism, thereby preserving their right to claim that only evidence can feature in doxastic deliberation. However, this would put their view within the firing range of the argument for agnosticism-directed pragmatism offered in this chapter.

A second implication of agnosticism-directed pragmatism is that formulations of transparency that are typically taken to be equivalent to each other turn out not to be. For example, consider the formulations of transparency found in Steglich-Petersen (2008) and Howard (2016):

> Transparency is the feature of doxastic deliberation that the deliberative question of *whether to believe that* **P** inevitably gets decided by answering a different question, namely that of *whether* **P**. (Steglich-Petersen 2008, p. 541, *italics* his)

> If you deliberatively determine that it would be prudentially (or morally) good for you to believe that **P**, your deliberation alone will not issue in a belief that **P**. (Howard 2016, p. 1192)

Notice that the focus of Steglich-Petersen's formulation of transparency is on the deliberative question of whether to believe that **P**. As we already noted, the deliberative question of whether to believe that **P** is elliptical for the deliberative question of *whether to believe that* **P**, and one of the ways to *not believe that* **P** is to be agnostic towards **P**. This means that Steglich-Petersen's formulation of transparency entails Agnosticism Transparency. Moreover, Agnosticism Transparency has been shown to be false by the SUSPICIOUS SAMANTHA example.

By contrast, Howard's formulation of transparency only entails Belief Transparency. That is, it assumes that one can deliberatively arrive at the belief that **P** only based on considerations that bear on the truth of **P** but it makes no claims about deliberation that issues in agnosticism towards **P**. This means that Howard's formulation of transparency is consistent with the SUSPICIOUS SAMANTHA example. This result is surprising since both Steglich-Petersen and Howard take their formulations to be equivalent to or mere elaborations of the account of transparency found in Shah (2006: 481): 'The deliberative question whether to believe that **P** inevitably gives way to the factual question whether **P**.' However, insofar as Steglich-Petersen's formulation of transparency shares the same defect as Shah's: namely both accounts of transparency entail Agnosticism Transparency, while Howard's formulation does not, it follows that the two formulations

8.5 Agnosticism and Evidentialism

of transparency are not equivalent to each other. This means that despite Howard's claims to the contrary, his formulation of transparency is not equivalent to or a mere elaboration of that found in Shah (2006). These are subtleties that are easily overlooked when we fail to distinguish between an agent's basis for believing and an agent's basis for not believing (i.e. adopting an attitude of agnosticism). Agnosticism-directed pragmatism better enables us to appreciate these nuances.

A third implication of agnosticism-directed pragmatism is that it brings into sharp relief an important, but often overlooked, distinction between pragmatism and the **uniqueness thesis**. According to evidentialism, only evidential considerations can be reasons for belief. According to the uniqueness thesis, there is only one rationally permissible doxastic response to a given body of evidence. The following passage from Dorit Ganson (2008) illustrates how the two theses are sometimes conflated:

> At issue is the tenability of evidentialism, a view that takes differences with respect to practical needs and interests to be relevant to epistemic assessment: if two subjects S and S′ have the same evidence for and against **P**, then S and S′ cannot differ with respect to whether they are epistemically justified in believing **P**. (443)

Notice that on Ganson's characterisation of evidentialism, the view entails the uniqueness thesis: the claim that two agents cannot have the same evidence for and against **P**, and yet differ in the doxastic attitude they are rationally permitted to have towards **P**.[18] However, one could be a weak evidentialist without being committed to the uniqueness thesis. Recall, according to weak evidentialism, only evidence can be a reason to believe **P**. This, we noted is consistent with agnosticism-directed pragmatism, the claim that pragmatic considerations may be reasons to be or remain agnostic. Now, suppose that S and S′ have the same evidence, but that S′ also has pragmatic considerations in support of agnosticism towards **P** while S fails to have such considerations. It would be possible for S to be

---

[18] Admittedly, there are theorists who distinguish between reasons for belief and epistemic justifications for belief, such that reasons for belief are not restricted to epistemic justifications for belief. Given such an approach, one may see Ganson's version of evidentialism as restricted to epistemic justification, and not a claim about reasons, simpliciter. However, understood in these terms, evidentialism is consistent with most versions of pragmatism. Since Ganson takes herself to be in conversation with the likes of Shah and given that she takes her version of evidentialism to be at odds with most (if not all) versions of pragmatism, it is doubtful that Ganson would allow that pragmatic considerations may be reasons to believe, even if they are not epistemic justifications for believing. Considering this, I will proceed under that assumption that Ganson's notion of epistemic justification is co-extensive with reasons for belief.

justified in believing **P**, while S′ is justified in agnosticism towards **P**, even though S and S′ have the same evidence. The upshot is that one may be a weak evidentialist without subscribing to the thesis that if two subjects have the same evidence, then they cannot differ with respect to the doxastic attitude they are justified in having.

Matters become even more complicated when we consider the two interpretations of the CAUTIOUS CARL case limned in Section 7.3.1. Recall, on both interpretations, pragmatic factors may make it rationally permissible for an agent to remain agnostic. In this respect, both interpretations are at odds with the uniqueness thesis as it is standardly understood. On the standard interpretation of the uniqueness thesis, there is only one rationally permissible doxastic attitude given a certain body of evidence. This means that the introduction of pragmatic factors should not matter as far as which doxastic attitude an agent is rationally permitted to have at a given time. Call the standard formulation of the uniqueness thesis evidential uniqueness.

Evidential Uniqueness: Given a certain body of evidence, e, at some time t, there is only one rationally permissible doxastic attitude one may have at t in response to e.

Evidential Uniqueness contrasts with versions of the uniqueness thesis that have to do with an agent's reasons as opposed to an agent's evidence. Call this version of the uniqueness thesis Reasons Uniqueness.

Reasons Uniqueness: Given an agent's total reasons, R, at some time t, there is only one rationally permissible doxastic attitude one may have at t in response to R.

Reasons Uniqueness maintains that there is only one doxastic attitude that an agent is rationally permitted to adopt at a given time, but it takes no stance on what may constitute a reason. Hence, in contradistinction to Evidential Uniqueness, Reasons Uniqueness is consistent with the claim that pragmatic considerations may be reasons. The result is that while Evidential Uniqueness is at odds with both the less permissive and more permissive interpretations of the CAUTIOUS CARL case, Reasons Uniqueness is only at odds with the more permissive interpretation. Recall, according to the less permissive interpretation, the only doxastic attitude Carl is permitted to have at t_2 is that of adopting an attitude of agnosticism towards the bank being open next Saturday. According to the less permissive interpretation, to arrive at a correct assessment of an agent's reasons, we must consider not only the evidence they have available but also certain salient pragmatic factors, such as the high cost attached to getting things wrong or the low cost of further inquiry. However, given Carl's total reasons at t_2 (which includes both evidential and pragmatic considerations), there is only one doxastic attitude (i.e. agnosticism) that Carl is rationally permitted to have at t_2. Contrast this with the more permissive interpretation, which states that Carl is rationally permitted to either continue to believe at t_2 that the bank will be open next Saturday or adopt an attitude of agnosticism at t_2 towards the bank being open next Saturday. Hence, the more permissive interpretation not only allows evidential and pragmatic considerations to constitute reasons, but it also holds that it may be rationally permissible for two agents with the same total reasons, to have different doxastic attitudes.

When we distinguish between Weak Evidentialism and Strong Evidentialism, on the one hand, and Evidential Uniqueness and Reasons Uniqueness, on the other hand, what emerges is a richer tapestry of the relationship between pragmatism and evidentialism and between pragmatism and the uniqueness thesis. First, while Strong Evidentialism is inconsistent with agnosticism-directed pragmatism, Weak Evidentialism is not. Hence, we can no longer simply say that evidentialism and pragmatism are mutually exclusive proposals. A great deal will depend on what kind of evidentialism and what kind of pragmatism one is talking about. Moreover, while Evidential Uniqueness is at odds with agnosticism-directed pragmatism, Reasons Uniqueness is not. Insofar as Reasons Uniqueness allows that Carl's reasons to remain agnostic may include pragmatic considerations, it is consistent with the less permissive interpretation of the CAUTIOUS CARL case. Hence, both Weak Evidentialism and Reasons Uniqueness turn out be consistent with agnosticism-directed pragmatism.

8.6 Conclusion

The aim of this chapter has been to reinstate the attitude of agnosticism in its proper place in the debate between evidentialists and pragmatists. Both sides of the debate have typically focused on the question of what kinds of considerations may be reasons to believe, but have largely neglected to consider the question of what kinds of considerations may be reasons not to believe (i.e. to be agnostic). Examples like that of CAUTIOUS CARL illustrate that it is not only possible for an agent to deliberatively arrive at agnosticism based on pragmatic considerations but also that it may be rationally permissible for an agent to do so. Several important consequences follow from this observation. First, the scope of transparency – as a descriptive constraint on doxastic deliberation – is restricted to only one aspect of doxastic deliberation (i.e. deliberatively arriving at believing **P**), but fails to extend to another aspect of doxastic deliberation (i.e. deliberatively arriving at agnosticism towards **P**). Second, the scope of arguments for evidentialism that rely on transparency (such as that advanced by Nishi Shah) is also restricted. At best, such arguments may establish that only evidence can be reasons for belief. But they cannot establish that only evidence can be reasons not to believe. Third, it underscores the need to distinguish between two versions of evidentialism: one that only applies to the kinds of considerations that may be reasons for belief (Weak Evidentialism) and another that applies to the kinds of considerations that may be reasons for doxastic attitudes in general (Strong Evidentialism). Furthermore, it is revealed that Strong Evidentialism is shown to be false by counterexamples like the CAUTIOUS CARL case. Finally, it reveals that the relationship between evidentialism and the uniqueness thesis is much more complicated than certain theorists have recognised. Specifically, there are versions of evidentialism (i.e. Weak Evidentialism) that do not entail the uniqueness thesis, and there are versions of the uniqueness thesis (i.e. Reasons Uniqueness) that are consistent with certain versions of pragmatism (i.e. agnosticism-directed pragmatism). Presumably, the preceding list of implications of this chapter's central claims is incomplete. However, I believe it is sufficient to establish that agnosticism-directed pragmatism – the thesis that pragmatic considerations may constitute reasons to be agnostic – deserves serious consideration by both sides of the debate between evidentialists and pragmatists.

CHAPTER 9

Agnosticism, Permissivism, and Peer Disagreement

9.1 Introduction

Permissivism is the thesis that it may be rationally permissible to adopt different doxastic attitudes towards a proposition in response to evidence bearing on the truth or falsity of that proposition. In this chapter, I will defend a moderate version of permissivism according to which there are situations in which it is rationally permissible to either believe **P** based on some body of evidence *e* or not believe **P** based on *e*. Since this version of permissivism is one that juxtaposes believing **P** with not believing **P**, without specifying which attitude, or attitudes, are included under the umbrella of 'not believing **P**', I will refer to it as **negative permissivism**. Negative permissivism fails to take a stand on whether it is ever rationally permissible to believe **P** and disbelieve **P**. In this respect, negative permissivism contrasts with the version of permissive endorsed by Miriam Schoenfield (2014): 'The kind of permissivist that I am interested in will sometimes want to say that it is permissible, given *e*, to believe **P** and permissible, given *e*, to believe ¬**P**' (199). I will refer to versions of permissivism that explicitly identify disbelieving **P** and/or believing ¬**P** as rationally permissible alternatives to believing **P** as **positive permissivism**. Hence, we arrive at the following definitions of negative and positive permissivism:

Negative Permissivism: Given some body of evidence, *e*, it may be rationally permissible for one to believe **P** based on *e* or not believe **P** based on *e*.

Positive Permissivism: Given some body of evidence, *e*, it may be rationally permissible for one to believe **P** based on *e*, disbelieve **P** based on *e*, or be agnostic towards **P** based on *e*.

Some of the arguments I will advance in favour of negative permissivism may also be marshalled, mutatits mutandis, in support of positive permissivism. However, one may consistently accept negative permissivism while also rejecting positive permissivism. Moreover, given that this a monograph on the attitude of agnosticism, I will be almost entirely concerned with putative permissive cases in which one of the permitted attitudes is that of agnosticism. To this end, I wish to remain non-committal on whether there are positive permissive cases – that is, instances in which it is rationally permissible to believe **P**, given *e*, and disbelieve **P**, given *e*.

The most glaring exception to the above restriction on the scope of this chapter will be my discussion of peer disagreement. Cases of peer disagreement are instances in which two subjects become aware that they are in a permissive case (or at least so I shall argue, below). The standard case of peer disagreement are ones in which one subject believes P and another subject disbelieves P based on some shared body of evidence, *e*. In keeping with the common practice in peer disagreement literature, my discussion of peer disagreement in the second half of this chapter will focus on standard cases of peer disagreement. Insofar as there are such cases, I shall argue that both subjects are rationally required to adopt an attitude of agnosticism in response to a discovered peer disagreement. This is what Michele Palmira (2013) has dubbed the **Agnostic Response** to peer disagreement. I conclude the chapter by considering cases of peer disagreement in which one of the subjects is agnostic. Pace Palmira, I argue that the Agnostic Response is rationally appropriate in such cases as well.

9.2 Agnosticism-Involving Permissivism

The main theoretical motivation for permissivism is the idea that it is implausible that there is a single, unique level of confidence we are allowed to have in a proposition, given some body of evidence. Schoenfield illustrates the intuitive appeal of this theoretical motivation by inviting her readers to consider the question of how many black ravens one must observe to be justified in believing that all ravens are black? It seems implausible to suggest that it is 200 as opposed to 199 or 201 – that is, that there is some exact number of observed black ravens that all rational subjects will agree on for the belief that all ravens are black to be justified. If there is no such precise number, then it is easy to imagine a case in which one subject comes to rationally believe that all ravens are black after observing 199 black ravens while another subject remains rationally agnostic after observing 199 black ravens.

While the preceding consideration offers some support for negative permissivism, it is less clear that it supports positive permissivism. What the raven example highlights is that the precise threshold of evidence necessary to move a rational subject from non-belief to belief will plausibly vary. However, this gives little reason to think that one subject may rationally believe that all ravens are black while another subject rationally disbelieves that all ravens are black, after observing a certain number of black ravens. Prior to any observation, the starting place would be one of agnosticism towards the proposition that all ravens are black. Given this starting point, observing a single non-black raven would be sufficient to justify disbelieving all ravens are black. However, if the first ten ravens one observed were all black, and then the next ten observed ravens were black, and so on, then at no point should one begin to disbelieve that all ravens are black. Hence, insofar as different subjects have different evidential thresholds for belief, there will inevitably come a point at which the subject with the lower threshold will begin to believe that all ravens are black while the subject with the higher threshold will continue to be agnostic about whether all ravens are black. The upshot is that if we allow different rational subjects to have different thresholds for belief, there will inevitably be agnosticism-involving permissive cases.

My attraction to permissivism is rooted in the idea that there may be multiple rationally permissible epistemic standards. I define an **epistemic standard** as the weight a subject assigns to some evidence or the threshold of support that a subject thinks some evidence must meet in order to justify a belief.[1] However, all of the arguments I will offer in support of my position in this chapter will be consistent with all of the conceptions of epistemic standards highlighted by Schoenfield in the following passage:

> What are a subject's epistemic standards? There are different ways of thinking of epistemic standards. Some people think of them as rules of the form "Given *e*, believe **P**!" Others think of them as beliefs about the correct way to form other beliefs. If you are a Bayesian, you can think of a subject's standards as her prior and conditional probability functions.[2]

All epistemic standards are not created equal. I hold that an epistemic standard is rationally permissible just in case (i) it reliably warrants believing **P** in cases in which **P** is true and reliably warrants not believing **P** in cases in which **P** is false and (ii) no other epistemic standard is known or

---

[1] Permissivists who hold that there may be multiple rationally permissible epistemic standards typically distinguish between factors like the weight that should be assigned to a piece of evidence, which may differ between rational subjects, and the norms governing belief formation that every rational subject should agree about, such as the logical principles of modus ponens and conjunction elimination. I will refer to norms governing belief formation that all rational subjects should agree on, irrespective of their epistemic standards, as rational norms. To avoid confusion, I will assume that epistemic standards stand in a disjunctive relationship to rational norms.
[2] Schoenfield (2014: 199).

justifiably believed to be more reliable. Furthermore, it seems prudent to conceive of the reliability of an epistemic standard in terms of how it handles non-misleading evidence. *Misleading evidence* is evidence that, taken at face value, supports a false proposition. For example, suppose that one of my co-workers, who is usually well-informed and honest, tells me that she saw the branch supervisor enter his office earlier this morning. However, the branch supervisor is out sick and the person my co-worker saw enter the supervisor's office is the supervisor's twin brother, who dropped by to collect a few things at the supervisor's request. Any positive weight I give to the evidence constituted by my co-worker's testimony would point me towards a false conclusion. Were I to arrive at a false belief in such a case, the problem would not be that my epistemic standard assigns an inappropriate weight to my co-worker's testimony (given that we have already stipulated that my co-worker is usually reliable), but that the evidence itself is misleading. It would be inappropriate to penalise an epistemic standard for prescribing a false belief in such a case. As such, it makes sense to frame the reliability requirement for a rationally permissible epistemic standard in terms of non-misleading evidence. Hence, I propose the following reliability requirement for an epistemic standard to be rationally permissible:

Reliability Requirement: An epistemic standard is rationally permissible for some subject, S, relative to some non-misleading evidence, e, if and only if: (i) it reliably warrants believing **P** based on e in cases in which **P** is true and not believing **P** based on e in case in which **P** is false and (ii) there is no competing epistemic standard that S knows or justifiably believes to be more reliable.

In principle, it is possible for there to be two equally reliable epistemic standards, ES_1 and ES_2, such that ES_1 has a threshold n for believing all ravens are black, while ES_2 has threshold n + 1 for believing all ravens are black. In such a case, both ES_1 and ES_2 would both satisfy the above reliability requirement. This means that it is possible for a subject, S_1, to rationally believe that **P** based on some body of evidence e, via the error-free application of a rationally permissible evidential standard, ES_1, and another subject, S_2, to be rationally agnostic towards **P** based on e, via the error-free application of some other rationally permissible evidential standard, ES_2. The same point applies, mutatis mutandis, to cases involving agnosticism towards **P** and disbelieving **P**. There is a further question as to whether two epistemic standards may both satisfy the reliability requirement even though one prescribes believing **P** based on e, while the other prescribes disbelieving **P** based on *e*. Given how differently two epistemic standards would need to weigh the same evidence for one to prescribe believing **P** and the other to prescribe disbelieving **P**, there is some reason to doubt that both could be reliable given the aforementioned disparity. This explains why one may wish to remain non-committal with respect to positive permissivism even if one endorses negative permissivism.

9.3 Nickel's Argument for Permissivism

In his paper, 'Voluntary Belief on a Reasonable Basis', Philip Nickel defends the thesis that there are agnosticism-involving permissive cases. Nickel describes a pair of examples in which a subject is rationally permitted to either believe or refrain from believing. Here is the first in Nickel's own words:

> [TRAIN CASE]: Suppose I have lived for three years in an area where I have never heard the sound of a train, although I have observed some seemingly unused train tracks. I do not know whether the train tracks have fallen into disrepair. One morning, as I am working, I hear the sound of a train whistle, and I feel the distinctive vibration of a locomotive…I may take the sound of the locomotive to provide adequate reason to believe that there is a locomotive, or I may take it not to provide adequate reason for that belief. Both responses are reasonable.[3]

And here is the second case, which I again present in Nickel's own words:

> [LIZARD CASE]: Suppose my roommate, a serious and sincere person, announces to me that he has just been outside and seen a three-foot lizard in the driveway. I have never seen such a large lizard in the area before, and I have some reason to doubt whether any lizards of that size live naturally in the area. Here again, I think, is a case in which I am in a position to take my roommate's testimony as providing adequate reason to believe that there was a three-foot lizard in the driveway, or to suspend belief and demand more evidence.[4]

What makes the above pair of cases permissive, according to Nickel, is the fact that they involve adequate but not conclusive evidence for the respective target propositions. Nickel defines conclusive and adequate evidence as follows:

Conclusive Evidence for P: The truth of **P** is implied by or reliably correlated with the information available to a subject, assuming normal background conditions.

---

[3] Nickel (2010: 313–314).   [4] Nickel (2010: 314).

Adequate Evidence for P: The truth of **P** is implied by or reliably correlated with the information available to a subject, assuming normal background conditions, but there is an unresolved, open question about whether normal background conditions obtain.

In the TRAIN CASE, the sound of a train whistle and the distinctive vibration of a locomotive is reliably correlated with there being a train nearby, assuming normal background conditions. However, Nickel maintains that the fact that I have not previously seen, heard, or felt a train in the area is sufficient to render it an open question whether normal background conditions obtain. Likewise, in the LIZARD CASE, the sincere testimony of my serious-minded roommate that there is a three-foot lizard in the driveway would be reliably correlated with there being such a reptile, assuming normal background conditions. However, the fact that I have never seen a three-foot lizard before and that I have reason to doubt that there are three-foot lizards indigenous to the area leaves it an open question whether normal background conditions obtain. In short, the subjects described in TRAIN CASE and LIZARD CASE have adequate evidence but lack conclusive evidence.

According to Nickel, since the subjects in the TRAIN CASE and LIZARD CASE have adequate evidence, it is rationally permissible for them to believe the respective target propositions. However, since they do not have conclusive evidence, it is also rationally permissible for them to be agnostic towards the respective target propositions. Nickel concludes his analysis of his two 'target cases' by offering the following recipe for agnosticism-involving permissive cases: 'take a case in which the evidence has decisive force if normal conditions obtain, and stipulate that the question of normal conditions obtaining has not been resolved' (316). All such cases, Nickel maintains, constitute agnosticism-involving permissive cases.

While I agree with Nickel's conclusion that there are agnosticism-involving permissive cases, I am sceptical about the argument he offers in support of said conclusion. Consider Nickel's formula for agnosticism-involving permissive cases: any situation in which our evidence would be decisive if normal conditions obtained but in which it is an open question whether such conditions obtain. Contra Nickel, I submit that if it is an open question whether normal background conditions obtain, then it is rationally impermissible to believe the relevant proposition. Agnosticism is the only rationally appropriate doxastic attitude in such cases. This point is illustrated by the following example:

DANCE CLUB: Philip is at a dance club and sees Blake at the other end of the room wearing what appears to be a bright green shirt. However, Philip is aware

9.3 Nickel's Argument for Permissivism

that many of the dance clubs in the area are equipped with special light filters that make white surfaces appear bright green. Although Philip is easily able to distinguish between white and green surfaces under normal lighting conditions, he is unsure whether such conditions obtain in the present case.

DANCE CLUB conforms to Nickel's recipe for an agnosticism-involving permissive case. Seeing someone wearing what appears to be a light-green shirt is reliably correlated with them wearing a light-green shirt, assuming normal background conditions. However, Philip's knowledge that some of the dance clubs in the area are equipped with special light filters that make white surfaces appear green entails that it is unresolved whether normal background conditions obtain. It follows from Nickel's recipe that DANCE CLUB is an agnosticism-involving permissive case. However, it would be rationally impermissible for Philip to believe that Blake is wearing a light-green shirt until he has eliminated the live possibility that the club is equipped with the special lighting that makes white surfaces appear green – that is, until it is no longer an open question whether normal conditions obtain. The upshot is that Nickel's recipe for generating agnosticism-involving permissive cases fails to do so consistently.

My diagnosis of where Nickel's analysis goes wrong is that his characterisation of adequate evidence is inadequate. If some evidence, *e*, is reliably correlated with **P** only if normal background conditions obtain, but it is an open question whether normal background conditions obtain, then *e* is not adequate to justify believing **P**. Hence, Nickel's conception of adequate evidence should be rejected. Specifically, Nickel appears to conflate the following two types of cases:

Unusual Situation Cases: Occasions where the *situation* in which a subject is considering a proposition is a departure from the norm.
Unusual Proposition Cases: Occasions where the *proposition* a subject is considering is a departure from the norm.

One difference between the two kinds of cases is that the discovery that one is in an Unusual Situation Case is enough to undermine the justificatory efficacy of one's evidence while the discovery that one is in an Unusual Proposition Case is not. For example, if Philip were to discover that the lights in the dance club had a colour-altering filter, then this would amount to the discovery that he was in an Unusual Situation Case. What makes DANCE CLUB an Unusual Situation Case is that someone equipped with the normal colour-discriminatory abilities of a human adult would be unable to perform the required colour discrimination. Moreover, one does not have to know that one is in an Unusual Situation Case for the justificatory efficacy of one's evidence to be undermined. Merely having reason to think that one *may* be in an Unusual Situation Case – such that it is an open question whether normal background conditions obtain – is enough to make agnosticism the rationally appropriate doxastic attitude. Hence, although, in DANCE CLUB, Philip does not know that he is in an Unusual Situation Case, the live possibility that he is in one is enough to undermine the efficacy of the evidence provided by his visual experience.

Nickel's TRAIN CASE, by contrast, is an example of an Unusual Proposition Case. Since a train has not been observed in the area within the last three years, there being a train nearby represents a departure from the norm. However, the fact that a train has not been seen in the last three years does not undermine the justificatory efficacy of hearing a train whistle or feeling the distinctive rumble of a locomotive. In this respect, failing to see a train in the area differs from being in a dance club with special light filters. Indeed, as we already observed, it merely has to be a live possibility that one is in a dance club with unusual lighting for the justificatory force of one's visual experience to be undermined. By contrast, the mere possibility that one may not have seen a train in the last three years does not undermine the justificatory efficacy of the perceptual evidence constituted by the sound of the train whistle and the distinctive rumble of a locomotive.

Saying that one's evidence is not undermined in Unusual Proposition Cases does not imply that such cases are no different from ones that do not involve unusual propositions. Consider the evidentialist cliché that extraordinary claims require extraordinary evidence. We may similarly declare that unusual propositions require an unusual (i.e. greater) amount of evidence. Hence, it may be argued that the fact that I have not seen a train in the last three years entails that more evidence is required to justify believing there is a train nearby than would be necessary if I saw a train three days ago. But notice that the mechanism that gives rise to the need for additional evidence in Unusual Proposition Cases like the TRAIN CASE is quite different from the one that gives rise to the need for additional evidence in DANCE CLUB. In DANCE CLUB, the possibility that I am in a situation for which my colour-discriminatory ability is poorly suited robs the evidence provided by my perceptual experience of their usual justificatory power. However, the fact that I have not seen a train in the last three years does not rob my perceptual experiences of the sound and feel of a locomotive of their usual justificatory power. At worst, it only demands that I have more such evidence by raising the bar of how much evidence is required for my belief to be justified.

The LIZARD CASE is also an example of an Unusual Proposition Case. However, in the LIZARD CASE, the evidence the subject has in support of the target proposition seems weaker than in the TRAIN CASE. In TRAIN CASE, the strength of the available evidence is a function of the reliability of my perceptual faculties along with my ability to identify the sound and vibrations of a train. In the LIZARD CASE, the strength of the available evidence is not only a function of the reliability of my perceptual faculties, but also a function of the reliability of my roommate's perceptual faculties, my roommate's discriminatory abilities, and my roommate's honesty on the occasion in question. This means that there are more opportunities for error in the LIZARD CASE. Because of this fact, it is less obvious whether the subject has adequate evidence in the LIZARD CASE. However, I do not believe this lack of clarity has the implication Nickel thinks it does. There is a difference between saying that we do not know what single doxastic attitude is rationally appropriate in a given example and saying that there is no single doxastic attitude that is rationally appropriate in a given example. Insofar as we are unsure whether it is rationally appropriate to believe or be agnostic in the LIZARD CASE, it may be argued that it is because we have not been given enough information to make a determination. In other words, the LIZARD CASE seems less like a case in which there is no single rationally permissible doxastic attitude and more like a case in which it is unclear what the single rationally permissible doxastic attitude is because we are unsure how much weight should be given to the roommate's testimony. But if the LIZARD CASE is going to establish that there are agnosticism-involving permissive cases, it is not enough that it represents a case in which we are unsure what doxastic attitude is rationally appropriate. It must represent a case in which more than one doxastic attitude is rationally appropriate. Unfortunately, Nickel has failed to establish that the LIZARD CASE is an instance of the latter.

The takeaway from the above discussion is not that agnosticism-involving permissive cases do not exist. What the failure of Nickel's argument reveals is the inadequacy of his strategy for arguing in support of the existence of agnosticism-involving permissive cases; a strategy that relies on Nickel's distinction between adequate and conclusive evidence. A better strategy would be one that appeals to the idea that there may be multiple rationally permissible epistemic standards. This is the strategy I will be presupposing in the remainder of this chapter.

9.4 Objections to Permissivism

To recap, I have adumbrated my motivation for holding that there are agnosticism-involving permissive cases and criticised the alternative argument in favour of agnosticism-involving permissive cases offered by Nickel. In this section, I will examine the two main objections to permissivism highlighted by Miriam Schoenfield (2014) and consider their implications, if any, for the existence of agnosticism-involving permissive cases.

9.4.1 The Evidence Pointing Problem

The first objection to permissivism Schoenfield discusses is the *Evidence Pointing Problem* identified by Sosa (2010) and White (2005). Here is Schoenfield's summary of the objection:

> The kind of permissivist that I am interested in will sometimes want to say that it is permissible, given *e*, to believe **P** and permissible, given *e*, to believe ¬**P**. But surely it should only be rationally permissible to have beliefs that the total body of evidence supports, and it is impossible for the evidence to support belief in both **P** and ¬**P**. After all, to whatever extent the evidence supports believing **P**, it supports disbelieving ¬**P**, and vice versa.[5]

Schoenfield claims that the evidence pointing problem mischaracterises the permissivist as being committed to the idea that a single body of evidence may point to both the truth and falsity of **P** at the same time. However, the most plausible versions of permissivism are rooted in the idea that there may be multiple rationally permissible epistemic standards. According to this approach, what the permissivist claims is that one epistemic standard, ES_1, may prescribe believing **P**, based on some evidence, *e*, and another epistemic standard, ES_2, may prescribe disbelieving **P**, based on *e*. However, the permissivist is not committed to the existence of a single rationally permissible epistemic standard that both justifies believing **P** and disbelieving **P** based on *e*.[6]

Unfortunately, Schoenfield's reply to the Evidence Pointing Problem fails to address what gives the objection its intuitive appeal. Once the notion of epistemic standards has been invoked, the Evidence Pointing Problem may be seen as rooted in the idea that an epistemic standard

---

[5] Schoenfield (2014: 199–200).   [6] Schoenfield (2014: 200).

9.4 Objections to Permissivism

should warrant believing **P** based on some evidence, *e*, only if *e* points to the truth of **P**. In other words, a rationally permissible epistemic standard should interpret the evidence as pointing in the direction that the evidence actually points. Since the same evidence cannot point in two different directions at the same time, it is impossible for two rationally permissible epistemic standards to point towards both **P** and ¬**P**.

It may be objected that the preceding argument rests on a mistake: namely that there is some fact of the matter as to whether *e* points to the truth of **P**, independent of some epistemic standard. But this, it may be claimed, is simply not the case. However, to say that *e* points to the truth of **P** simply means that *e* is reliably correlated with **P** (and not reliably correlated with ¬**P**). Moreover, whether *e* is reliably correlated with **P** is an objective fact about the world, not a psychological fact about a subject or the significance a subject attaches to *e*. For example, the fact that Koplik spots are reliably correlated with measles is completely independent of the epistemic standards of any particular subject. Hence, we can say that the fact that someone has Koplik spots points to the truth of the proposition that they have measles without invoking the epistemic standards of a particular subject. Admittedly, there will be cases in which a certain consideration is reliably correlated with both **P** and ¬**P**. However, in such cases, we may safely conclude that that consideration is neither evidence for **P** nor ¬**P**. For example, insofar as being composed of atoms is reliably correlated with an object being animate and an object being inanimate, the fact that an object is composed of atoms cannot be evidence that it is animate or evidence that it is inanimate. In sum, it may be argued that it is a minimum requirement for a consideration to be properly considered evidence for **P** that it be reliably correlated with **P** and not reliably correlated with ¬**P**.

Once it is granted that there is some fact of the matter as to whether *e* is reliably correlated with **P**, independent of the epistemic standards of a particular subject, it becomes clear that Schoenfield has failed to address the central worry raised by the Evidence Pointing Problem. Let us assume that the permissivist is correct in holding that there is more than one rationally permissible epistemic standard. Call a putative permissive case in which one epistemic standard prescribes believing **P** and another epistemic standard prescribes disbelieving **P** a *positive permissive case*. Since some consideration cannot be reliably correlated with both **P** and ¬**P** and retain its status as evidence for either, it follows that in a would-be positive permissive case, at least one of the implicated epistemic standards is not rationally permissible. Given the assumption that one cannot rationally believe or disbelieve **P** based on a rationally impermissible epistemic standard, it follows that in all would-be positive permissive cases, at least one of the subjects is being irrational. The upshot is that there will be no case in which one subject rationally believes **P** based on some body of evidence, *e*, and another subject rationally disbelieves **P** based on *e*. Call the preceding argument the *Revised Evidence Pointing Problem*.

Two points are worth noting about the Revised Evidence Pointing Problem. First, it does not presuppose that there is a special set of epistemic standards that warrant both believing **P** and disbelieving **P**, based on *e*. On the contrary, it is entirely consistent with the rationale for permissivism offered by Schoenfield:

> [T]he reason it can be permissible for Anna to believe **P**, and Bob to believe ¬**P**, is not that there is a special set of epistemic standards, such that according to these standards, it is reasonable to believe **P** and reasonable to believe ¬**P**. Rather, the permissivist thinks that what it is reasonable to believe about **P** needs to be understood relative to some set of epistemic standards.[7]

Even if we grant that what it is reasonable to believe is always relative to some epistemic standard, there remains the further question of whether an epistemic standard may be rationally permissible even if it warrants believing **P** based on *e* in cases in which *e* is not reliably correlated with **P**. The intuition motivating the Revised Evidence Pointing Problem is that a rationally permissible epistemic standard should always interpret the evidence as pointing in the direction that the evidence actually points, and this precludes two rationally permissible epistemic standards pointing in opposite directions. This is an intuition that Schoenfield simply fails to address.

Second, the Revised Evidence Pointing Problem poses no threat to agnosticism-involving permissivism. Recall, the Revised Evidence Pointing Problem takes as its point of departure the idea that an epistemic standard is rationally permissible only if it warrants believing **P** based on *e* in cases in which *e* is reliably correlated with **P**. If one epistemic standard, ES_1, prescribes believing that all ravens are black only if one has observed 199 or more black ravens and another epistemic standard, ES_2, prescribes believing all ravens are black only if one has observed 201 or more black ravens, it remains true that both ES_1 and ES_2 prescribe believing that all ravens are black based on some evidence, *e*, only if *e* is reliably correlated

---

[7] Scheonfield (2014: 200).

with the truth of the proposition that all ravens are black. Even though ES_1 and ES_2 imply different thresholds for warranted belief given some evidence, e, they both agree on whether e points towards **P** or ¬**P**. This means that both ES_1 and ES_2 may qualify as rationally permissible epistemic standards according to the Revised Evidence Pointing Problem. I conclude that the Revised Evidence Pointing Problem fails to pose a challenge to negative permissivism.

9.4.2 The Arbitrariness Objection

The second major objection to permissivism highlighted by Schoenfield is what is commonly called the *Arbitrariness Objection*, the complaint that once a subject recognises that the epistemic standard upon which her belief is based is one among the rationally permissible many, there is no reason for her to follow her epistemic standard's prescription to believe **P** in cases in which another rationally permissible standard prescribes not believing **P**. We may expand the arbitrariness objection to include agnosticism-involving permissive cases by noting that if our epistemic standard prescribes believing **P** and we are aware that there is some other rationally permissible epistemic standard that prescribes agnosticism towards **P**, there is nothing to stop us from switching to the agnosticism-prescribing epistemic standard. Hence, our decision to remain with our belief-prescribing epistemic standard seems arbitrary. The upshot is that the Arbitrariness Objection appears to pose a challenge to agnosticism-involving permissivism.

Significantly, the Arbitrariness Objection targets what Ginger Schultheis (2018) refers to as the *clear-eyed permissivist*, 'someone who believes, of a certain case, that it is a permissive one' (868). The Arbitrariness Objection alleges that the clear-eyed permissivist has no reason to stick to the attitude prescribed by their epistemic standard given that they are aware that there is some other rationally permissible epistemic standard that prescribes a different doxastic attitude. However, this problem fails to arise in cases in which a subject is unaware that they are in a permissive case. Hence, the Arbitrariness Objection is not a direct refutation of the claim that there are permissive cases. What gives the Arbitrariness Objection its dialectical force is that it identifies a problem that only arises if we hold that there may be multiple rationally permissible epistemic standards. If, by contrast, we hold that there is one rationally permissible epistemic standard, then the question of whether a subject needs to switch to a competing standard simply never arises. The upshot is that, all things being equal, holding that there is a single rationally permissible epistemic standard is preferable to holding that there are multiple rationally permissible epistemic standards.

One limitation of the Arbitrariness Objection is that it does not seem to apply to most real-world permissive cases. Most real-world permissive cases are less like clear-eyed permissive cases and more akin to the following example:

> COMPETING STANDARDS: Seth's epistemic standard, ES_1, prescribes believing **P**, given some body of evidence, e. As far as Seth can tell, ES_1 has a track record of generating true beliefs and avoiding false ones. To wit, on those occasions on which Seth has been able to verify whether ES_1 prescribed the correct doxastic attitude, it has almost always gotten things right. However, during a conversation with a co-worker, Lin, Seth learns that Lin is agnostic towards **P** based on e. This suggests that Lin either gives e less weight in support of **P** than he does or that Lin has a higher evidential threshold for believing **P**. However, because Seth has heretofore only employed his own epistemic standard, he knows relatively little about what the track record of success of Lin's epistemic standard has been like. Consequently, Seth has no reason to think that Lin's epistemic standard is more reliable than his own.

Arriving at an accurate assessment of one's own epistemic standard is no easy matter. Doing so requires paying careful attention to our own track record of forming true beliefs and avoiding false ones. We have all had the experience of discovering that certain of our beliefs – some recently formed, some long-standing – are false. This suggests that we are not entirely at the mercy of our current epistemic standards. If we notice ourselves frequently arriving at false beliefs in a certain domain, this may lead us to wonder if we need to amend our epistemic standard. Indeed, this was my own experience with the faith-based epistemic standard I acquired from my fundamentalist Christian religious upbringing. Repeatedly discovering that many of my recently formed and long-standing beliefs were false prompted me to question and ultimately reject the reliability of said faith-based epistemic standard. It is often assumed by theorists that critically evaluating one's epistemic standard is impossible since one can only evaluate one's epistemic standard via an appeal to that very epistemic standard. This assumption is mistaken and the preceding biographical anecdote hints at one reason why. It is undeniable that many people do shift from one epistemic standard to another and a subset of such cases include individuals whose reason for adopting a new epistemic standard is that they believed their initial epistemic standard was unreliable.

While assessing the reliability of one's own epistemic standard is possible, doing so requires intimate familiarity with the track record of said epistemic standard. However, barring extreme cases, we would not have access to the track record of someone else's epistemic standard unless we have ourselves employed that standard. Moreover, in most real-life permissive cases, we would not have employed the alternative standard at issue. It is for this reason that I claim that, more often than not, our position would be like that of Seth, who is unaware of the comparative reliability of Lin's epistemic standard. If this is right, then in many (if not most) real-world permissive cases, we may not be able to say for sure whether an alternative epistemic standard to our own is in fact reliable. The upshot is that, given the Reliability Requirement, we would not know for sure whether the alternative epistemic standard is rationally permissible and, consequently, whether we are in a permissive case. Moreover, even on those occasions on which we have a vague sense that someone else's epistemic standard is minimally reliable, we are nevertheless unable to determine if it is more reliable than our own. The upshot is that, given the Reliability Requirement, there is no obligation that we switch from our epistemic standard to that of someone else. In light of the preceding points, I submit that most real-world permissive cases have more in common with examples like COMPETING STANDARDS, where one is unaware of the comparative reliability of an alternative epistemic standard, than clear-eyed permissive cases.

Thus far, my strategy for responding to the Arbitrariness Objection has been to claim that most real-world permissive cases are not like that of the clear-eyed permissivist. Nevertheless, there will be exceptional cases in which we do know, justifiably believe, or have most reason to think that some other epistemic standard is more reliable than our own. Consider the epistemic standard that holds that a literal interpretation of the King James Version of the Bible is a source of inerrant truths about the world. One way someone who held to such an epistemic standard may come to doubt its reliability is the discovery of inconsistencies in biblical pronouncements. One banal example of such inconsistency is the biblical declaration that Michal, the daughter of Saul, had 'no child unto the day of her death' (2 Samuel 6:23, KJV) and the later reference to 'the five sons of Michal the daughter of Saul' (2 Samuel 21:8, KJV). Insofar as it cannot both be true that Michal, the daughter of Saul, had no children up until the day of her death and that she also had five sons, it follows that at least one of the beliefs prescribed by the epistemic standard that regards the Bible as a source of inerrant truths must be false. Repeatedly discovering such inconsistencies may lead one to regard an epistemic standard that prescribed believing every literal declaration found in the King James Version of the Bible as less reliable than one which held that the King James Version of the Bible should be held to the same or similar critical standards as other comparable modern translations of ancient texts. Recognition of this fact may lead someone to switch from the former to the latter epistemic standard.

The preceding example is noteworthy in at least three respects. First, the epistemic standard described is not merely a theoretical invention since it is one that is embraced by many actual religious communities. Indeed, I hail from one such community myself. Second, it illustrates one way one may be led to question the reliability of one's own epistemic standard. Indeed, noticing such inconsistencies was the first step along a long path that led to my eventual rejection of a literal inerrantist biblical epistemic standard. Third, the example underscores the need to make room for the possibility of discovering that one's epistemic standard either fails to meet some minimal threshold of reliability or discovering that one's epistemic standard is less reliable than some alternative epistemic standard. Indeed, it was my coming to believe that the literal inerrantist biblical standard with which I was raised was less reliable than one that regarded the Bible no less critically than a comparable ancient text that led to my adoption of the latter epistemic standard. In light of this, it is worthwhile to consider how we should respond to the discovery that an alternative epistemic standard is less, more, or equally reliable to our own. Here is my analysis of each of the three cases:

Case 1: Less Reliable Alternative Standard

The first putative clear-eyed permissivist case is one in which two subjects, S_1 and S_2, both have epistemic standards that satisfy the minimum reliability threshold and in which S_1 knows, justifiably believes, or has most reason to believe that the alternative epistemic standard of S_2 is less reliable than their own. For this to qualify as a genuine permissive case, S_2 must not know, believe, or have most reason to believe that their standard is less reliable than that of S_1. (For example, we can imagine an alternative version of Competing Standards in which Seth knows that his epistemic standard is more reliable than that of Lin, but in which Lin is unaware that Seth's epistemic standard is less reliable than her own. Were Lin to learn that her epistemic standard was less reliable than that of Seth, her epistemic standard would no longer qualify as rationally permissible, according to the Rationality Requirement. Hence, the revised version of Competing Standards' status as a permissive case is contingent on Lin's being blamelessly ignorant of the fact that Seth's epistemic standard is more reliable than her own.) Insofar as S_1 is aware that S_2's epistemic standard is less reliable than their own, S_1 is rationally permitted to maintain the doxastic attitude prescribed by their epistemic standard. And insofar as S_2 is blamelessly ignorant of the fact that their epistemic standard is less reliable than that of S_1, S_2 is also rationally permitted to maintain the doxastic attitude prescribed by their epistemic standard.

Case 2: More Reliable Alternative Standard

The second putative clear-eyed permissivist case is one in which the epistemic standard of a subject, S_1, satisfies the minimum reliability threshold and in which S_1 knows, believes, or has most reason to believe that an alternative epistemic standard is more reliable than their own. Since, according to the Reliability Requirement, an epistemic standard is rationally permissible only if the subject does not know or have most reason to believe that there is an alternative standard that is more reliable, it follows that S_1's epistemic standard is no longer rationally permissible once they discover that there is a more reliable alternative. Hence, what may have begun as a genuine permissive case, prior to the subject's discovery of a more reliable epistemic standard, ceases to be a genuine permissive case. The upshot is that according to the account presently on offer – that is, one that presupposes the Reliability Requirement for a rationally permissible epistemic standard – there are no genuine clear-eyed permissive cases in which one knows, believes, or has most reason to believe that a competing epistemic standard is more reliable.

Case 3: Equally Reliable Alternative Standard

The third putative clear-eyed permissivist case is one in which a subject knows that an alternative epistemic standard is equally reliable to their own. Two points are worth noting about the present case at the outset. First, it is exceedingly unlikely that we will find ourselves in the position of knowing, justifiably believing, or having most reason to believe that an alternative standard is equally reliable as our own. Second, the question of how we should respond to the discovery that a competing epistemic standard is equally reliable to our own turns out to be the central question of the peer disagreement debate: how one should respond to the discovery that a putative epistemic peer has arrived at the opposite conclusion to you based on the same evidence. In most discussions of peer disagreement, it is not explicitly stated that the parties to the debate have different epistemic standards. However, since it is typically stipulated that the parties to the debate have the same (or nearly the same) evidence, then the explanation of why they disagree must be that they have different epistemic standards. After all, if they had exactly the same epistemic standards, then they would presumably arrive at the same conclusion given the same evidence. Furthermore, since both parties to the debate are peers, we can assume that, as far as the parties to the disagreement are concerned, their epistemic standards have roughly the same reliability. Were it discovered that one of the parties to the debate had a less reliable epistemic standard, then we could dispense with the assumption that they are epistemic peers. The upshot is that the case in which one discovers that a competing epistemic standard is equally reliable is merely a case of peer disagreement and our response to cases of peer disagreement will apply to such cases. In light of the preceding observations, I will devote the remainder of this chapter to a discussion of how we should respond to putative cases of peer disagreement.

9.5 The Requirements for Epistemic Peerhood

The following is a standard case of peer disagreement: Lisa and Jeanie are life-long best friends and first-year college students at the same school. They are enrolled in an introduction to philosophy course in which they are confronted with the freewill debate for the first time. They consider each other to be equally intelligent, honest, and competent reasoners. Moreover, they have been exposed to all the same information and arguments on the subject; neither takes herself to be more informed on the matter than the other. In short, they are and take themselves to be *epistemic peers*.[8] However, during a conversation after class, they discover that they have opposing views on the subject: Lisa believes we have freewill while Jeanie believes we do not. After a lengthy conversation, they are able to confirm that neither has overlooked any of the arguments the other has considered. Moreover, neither has any special reason to believe that the other has made a performative error in their reasoning. And yet, the disagreement remains. How should Lisa and Jeanie respond to the revelation that they disagree?

According to *Conciliationism*, both Lisa and Jeanie should decrease their confidence in their original position.[9] The view that Conciliationism is

---

[8] See and cf. Feldman and Warfield (2010: 2).   [9] See and cf. Elga (2010).

mistaken and that we should remain steadfast in the face of revealed peer disagreement is known as *Steadfastness*. Conciliationists may differ in terms of how much Lisa and Jeanie should reduce their respective levels of confidence. For example, David Christensen (2007) holds that in cases of peer disagreement, both parties should reduce their level of confidence in their original position, but not necessarily to the point of being agnostic. Pace Christensen, I wish to defend an extreme form of Conciliationism, according to which the only rationally appropriate doxastic attitude one may adopt in revealed cases of peer disagreement is agnosticism.[10] Following Michele Palmira (2013), I will refer to this response to revealed peer disagreement as the *Agnostic Response*.

Before I get to my defence of the Agnostic Response, it would be helpful to get clearer on what it means to regard someone as our epistemic peer and when the belief that someone is our epistemic peer is justified. Specifically, I wish to flag three features of the conception of epistemic peerhood implicated in the arguments to follow that at least partly explain some of the ways in which the intuitions of the defenders of the Agnostic Response tend to differ from that of advocates of Steadfastness. This will hopefully better equip the reader to assess the relative merits of the competing views.

9.5.1 The Equal Fallibility Requirement

In the discussion that follows, we will be concerned with cases in which two individuals are and take themselves to be epistemic peers with respect to whether some proposition, **P**, is true. To say that someone is our epistemic peer with regards to whether **P**, in the semi-technical sense in which the expression is currently being employed, entails that we are no more likely or well positioned to arrive at the truth about whether **P** than that individual. On this view, if someone who disagrees with us is our epistemic peer, then it is equally likely that we have unwittingly made an error in our reasoning as it is that they have. This conception of epistemic peerhood implies the following requirement:

> **Equal Fallibility Requirement:** One considers S to be one's epistemic peer with respect to whether **P** only if in cases in which one disagrees with S about whether **P**, one believes it is equally likely that one is mistaken about whether **P** as it is that S is mistaken about whether **P**.

---

[10] See and cf. Feldman (2006, 2007), Christensen (2007), and Kornblith (2010).

The equal fallibility requirement makes the present notion of an epistemic peer more restrictive than that implicitly assumed in some discussions of peer disagreement. For example, when discussing an instance of peer disagreement between two palaeontologists, Jack and Jill, about the fate of Neanderthals, Catherine Elgin summarises the Steadfastness position as follows:

> Advocates of [Steadfastness] maintain that Jack should hold fast to his belief. To do otherwise would be spineless. Since Jack believes that his reasons are sufficient to support his conclusion, he thinks that Jill is wrong about the Neanderthals. This is compatible with her being, and his recognising her as, his epistemic peer. Everyone makes mistakes.[11]

In the above passage, it is assumed that we may regard someone as our epistemic peer even if we take ourselves to be correct and take them to be mistaken with respect to the proposition the disagreement is about. What this conception of epistemic peerhood overlooks is that the 'everyone makes mistakes' slogan applies as much to us as it does to others. This means that unless we have some special reason to believe we have reasoned more soundly than our putative peer, it would be unwarranted to assume that it is our epistemic peer, rather than ourselves, that made the mistake. In other words, Jack would justifiably believe that Jill made an error in her reasoning, while he did not, only if he justifiably believed that Jill's reasoning was inferior in quality to his own. But if Jack justifiably believes that Jill's reasoning is inferior in quality to his own with respect to the fate of Neanderthals, then there is a natural and intuitive sense in which he does not regard Jill as his epistemic peer with respect to the fate of Neanderthals. It is this intuitive sense of epistemic peerhood that the equal fallibility requirement aims to capture.

9.5.2. *The Evidence of Peerhood Requirement*

The claim that someone is our epistemic peer is an empirical proposition, and like all empirical propositions we are justified in believing that someone is our epistemic peer only if we have sufficient evidence to establish that they are. Hence, it would be rationally inappropriate to assume, without evidence, that a stranger or someone we are meeting for the first time is our epistemic peer. This is why the example with which we began our discussion of peer disagreement – that is, the differing views of Lisa

---

[11] Elgin (2010: 54–55).

and Jeanie on the question of freewill – included the specification that they were life-long friends. The implication is that they had ample opportunity to acquire the evidence necessary to justifiably believe themselves to share epistemic virtues like honesty, carefulness, etc. However, being aware that someone is equally epistemically virtuous as ourselves is not enough to justify the belief that they are our epistemic peer with respect to some proposition. We must also have evidence that they are equally informed on the subject the proposition is about as we are. Therefore, it was also built into the Lisa and Jeanie example that they were enrolled in the same introduction to philosophy course, that they were familiar with all the same arguments, and that they took the time to ensure that there were not salient factors that the other had failed to consider. In sum, justifiably believing that someone is our epistemic peer requires that we possess evidence that they are not only equally epistemically virtuous, but also that they are equally well-informed on the topic as we are. In the absence of such evidence, our default stance should be one of agnosticism regarding their epistemic peerhood. Call this the *Evidence of Peerhood Requirement*.

> **Evidence of Peerhood Requirement**: One justifiably believes S to be one's epistemic peer with respect to whether **P** only if one has sufficient evidence to establish that it is equally likely that one is mistaken about whether **P** as it is that S is mistaken about whether **P**.

My endorsement of the Evidence of Peerhood Requirement sheds light on why my intuitions tend to differ from that of those who hold that the rationally appropriate response to revealed peer disagreement is (often) to revise our belief that the other person is our epistemic peer. Consider the position of David Enoch (2010), who argues that revealed peer disagreement should typically be taken not as evidence that we may be mistaken, but as evidence that the person is not our epistemic peer.[12] If the belief that someone is our epistemic peer is justified only if we have evidence that we are as likely to be mistaken as they are, then responding to a case of revealed peer disagreement by simply revising our belief that the person is our epistemic peer would entail ignoring the evidence that justified our belief in their epistemic peerhood in the first place. Insofar as we justifiably believe someone to be our epistemic peer, then (given the Evidence of Peerhood Requirement) it follows that we have sufficient evidence to establish that we are as likely to be mistaken as they are. Given this fact,

---

[12] See Enoch (2010: 983).

it would be rationally inappropriate for us to simply assume that it is our epistemic peer, rather than ourselves, that has reasoned unsoundly.

9.5.3 Specific versus Independent Evidence

Contra the line of argument in Section 9.5.2, it may be objected that, as a matter of fact, we often do respond to revealed peer disagreement by revising our belief that the other person is our epistemic peer and that this practice is at least in some instances justified. This point may be illustrated by the following case:

> CLIMATE CHANGE: Christine is a long-time, trusted friend and I regard her as my epistemic peer on a host of issues, including the topic of climate change. During a family cookout, I discover that Christine does not believe that climate change is real. However, this discovery does not prompt me to lower my confidence in the reality of climate change. Instead, it causes me to rethink my assumption that Christine is my epistemic peer with respect to the topic at hand.

The cogency of the preceding example lies in the fact that it accurately describes how many of us, as a matter of fact, would respond to the discovery that a close friend did not believe in the reality of climate change. As such, CLIMATE CHANGE helpfully blurs the line between the actual and merely theoretical in a way that allows us to get a better handle on our actual attitudes and practices. Moreover, it does not seem as though we would be irrational to remain steadfast in a case like CLIMATE CHANGE. If this is right, then it is not only true that we often respond to putative cases of revealed peer disagreement by revoking the peerhood status of the person with whom we disagree, but it also seems true that we are often justified in so doing.

I grant that there are cases in which we are justified in responding to a putative case of peer disagreement by revising our belief that the person is our epistemic peer rather than lowering our confidence in the target proposition. However, I hold that this response to a putative case of peer disagreement would only be warranted if we have specific evidence that the other person is more likely to be mistaken.[13] For example, if there is a putative case of peer disagreement between two individuals, Pro and Con, and we learn that Con had unwittingly been given a powerful drug that significantly compromises people's reasoning abilities, then this would

---

[13] See and cf. Christensen (2009: 758–761).

9.5 The Requirements for Epistemic Peerhood

constitute specific evidence that Con is more likely to have made a mistake than Pro. Likewise, if we know that most experts agree with Pro, then the expert consensus against Con constitutes specific evidence that Con is more likely to be mistaken than Pro.

CLIMATE CHANGE is an example of the second kind of case. When I discover that Christine and I disagree about the reality of climate change, the information I have available is not limited to the shared first-order evidence for and against the reality of climate change. I also have the higher-order evidence supplied by my knowledge that the overwhelming majority of scientists with expertise on the topic agree that climate change – is real. This fact makes it more likely that Christine is mistaken and therefore constitutes evidence that she is not my epistemic peer when it comes to the matter of climate change. Hence, even if I believed Christine to be my epistemic peer prior to discovering our disagreement, I would be justified in revising my belief once I learned that she held a position opposed by most experts on the matter.

While I maintain that we need specific evidence that the other party to a dispute is more likely to be mistaken to be justified in revising our justified belief that they are our epistemic peer, I do not claim that this evidence needs to be 'independent', in the sense that it consists of information that neither party to the dispute considered prior to the revelation of the disagreement. This position is at odds with the standard Conciliationist approach, which includes some kind of independence principle. Consider, for example, the independence principle defended by Christensen:

Independence: In evaluating the epistemic credentials of another person's belief about **P**, to determine how (if at all) to modify one's own belief about **P**, one should do so in a way that is independent of the reasoning behind one's own initial belief about **P**.[14]

According to Independence, our assessment of someone's epistemic credentials should be based on considerations that did not feature in the reasoning leading to our pre-disagreement belief. One of the primary motivations for adopting a principle like Independence appears to be a double-counting worry. Consider the following case:

DOUBLE-COUNTING: Louise is attempting to calculate the probability of getting at least one 6 on a pair of fair dice. She knows that each die has a 1/6 chance of landing on 6. She therefore infers that the probability of getting 6 at least once on a pair of dice is $1/6 + 1/6 = 1/3 = 12/36$. However, Louise's

---

[14] Christensen (2009: 758).

calculation overlooks that the dice roll in which 6 shows up on both dice only represents one out of the possible 36 outcomes. Hence, she is double-counting the instance in which 6 shows up on both dice. The actual probability of getting at least one 6 on a pair of dice is 11/36.

It may be argued that there is a similar kind of double-counting taking place when I appeal to the expert consensus on the matter to support both my belief that climate change is real and my belief that Christine is not my epistemic peer. Just as a single consideration – that is, the case in which both dice land on 6 – is counted twice in Louise's calculation, a single consideration – that is, the scientific consensus in support of the reality of climate change – is being counted twice in CLIMATE CHANGE.

However, the preceding objection overlooks an important difference between DOUBLE COUNTING and CLIMATE CHANGE. In DOUBLE COUNTING, the same consideration is being invoked twice to settle a single question: what is the probability of getting at least one 6 when rolling a pair of dice? By contrast, in CLIMATE CHANGE, the same consideration is being invoked to answer two different questions:

(1) Is climate change real?
(2) Is Christine my epistemic peer?

I submit that we are guilty of double-counting only if a single consideration is invoked multiple times in support of one and the same proposition. However, it would be absurd to suggest that because a consideration is part of our basis for believing one proposition, it cannot subsequently be regarded as evidence in support of another proposition.

I believe the immediately preceding point highlights a fundamental problem with Independence; namely it makes whether some consideration, F, qualifies as evidence for some proposition, P, dependent on when we happen to first consider F or whether F – is also evidence for some other proposition, Q. Consider Christensen's example in which two individuals, let us call them Dave and Tom, who are equally adept at mental arithmetic, attempt to calculate in their heads how much each person at the table would need to pay when splitting a 20% tip. While Dave arrives at $45, Tom arrives at $43. However, let us modify Christensen's example so that Dave and Tom happen to be having dinner with four participants in a local arithmetic competition, all of whom are significantly better at mental calculations than Dave and Tom. Suppose further that all four expert arithmeticians arrive at $45. Intuitively, the fact that the expert arithmeticians agree with Dave suggests that Tom is the one who is more likely to have reasoned unsoundly. However, according

9.5 The Requirements for Epistemic Peerhood

to Independence, whether the expert consensus in favour of $45 constitutes evidence that Tom is more likely to be mistaken depends on when Dave learns about the expert consensus in favour of $45. If the four experts reveal the results of their calculation after Dave and Tom discover their disagreement, then the expert consensus does give Dave reason to revise his assessment of Tom's epistemic credentials. However, suppose that the four experts announced their responses before Dave and Tom, and that Dave based his belief that $45 is the correct answer based not only on his own mental calculation, but also on the fact that the expert arithmeticians also arrived at $45. According to Independence, the fact that the four other people at the table arrived at $45 can no longer constitute a reason to believe that, of the two, Tom is more likely to be mistaken. Hence, Independence has the implausible implication that whether consideration F – that is, the expert consensus in favour of $45 – qualifies as evidence that Tom is more likely to be mistaken depends on whether Dave considered the expert consensus when forming his initial belief that $45 is the right answer. However, intuitively, the fact that Dave partly based his belief that $45 is the right answer on the expert consensus does not change the fact that Tom's arriving at an answer that is out of step with the expert consensus constitutes evidence that he is more likely to be wrong. In sum, if some consideration gives us reason to believe that it is likely someone reasoned unsoundly, then it should not matter when we first become aware of said consideration or whether there are other propositions for which said consideration is a reason. In light of the above, I believe Independence should be rejected.

In lieu of Independence, I propose the following criterion for reassessing our belief that someone is our epistemic peer:

Evidence of Relative-Reliability Requirement: One's assessment of whether someone is one's epistemic peer with respect to whether **P** should only be based on evidence that bears on whether they are more (or less) likely than one is to be mistaken about the truth or falsity of **P**.

I submit that the initial plausibility of the suggestion that we are justified in revising our assumption that someone is our epistemic peer in the face of a disagreement with them is driven by the fact that in many cases of disagreement, we have higher-order evidence suggesting that the other person is more likely to be mistaken. This is true in cases like CLIMATE CHANGE, in which I learn that a putative epistemic peer held a view that is at odds with the expert consensus on the matter.

9.6 An Argument for the Agnostic Response

The primary motivation behind my commitment to Conciliationism is the idea that the discovery of disagreement with an epistemic peer constitutes higher-order evidence that our assessment of our first-order evidence may be unreliable. On the present suggestion, cases of revealed peer disagreement are merely an instance of the more general phenomenon of a subject encountering a defeater that casts doubt on the reliability of their reasoning. Consider the following case:

LITMUS TEST: Chris is employing blue litmus paper to determine the pH of a mystery substance, **X**. He is informed that the blue litmus paper will turn red if **X** is acidic, but will remain blue if it is not. When Chris applies the litmus test to **X**, the litmus paper appears to turn red. This prompts Chris to form the belief that **X** is acidic. Shortly thereafter, Chris is informed that he is actually part of a secret psychology experiment in which half of the participants were given a perception-warping drug that makes blue objects appear red. However, he is not told which half of the participants he falls into – the drugged or the sober. Chris concludes that there is a 50% chance that his assessment of the evidence that led him to believe that **X** is acidic is unreliable.

In the above example, the litmus paper constitutes Chris's first-order evidence regarding the pH of **X**. The discovery that he may have imbibed a hallucinogen that makes blue objects appear red constitutes higher-order evidence suggesting that his assessment of his first-order evidence may be unreliable. How should Chris respond to this higher-order evidence?

Clearly, it would be wrong for Chris to simply replace his belief that **X** is acidic with the opposing belief that **X** is not acidic. After all, there is only a 50% chance that he imbibed the hallucinogen, which means he cannot be sure that he is being unreliable in his assessment of his first-order evidence. However, it also seems true that it would be irrational for Chris to continue believing that **X** is acidic. After all, there is a 50% chance that he ois one of the participants that unwittingly imbibed the hallucinogen. Hence, the only rationally permissible doxastic attitude for Chris to take towards the proposition that **X** is acidic following the discovery that he may have imbibed a powerful hallucinogen is one of agnosticism.

I believe that LITMUS TEST is analogous to the case of revealed peer disagreement in all respects that are salient to the current debate. Chris's initial assessment that substance **X** is acidic based on the litmus paper is analogous to our initial assessment based on our first-order evidence. When Chris learns that there is a chance that he imbibed a hallucinogen, this is analogous to our discovery that an epistemic peer has arrived at the opposite conclusion. Given that we believe the other person is equally likely to be mistaken as we are, it follows that there is a 50% chance that our assessment of our first-order evidence is unreliable. Hence, the revealed peer disagreement constitutes higher-order evidence that there is a 50% chance that we were unreliable in our assessment of our first-order evidence. This is analogous to Chris's discovery that there is a 50% chance that he was unreliable in his assessment of his first-order evidence. Hence, while the details of LITMUS TEST differs in obvious ways from the standard case of revealed peer disagreement, both are instances of the broader phenomenon of a subject acquiring higher-order evidence indicating that there is a 50% chance that their assessment of their first-order evidence is unreliable. Moreover, I submit that the only doxastic attitude that is rationally appropriate in all cases that display this general structure is that of agnosticism.

9.7 Palmira's Objection to the Agnostic Response

According to Palmira (2013), the Agnostic Response generates a puzzle in cases in which one of the parties to the disagreement is already agnostic. Consider three subjects who disagree on the question of God's existence:

THEO SAYS : "God exists"
ATHOS SAYS : "God does not exist"
AGNOS SAYS : "I've made up my mind to suspend judgment on whether God exists or not."

According to the Agnostic Response, if Theo and Athos believe themselves to be epistemic peers, then they should adopt an agnostic attitude towards the existence of God. But what would be the Agnostic Response to a case of peer disagreement between Athos and Agnos? Insofar as the Agnostic Response is defined as the position that the rational response to all cases of revealed peer disagreement is for both parties to be agnostic about the disputed proposition, then there is only one thing that the advocate of the Agnostic Response can say: namely that both Athos and Agnos should be agnostic about whether God exists. Therein, according to Palmira, lies the problem. The Agnostic Response implies that Agnos, and only Agnos, should 'stick to his guns'.[15] This amounts to an instance

---

[15] Palmira (2013:1258).

of what Feldman calls 'one way rationality' – that is, the thesis that 'it's reasonable for one side but not the other to maintain belief'.[16]

According to the one-way rationality approach to peer disagreement, if one of the two sides in a case of peer disagreement is objectively right in their assessment of the conclusion the available evidence supports, then that side to the disagreement is rationally permitted to maintain their view. Let us call the two parties in a case of peer disagreement Pro and Con, with Pro holding that **P** and Con holding that ¬**P**. And let us suppose that the body of evidence, e, that Pro and Con share offers conclusive support for **P**. Insofar as Pro happens to be objectively correct, then she is rationally permitted to maintain her belief that **P** after her disagreement with Con is revealed, while Con is rationally required to amend his epistemic position. The problem with this suggestion, according to Feldman, is that it fails to consider the way a subject's total body of evidence changes once an instance of peer disagreement is revealed. Even if we grant that Pro is correct in her assessment that e conclusively supports **P**, following the revelation of her disagreement with Con, and given the assumption that Pro takes Con to be her epistemic peer, her evidence is no longer e but $e*$, where $e*$ includes the higher-order evidence that Pro may have made a mistake in concluding **P** based on e. Moreover, while may offer conclusive support for **P**, $e*$ does not. Hence, once her disagreement with Con comes to light, Pro's new total body of evidence, $e*$, no longer provides conclusive support for **P**.

Palmira maintains that Feldman's argument against the one-way rationality approach may be extended to cases of agnostic disagreement. He puts the point as follows:

> Since the Agnostic Response subscribes to the thesis that peer disagreement counts as higher-order defeating evidence, Agnos cannot rationally retain his initial doxastic attitude. A prima facie agnostic is thus unjustified in retaining his attitude in order to correctly respond to disagreement.[17]

By Palmira's lights, even if agnosticism is the justified attitude for Agnos to take based on his initial body of evidence, e, once he is made aware that his epistemic peer, Athos, has arrived at an opposing conclusion based on e, this fact constitutes higher-order evidence that Agnos' assessment of e is unreliable. When this higher-order evidence is combined with the first-order evidence for and against the existence of God, we arrive at Agnos's new body of evidence, $e*$. Since $e*$ includes the higher-order defeating

---

[16] Feldman (2006: 230).   [17] Palmira (2013: 1259).

evidence, it fails to justify the same attitude as *e*. Hence, Palmira concludes that agnosticism is not the justified attitude for Agnos to take based on *e**. The upshot is that the Agnostic Response fails in cases of agnostic disagreement.

9.7.1 Reply to Palmira's Objection

Curiously, when concluding that Agnos is unjustified in retaining his attitude of agnosticism, Palmira never explicitly discusses which doxastic attitude Agnos would be justified in adopting based on *e**. This, it seems to me, is a glaring lacuna in Palmira's argument against the Agnostic Response. After all, even if Agnos is in a different evidential state after discovering the peer disagreement from the evidential state he was in before doing so, it is possible that his new post-disagreement evidential state also warrants being agnostic. Indeed, I shall argue that this is in fact the case: agnosticism is precisely the right attitude for Agnos to have based on *e**.

Let us grant that after being made aware of their disagreement, Agnos's total body of evidence becomes updated from *e*, which consists in his first-order evidence for and against the existence of God, to *e**, which consists in the combination of *e* and the higher-order evidence that his assessment of *e* may have been unreliable. Recall that the driving intuition behind the need to update our doxastic state in cases of revealed peer disagreement is the recognition that it is just as likely that we are mistaken as it is that our epistemic peer is mistaken. However, the inverse of this is also true: it is just as likely that our epistemic peer is mistaken as it is that we are mistaken. In short, the higher-order evidence does not conclusively establish that our original position was mistaken. Rather, it suggests that there is a 50% chance that our assessment of our first-order evidence is mistaken. This means that Agnos's overall epistemic state is one of uncertainty about his reliability in the assessment of his first-order evidence. The question now becomes this: what doxastic attitude should one take towards **P** if the reliability of one's assessment of one's first-order evidence with respect to **P** is in question?

To help answer this question, let us consider the following revised version of LITMUS TEST.

REVISED LITMUS TEST: Chris is employing white litmus paper to determine the pH of some mystery substance, **X**. The white litmus paper turns red if a substance is acidic and turns blue if it is not. However, if the litmus test is unable to determine whether a substance is acidic, it turns purple. When Chris applies the litmus test to **X**, it appears purple, leading Chris to adopt an agnostic stance on whether **X** is acidic. However, Chris is informed that he is actually part of a secret psychology experiment in which half of the participants were given a perception-warping drug that makes red objects appear purple. However, he is not told which half of the participants he falls into – the drugged or the sober group. Given that there is a 50% chance that if the paper were red, it would still appear purple, Chris is unsure he has reliably ascertained the colour of the litmus paper.

Given the information he has available, it would clearly be unreasonable for Chris to believe that substance **X** is not acidic. After all, he has not been given any reason to believe the litmus paper is blue. But this still leaves the question of whether it would be reasonable for him to believe that **X** is acidic. Again, the answer seems to be no. There is a 50% chance that, despite appearing purple, the litmus paper is actually red. However, this fact alone is not enough to justify his believing that the litmus paper is red – that is, that **X** is acidic. Given all the information Chris has available, it seems rationally appropriate for him to remain agnostic about whether **X** is acidic. Learning that there is a 50% chance that he may have imbibed a perception-warping drug only deepens, rather than removes, the uncertainty that initially justified his attitude of agnosticism.

I believe that REVISED LITMUS TEST is analogous to the case of revealed peer disagreement in which one of the parties to the disagreement is initially agnostic. Like Agnos, Chris evaluates his first-order evidence as inconclusive with respect to the target proposition. And like Agnos, Chris later receives a higher-order defeater casting doubt on the reliability of his assessment of his first-order evidence. The two cases differ only in that the higher-order defeater is constituted by the discovery of peer disagreement, in the one case, and the possibility of a perception-warping drug, in the other case. But how we come to question the reliability of our assessment of our first-order evidence should not matter as far as which attitude is rationally appropriate is concerned. All cases in which our assessment of our first-order evidence is in question should be governed by a single general principle. Moreover, the general principle that seems to apply to all such cases is that the higher-order evidence leaves us no better positioned than before to assess the truth of the target proposition. Hence, if an attitude of agnosticism was justified prior to Agnos and Chris receiving the higher-order evidence suggesting they may be unreliable reasoners, then it continues to be justified after they received the higher-order evidence suggesting that they may be unreliable reasoners. Simply put, agnosticism is the attitude we ought to adopt if we are unsure we are reliable reasoners.

To sum up, I claim that Palmira ultimately drops the ball by failing to ask what doxastic attitude is justified by Agnos's total body of evidence once his disagreement with Athos comes to light. Had he asked this question, it would ultimately become clear that agnosticism is the only plausible candidate doxastic attitude for Agnos to have based on his updated body of evidence, $e\,*$. This has everything to do with the conception of agnosticism as the rationally appropriate doxastic attitude if the reliability of our assessment of our first-order evidence is in question. This normative feature of the attitude of agnosticism makes it far more promiscuous in terms of the evidential contexts in which it may be rationally appropriate than either belief or disbelief. Palmira appears to overlook this important asymmetry between belief and disbelief, on the one hand, and agnosticism, on the other hand; namely that while belief and disbelief are rationally impermissible if the reliability of our assessment of our first-order evidence is in question, the same is not true of agnosticism, which is precisely the doxastic attitude one should adopt under such circumstances.

It should also now be clear why Agnos's post-disagreement agnosticism is not merely a case of one-way rationality. The claim that Agnos should remain agnostic does not start with the assumption that one of the parties to the dispute is objectively right in their assessment of what the evidence establishes. Indeed, we may assume that Theo is right and that both Agnos and Athos are mistaken. It remains true that upon discovering the peer disagreement, both Agnos and Athos have had the reliability of their assessment of their first-order evidence called into question. Consequently, they are rationally required to adopt the one and only doxastic attitude that is rationally appropriate when we are uncertain about our reliability as assessors of our first-order evidence with respect to whether **P** – namely, the attitude of agnosticism about whether **P**.

9.8 Conclusion

The goal of this chapter has been twofold. First, I have argued in defence of a moderate version of permissivism that I call negative permissivism: the claim that there are instances in which it is rationally permissible to (dis)believe P based on some body of evidence, e, or be agnostic towards **P**, based on e. My commitment to negative permissivism is motivated by the intuition that different rationally permissible evidential standards may prescribe different evidential thresholds for justifiably believing a proposition. Given this fact, there will always be a potential for one epistemic standard to prescribe believing **P** based on some evidence, e, while another prescribes remaining agnostic towards **P** based on *e*. Moreover, I claim that clear-eyed permissive cases in which one knows, justifiably believes, or has most reason to believe that a competing epistemic standard is equally reliable as one's own may be conceived of as cases of peer disagreement. Second, I have argued that the rationally appropriate response to cases of peer disagreement is for both parties to the disagreement to adopt an attitude of agnosticism. If this is right, then agnosticism turns out to be the rationally appropriate attitude for a much wider range of cases than philosophers have often countenanced.

CHAPTER 10

Conclusion

I began this monograph with a biographical anecdote that partly explains why the topic of agnosticism is of deep personal interest. It has been over two decades since my agnosticism with respect to the existence of God forced me to give up my ministerial career. Theological questions no longer hold my interest. I am now a self-described *apatheist*; someone who is apathetic or uninterested in either accepting or rejecting the claim that God exists. But my religious agnosticism remains. I have serious reservations about the truth of the claim that God exists and also about the claim that God does not exist. My competently considered evidence has been insufficient to establish either claim. This straightforward self-description is one that the account of agnosticism offered by Friedman appears to preclude. To be genuinely agnostic about whether God exists, I must have the aim of answering the question. Hence, my apatheism is, on Friedman's account, metaphysically inconsistent with my agnosticism. It is this aspect of Friedman's view – the fact that it appears to deem impossible what I take to be my current lived reality – that first sparked my interest in the contemporary philosophical attempts to arrive at a descriptive account of agnosticism.

The central motivating intuition for my descriptive account of agnosticism is the idea that it should be metaphysically possible and rationally permissible to be agnostic about whether **P** irrespective of whether or not one has the aim of settling whether **P**, so long as one's competently considered evidence fails to establish **P**. To this end, I have offered a sustained defence of the thesis that agnosticism is best conceived of as the rationally appropriate attitudinal response to some proposition, **P**, in cases in which one's competently considered evidence is insufficient to determine whether **P**. Call this *my central thesis*. The defining features of my positive view – the questioning-attitude account – all support some aspect of my central thesis. The aim of this concluding chapter is to tie together the major threads of the arguments advanced in this volume in order to

10.1 Agnosticism as Sui Generis Attitude

The chapters of this monograph may be grouped under two broad themes, each of which goes some distance towards defending my central thesis. The first broad theme involves the defence of the claim that agnosticism is a sui generis attitude on par with believing and disbelieving. Call this the *attitudinal thesis*. The most compelling reason for holding to the attitudinal thesis is that it is the only way to preserve the possibility of agnosticism-involving doxastic inconsistency, instances in which an irrational subject both believes **P** and is agnostic towards **P** at some time, t, or both disbelieves **P** and is agnostic towards **P** at t. Moreover, preserving this possibility is essential for explaining how certain courses of action, like those described in my biographical anecdote in Section 2.6, are both possible and rationally problematic. However, if we hold that either agnosticism or the neutrality implicated by agnosticism consists in the absence of belief and disbelief, we are left with no way to preserve the possibility of agnosticism-involving inconsistency. I take this to be the main lesson of Chapter 2.

Furthermore, the attitudinal thesis makes room for an attitudinal notion of neutrality. Except for Friedman's question-directed attitude account, all the major theoretical approaches to agnosticism examined in this volume conceive of doxastic neutrality in purely negative terms: the absence of belief and disbelief. However, I have argued for a positive conception of doxastic neutrality, one that conceives of neutrality as a distinct mental stance on par with the affirming and denying implicated by the attitudes of believing and disbelieving, respectively. Drawing inspiration from Friedman's question-directed attitude account, I maintain that the positive neutral stance implicated by agnosticism may be unpacked in terms of having reservations about (or what I refer to as 'sceptically questioning') both the truth and falsity of a proposition. Hence, while I agree with Friedman that the tendency of agnosticism to take an interrogative complement highlights that it has a questioning component, I maintain that the 'interrogativeness' of agnosticism is located in the mental stance implicated by the attitude itself, as opposed to the attitude's content. This not only preserves the parity between the content of all three doxastic attitudes, but also allows for a more consistent philosophy of mind, with the affirming, denying, and questioning valence of each doxastic attitude identified with a kind of mental stance. I take this to be the main lesson of Chapters 3 and 4.

10.2 Agnosticism's Rational Appropriateness

The second broad theme of this monograph is that agnosticism towards **P** is rationally appropriate if one's competently considered evidence is insufficient for determining whether **P**. Call this the *appropriateness thesis*. The appropriateness thesis is at odds with Friedman's claim that one is agnostic about whether **P** only if one is in an inquiring state of mind about whether **P**. Given that it is possible for one's competently considered evidence to be insufficient to determine whether **P** and yet one be unmotivated to adopt or maintain the aim to resolve whether **P**, there will be cases in which one is both motivated and justified in being agnostic towards **P** despite being unmotivated to have an inquiring mental stance about whether **P**. I take this to be the main lesson of Chapter 5.

The appropriateness thesis is also at odds with McGrath's claim that there are cases in which one has a reason to suspend judgement but lack a reason to be agnostic. Specifically, McGrath claims that the fact that one may be in a better position to judge later (either because one is temporarily cognitively impaired or because one will have better evidence available later) gives one a reason to suspend judgement but no reason to be agnostic. However, McGrath's argument overlooks two important points. First, if one is too cognitively impaired to assess one's evidence, then it immediately follows that one's competently considered evidence is insufficient to determine whether **P**. Second, if one's competently considered evidence is already sufficient to establish the truth or falsity of **P**, then the mere fact that one will have additional evidence later would not justify failing to believe or disbelieve **P**, respectively. Hence, if one has a reason to suspend judgement because one will get additional evidence later, it is only because the evidence already available is insufficient to determine whether **P**. In either case, the appropriateness thesis implies that one has a reason to suspend judgement only if one also has a reason to be agnostic. The upshot is that, contra McGrath, we are able to preserve a univocal normative characterisation of doxastic neutrality. I take this to be the main lesson of Chapter 6.

Significantly, there is no praxistic analogue to the aforementioned appropriateness norm. If one's competently considered practical reasons are insufficient to determine whether one should do **X** or not do **X**, one is rationally free to pick; one may either intend to do **X** or intend not to do **X**. This demonstrates that there is no praxistic attitude that is the practical analogue of agnosticism. If there were such an attitude, then it would be the only rationally permissible praxistic attitude in cases in which one's practical reasons are perfectly counterbalanced. This disanalogy between belief, on the one hand, and intention, on the other hand, poses a significant, but almost entirely overlooked, challenge to *strong cognitivism*; the thesis that intentions are a kind of belief. I take this to be the primary lesson of Chapter 7.

The appropriateness thesis only specifies a sufficient condition for the rational appropriateness of agnosticism. This is because there may be pragmatic reasons to be agnostic. Insofar as raising the cost of getting things wrong, while keeping one's competently considered evidence fixed, may make it rationally impermissible to believe and rationally appropriate to be agnostic, there will be cases in which one's competently considered evidence is, strictly speaking, sufficient to establish that **P**, but in which it is rationally appropriate to be agnostic towards **P**. It follows that having one's competently considered evidence be insufficient to determine whether **P** is not a necessary condition for it to be rationally appropriate to be agnostic towards **P**. I take this to be the main lesson of Chapter 8.

Which attitude is prescribed by our competently considered evidence will partly depend on our evidential standards. These will differ from subject to subject. Even so, plausibly, there are limits on the degree to which rationally permissible evidential standards may differ. One suggestion that arises from an examination of the evidence-pointing problem is that rationally permissible evidential standards should agree about whether some evidence, e, supports **P** or ¬**P**. However, even if we impose this restriction on which rational standards qualify as rationally permissible, there will inevitably arise cases in which the threshold of evidential support necessary for believing **P** to be justified will vary between rationally permissible evidential standards. Specifically, there will be cases in which one rationally permissible evidential standard prescribes believing **P** while another prescribes remaining agnostic towards **P**. In cases in which one discovers that one disagrees with someone one justifiably believes or knows to be one's epistemic peer about which attitude towards **P** is justified, I maintain that adopting or maintaining an attitude of agnosticism towards **P** is the rationally appropriate response. I take the preceding points to be the main lessons of Chapter 9.

10.3 Giving Agnosticism Its Due

Many of the errors identified in the competing theories of agnosticism considered in this monograph may be traced back to a conception of agnosticism as, in some sense, occupying a lower status to the other two members of the doxastic triad. This is most explicit in the non-attitudinal accounts of Crawford and Russell, which conceive of agnosticism as more or less the absence of the other two doxastic attitudes. However, it is also true of the reductionist views of Masny and Raleigh, which conceive of agnosticism as merely a special kind of higher-order belief or some combination of higher-order beliefs and intentions. Perhaps more surprisingly, this tendency also appears to motivate certain problematic aspects of Friedman's sui generis account. Consider the train of thought that eventually leads Friedman to conclude that one is agnostic about whether **P** if and only if one is inquiring into whether **P**:

> Why suspend judging? I take it that one sort of answer that people are initially tempted to give is something about one's deficient epistemic standing on some matter. Why suspend judgment? Because one is not in the position to know or because one's evidence fails to settle some matter or because one has insufficient reason to believe, and so on. But this sort of answer feels inadequate once we admit that suspending is a matter of taking up some attitude rather than merely not having some... [I]f suspending is different from merely not believing, then the claim that I should not believe those propositions is not equivalent to the claim that I should suspend judgment.[1]

Friedman is dissatisfied with the suggestion that agnosticism is fundamentally a response to having insufficient reason to believe, claiming that this is an inadequate basis for holding that agnosticism is more than merely not believing. What Friedman overlooks is how much may potentially go into saying that agnosticism is the rationally appropriate doxastic response to having insufficient reason to both believe and disbelieve. If we hold that doxastic responses to competently considered evidence are commitment-involving, then one would need to say in virtue of what is agnosticism a commitment-involving mental state. This seems to require some positive stance on the part of a subject, as opposed to the mere absence of belief or disbelief. Moreover, insofar as it is possible to have inconsistent doxastic commitments, one would also need to explain how the neutrality implicated by agnosticism is compossible with believing and disbelieving and

---

[1] Friedman (2017a: 303–304).

what makes a subject count as being committed to said neutrality in such cases. This can only be done if we hold that the neutrality implicated by agnosticism is a positive feature of a subject as opposed to the mere absence of certain attitudes. Hence, holding that agnosticism is fundamentally tied to an inquiring state of mind is not necessary to ground the idea that agnosticism is an attitude.

In summation, I maintain that agnosticism need not involve higher-order beliefs, intentions, or an inquiring state of mind. The attitude of agnosticism stands on its own two feet as the rationally appropriate, commitment-involving, doxastic response to inconclusive evidence.

References

Anscombe, G. E. M. (1963). *Intention*, 2nd ed. Oxford: Blackwell.
Archer, A. (2016). Reconceiving Direction of Fit. *Thought: A Journal of Philosophy,* **4** (2): 171–180.
  (2018). Wondering about What You Know. *Analysis,* **78** (4): 596–604.
  (2019). Agnosticism, Inquiry, and Unanswerable Questions. *Disputatio,* **11** (53): 63–88.
  (2021). The Aim of Inquiry. *Disputatio,* **13** (61): 95–119.
  (2022). The Questioning-Attitude Account of Agnosticism. *Synthese,* **200** (6): 1–15.
  (2023). Agnosticism-Involving Doxastic Inconsistency. *Erkenntnis.* https://doi.org/10.1007/s10670-023-00745-9.
Atkins, P. (2017). A Russellian Account of Suspended Judgment. *Synthese,* **194**: 3021–3046.
Bendaña, J. and Mandelbaum, E. (2021). The Fragmentation of Belief. In C. Borgoni, D. Kindermann, and A. Onofri (eds.), *The Fragmented Mind.* Oxford: Oxford University Press: 419–436.
Bergmann, M. (2005). Defeaters and Higher-Level Requirements. *The Philosophical Quarterly,* **55**: 419–436.
Booth, A. R. (2007). The Two Faces of Evidentialism. *Erkenntnis,* **67** (3): 401–417.
Bratman, M. (1992). Practical Reasoning and Acceptance in a Context. *Mind,* **101** (401): 1–15.
Broome, J. (1999). Normative Requirements. *Ratio,* **12**: 389–419.
  (2009). The Unity of Reasoning? In S. Robertson (ed.), *Spheres of Reason: New Essays in the Philosophy of Normativity.* Oxford: Oxford University Press: 62–91.
  (2013). *Rationality through Reasoning.* Oxford: Blackwell.
Brown, G. (2016). *The Universal Declaration of Human Rights in the 21st Century: A Living Document in a Changing World.* vol. 2. Cambridge: Open Book Publishers.
Brown, J. (2008). Subject-Sensitive Invariantism and the Knowledge Norm for Practical Reasoning. *Noûs,* **42**: 167–189.
Brunero, J. (2014). Cognitivism about Practical Rationality. In R. Shafer-Landau (ed.), *Oxford Studies in Metaethics.* Oxford: Oxford University Press: 18–44.

Brunero, J. and Kolodny, N. (2013). Instrumental Rationality. In E. Zalta (ed.), *Stanford Encyclopedia of Philosophy*. URL = <https://plato.stanford.edu/archives/sum2023/entries/rationality-instrumental/>.

Cassam, Q. (2010). Judging, Believing and Thinking. *Philosophical Issues*, **20**: 80–95.

Chisholm, R. (1976). *Person and Object*. La Salle, IL: Open Court.

(1989). *Theory of Knowledge*. 3rd ed. Englewood Cliffs, NJ: Prentice Hall.

Christensen, D. (2009). Disagreement as Evidence: The Epistemology of Controversy. *Philosophy Compass*, **4**: 756–767.

(2007). Epistemology of Disagreement: The Good News. *Philosophical Review*, 116 (2):187–217.

Ciardelli, I., Groenendijk, J., and Roelofsen, F. (2018). *Inquisitive Semantics*. Oxford: Oxford University Press.

Cohen S. (1999). Contextualism, Skepticism, and the Structure of Reasons. *Philosophical Perspectives*, **13**: 57–89.

(2016). Theorizing about the Epistemic. *Inquiry: An Interdisciplinary Journal of Philosophy*, 59 (7–8):839–857.

Conee, E. and Feldman, R. (1985). Evidentialism. *Philosophical Studies*, **48** (1): 15–34.

Crawford, S. (2004). A Solution for Russellians to a Puzzle about Belief. *Analysis*, **64** (3): 223–229.

DeRose, K. (1992). Contextualism and Knowledge Attributions. *Philosophy and Phenomenological Research*, **52**: 913–923.

Elga, A. and Rayo, A. (2021). Fragmentation and Information Access. In C. Borgoni, D. Kindermann, and A. Onofri (eds.), *The Fragmented Mind*. Oxford: Oxford University Press: 37–53.

(2022). Fragmentation and Logical Omniscience. *Noûs*, **56** (3): 716–741.

Elgin, C. Z. (2010). Persistent Disagreement. In Richard Feldman & Ted A. Warfield (eds.), *Disagreement*. Oxford: Oxford University Press: 53–68.

Enoch, D. (2010). Not Just a Truthometer: Taking Oneself Seriously (But Not Too Seriously) in Cases of Peer Disagreement. *Mind*, 119 (476): 953–997.

Falbo, A. (2021). Inquiry and Confirmation. *Analysis*, **81** (4): 622–631.

Fantl, F. and McGrath, M. (2002). Evidence, Pragmatics, and Justification. *The Philosophical Review*, **3** (1): 67–94.

Feldman, R. (2002). Epistemological Duties. In P. K. Moser (ed.), *The Oxford Handbook of Epistemology*. Oxford: Oxford University Press: 362–384.

(2003). *Epistemology*. Upper Saddle River, NJ: Prentice-Hall.

(2005). Respecting the Evidence. *Philosophical Perspectives*, **19**: 95–119.

(2006). Epistemological Puzzles about Disagreement. In Stephen Hetherington (ed.), *Epistemology Futures*. Oxford: Oxford University Press: 216–236.

(2007). Reasonable Religious Disagreements. In L. Antony (ed.), *Philosophers without Gods*. Oxford: Oxford University Press: 194–214.

Feldman, R. and Conee, E. (2018). Between Belief and Disbelief. In K. McCain (ed.), *Believing in Accordance with the Evidence*. Synthese Library, **398**: 71–89.

Feldman, R. and Warfield, T. A. (eds.) (2010). *Disagreement*. Oxford, GB: Oxford University Press.
Ferrari, F. and Incurvati, L. (2022). The Varieties of Agnosticism. *The Philosophical Quarterly*, **72** (2): 365–380.
Friedman, J. (2013a). Question-Directed Attitudes. *Philosophical Perspectives*, **27**: 145–174.
   (2013b). Rational Agnosticism and Degrees of Belief. In D. Gendler and J. Hawthorne(eds.), *Oxford Studies in Epistemology*, vol 4, Oxford: Oxford University Press: 57–81.
   (2013c). Suspended Judgement. *Philosophical Studies*, **162** (2): 165–181.
   (2017). Why Suspend Judging? *Noûs*, **51** (2): 302–326.
Festinger, L. (1957). *A Theory of Cognitive Dissonance*. Stanford, CA: Stanford University Press.
Friedman, J. (2019a). Checking Again. *Philosophical Issues*, **29**: 84–96.
   (2019b). Inquiry and Belief. *Noûs*, **53**: 296–315.
Ganson, D. (2008). Evidentialism and Pragmatic Constraints on Outright Belief. *Philosophical Studies*, **139**: 441–458.
Greco, D. (2015). Iteration and Fragmentation. *Philosophy and Phenomenological Research*, **91** (3): 656–673.
Grice, H. P. (1971) Intention and Uncertainty. *Proceedings of the British Academy*, **57**: 263–279.
Groenendijk, J., and Stokhof, M. (1984). Studies on the Semantics of Questions and the Pragmatics of Answers (Unpublished doctoral dissertation). University of Amsterdam.
Hamblin, C. L. (1973). Questions in Montague English. *Foundations of Language*, **10** (1): 41–53.
Harman, G. (1976). Practical Reasoning. *The Review of Metaphysics*, **29** (3): 431–463.
Hájek, A. (1998). Agnosticism Meets Bayesianism. *Analysis*, **58** (3): 199–206.
Hieronymi, P. (2006). Controlling Attitudes. *Pacific Philosophical Quarterly*, **87** (1): 45–74.
Howard, C. (2016). Transparency and the Ethics of Belief. *Philosophical Studies*, **173** (5):1191–1201.
Huxley, T. (1889). Agnosticism. *The Nineteenth Century* **25**: 169–194.
Kapitan, T. (1986). Deliberation and the Presumption of Open Alternatives. *The Philosophical Quarterly,*. **36** (143): 230–251.
Kaplan, M. (1981). A Bayesian Theory of Rational Acceptance. *The Journal of Philosophy,*. **78** (6): 305–330.
Karttunen, L. (1977). Syntax and Semantics of Questions. *Linguistics and Philosophy,*. **1**: 3–44.
Kearns, S. and Star, D. (2008). Reasons: Explanations or Evidence. *Ethics*, **119** (1): 31–56.
   (2009). Reasons as Evidence. *Oxford Studies in Metaethics*, 4:215–242.
Kelly, T. (2005). The Epistemic Significance of Disagreement. *Oxford Studies in Epistemology*, **1**: 167–196.

(2010). Peer Disagreement and Higher Order Evidence. In R. Feldman and T. Warfield (eds.), *Disagreement*. Oxford: Oxford University Press: 111–174.

Kelp, C. (2020). Theory of Inquiry. *Philosophy and Phenomenological Research*, **103**: 359–384.

(2021). *Inquiry, Knowledge, and Understanding*. Oxford: Oxford University Press.

Lasonen-Aarnio, M. (2014). Higher-Order Evidence and the Limits of Defeat. *Philosophy and Phenomenological Research*, **88** (2): 314–345.

Lilly, W. (2019). Constitutive Reasons and the Suspension of Judgement. *Dialogue*, **58** (2): 215–224.

Lord, E. (2020). Suspension of Judgment, Rationality's Competition, and the Reach of the Epistemic. In S. Schmidt and G. Ernst (eds.), *The Ethics of Belief and Beyond. Understanding Mental Normativity*. Routledge: 126–145.

Lord, E., and Sylvan, K. (2021). Suspension, Higher-Order Evidence, and Defeat. In M. Simion and J. Brown (eds.), *Reasons, Justification, and Defeat*. Oxford: Oxford University Press: 116–145.

Markman, A. and Duke, R. (2016). *Brain Briefs: Answers to the Most (and Least) Pressing Questions about Your Mind*. New York: Sterling.

Marušić, B. & Schwenkler, J. (2018). Intending is Believing: A Defense of Strong Cognitivism. *Analytic Philosophy*, 59 (3):309–340.

Masny, M. (2020). Friedman on Suspended Judgment. *Synthese*, **197** (11): 5009–5026.

McGrath, M. (2020). Being Neutral: Agnosticism, Inquiry and the Suspension of Judgment. *Noûs*, **55** (2): 463–484.

Millson, J. (2021). Seeking Confirmation: A Puzzle for Norms of Inquiry. *Analysis*, **80** (4):683–693.

Nickel, P. J. (2010). Voluntary Belief on a Reasonable Basis. *Philosophy and Phenomenological Research*, **81** (2):312–334.

Olsson, E. and Westlund, D. (2006). On the Role of the Research Agenda in Epistemic Change. *Erkenntnis*, **65**(2): 165–183.

Palmira, M. (2013). A Puzzle about the Agnostic Response to Peer Disagreement. *Philosophia*, **41**(4): 1253–1261.

(2020). Inquiry and the Doxastic Attitudes. *Synthese*, **197**:4947–4973.

Raleigh, T. (2021). Suspending Is Believing. *Synthese*, **198**: 2449–2474.

Raz, J. (1975). *Practical Reason and Norms*. London: Hutchinson & Co.

Roeber, B. (2016). Reasons to Not Believe (and Reasons to Act). *Episteme*, **13** (4): 439–448.

Rosa, L. (2019). Logical Principles of Agnosticism. *Erkenntnis*, **84**: 1263–1283.

Rosenkranz, S. (2007). Agnosticism as a Third Stance. *Mind*, **116**: 55–104.

Ross, J., (2009). How to Be a Cognitivist about Practical Reason. *Oxford Studies in Metaethics* **4**: 243–281.

Russell, B., and Full, B. (1921). *The Analysis of Mind*. London: G. Allen & Unwin Ltd.

Russell, B. (1997). What Is an Agnostic? In J. Slater (Ed.), *Bertrand Russell: His Works, volume 11: Last Philosophical Testament*. London: Routledge: 1943–1968.

Ryan, S. (2010). Doxastic Voluntarism. In J. Dancy, E. Sosa, and M. Steup *(ed.)*, *A Companion to Epistemology*, 2nd ed. Malden, MA.: Wiley-Blackwell: 322–324.

Schoenfield, M. (2014). Permission to Believe: Why Permissivism Is True and What It Tells Us about Irrelevant Influences on Belief. *Noûs*, **48**: 198–218.
Schroeder, M. (2012). The Ubiquity of State-Given Reasons. *Ethics*, **122** (3): 457–488.
Schultheis, G. (2018). Living on the Edge: Against Epistemic Permissivism. *Mind*, **107** (507): 863–879.
Setiya, K. (2003). Explaining Action. *The Philosophical Review*, **112**: 339–393.
  (2007). Cognitivism about Instrumental Reason. *Ethics*, **117** (4): 649–673.
  (2008). Practical Knowledge. *Ethics*, **118**: 388–409.
Shah, N. and Velleman, D. (2005). Doxastic Deliberation. *The Philosophical Review*, **114** (4): 497–534.
Shah, N. (2006). A New Argument for Evidentialism. *The Philosophical Quarterly*, **56** (225), 481–498.
Sosa, E. (1991). *Knowledge in Perspective: Selected Essays in Epistemology*. Cambridge: Cambridge University Press.
  (2010). The Epistemology of Disagreement. In A. Haddock, A. Millar and D. Pritchard (eds.), *Social Epistemology*. Oxford, UK: Oxford Academic: 278–297.
Staffel, J. (2019). Credences and Suspended Judgments as Transitional Attitudes. *Philosophical Issues*, **29** (1), 281–294.
Steglich-Petersen, A. (2008). Does Doxastic Transparency Support Evidentialism? *Dialectica*, **62** (4): 541–547.
Steup, M. (2008). Doxastic Freedom. *Synthese*, **161** (3): 375–392.
  (1988). The Deontic Conception of Epistemic Justification. *Philosophical Studies*, **53** (1): 65–84.
Sylvan, K. (2016). The Illusion of Discretion. *Synthese*, **193** (6): 1635–1665.
Turri, J. (2012). A Puzzle about Withholding. *Philosophical Quarterly*, **62** (247): 355–364.
Ullmann-Margalit, E. and S. Morgenbesser. (1977). Picking and Choosing. *Social Research*, **44** (4): 757–785.
Velleman, D. (1985). Practical Reflection. *The Philosophical Review*, 94: 33–61.
  (1989/2007). *Practical Reflection*. CSLI Publications.
Wagner, V. (2021). Agnosticism as Settled Indecision. *Philosophical Studies*. https://doi.org/10.1007/s11098-021-01676-3.
Way, J. (2017). Reasons as Premises of Good Reasoning. *Pacific Philosophical Quarterly*, **98** (2): 251–270.
Wedgwood, R. (2002). The Aim of Belief. *Philosophical Perspectives*, **16**:267–297.
Weintraub, R. (1990). Decision-Theoretic Epistemology. *Synthese*, **83** (1): 159–177.
White, R. (2005). Epistemic Permissiveness. *Philosophical Perspectives*, **19** (1): 445–459.
Williams, S. G. (1989). Belief, Desire and the Praxis of Reasoning. *Proceedings of the Aristotelian Society*, **90**: 119–142.
Yamada, M. (2010). A New Argument for Evidentialism? *Philosophia*, **38**: 399–404.
Zinke, A. (2021). Rational Suspension. *Theoria*, **87** (5): 1050–1066.

Index

Absent Positive Evidence, 77, 110
acceptance, 145
Agnostic Astronomer, 94–95, 97
agnosticism, 1, 3
   non-evidential reasons for, 163–164
agnosticism permissibility norm, 101
agnosticism permissibility thesis, 155
agnosticism towards p, 71
agnosticism transparency, 154
agnosticism-ascriptions, 62, 81
agnosticism-entails-inquiry thesis, 84, 91, 96
alethic commitment, 76
Anscombe, Elizabeth, 148
answer-seeking, 98
anti-interrogative attitude, 130
appropriateness criterion, 39–42, 53, 57, 81
appropriateness norm
   for agnosticism, 134
   for practical agnosticism, 137, 141
   for believing, 133
   for disbelieving, 134
   for intending, 135
appropriateness thesis, 205
arbitrariness objection, 183, 185
Astronomical Body, 49, 160
attention-holding, 98
attitudinal thesis, 204

basic picking, 140
belief-ascriptions, 62
belief-opportunity, 46
believing that p, 60
BICON, 84, 91
Booth, Anthony, 165
Brown, Jessica, 86
Buridan's ass, 140

Cautious Carl, 124, 156–157, 169
Certainty Seeker, 89, 91, 129
Chisholm, Roderick, 7
Christensen, David, 189

clearer and better evidence, 109
climate change, 192, 195
Cohen, Stewart, 156, 160
commitment criterion, 32, 34, 40–43, 48, 50–51, 53–55, 57, 80
Competing Standards, 184
Cognitive Contact Criterion, 7, 39, 41, 49, 53, 57, 79
   strongly considering, 9
   weakly considering, 9
contextualism, 156
Counterbalanced Positive Evidence, 77
Crawford, Sean, 2, 41
   Crawford's Metacognitive Account, 44, 47
Crawford's Metacognitive Account, 43, 48

Dance Club, 177
Defeated Positive Evidence, 78
Delayed Flight, 44–45, 47
deliberative constrain on reasons, 153
DeRose, Keith, 156
descriptive thesis, 92
disbelieving that p, 61
double-checking, 86–87
double-checking objection, 87
Double-Counting, 193
doxastic attitude, 61
doxastic deliberation, 3, 151–152
doxastic inconsistency
   agnosticism-involving, 204
doxastic indecision, 52
doxastic neutrality, 3, 34, 49, 51, 53–55
   bipartite act-attitude account, 3, 107, 122, 125, 131
Duke, Bob, 13, 15, 17

Elgin, Catherine, 190
Enoch, David, 191
epistemic humility objection, 103
epistemic peerhood, 188–191

epistemic standards, 173–174, 186
  reliability requirement, 174
Equally Reliable Alternative Standard, 187
Everest Summit, 43
evidence pointing problem, 180
  revised, 182
evidential standards
  reliability requirement, 185
evidentialism, 151, 167
  strong, 165
  weak, 165
Expert Surgeon, 86
Extraterrestrial Enthusiast, 89, 91

Falbo, Arianna, 86
Feldman, Richard, 198
Ferrari, Filippo, 63
Festinger, Leon, 14
forensic questioning, 67
Friedman, Jane, 1, 6, 39, 41, 56, 59, 83
  Friedman Criteria, 41

Ganson, Dorit, 167
goal-inspired openness, 103
Gödel's incompleteness theorem, 92

Hieronymi, Pamela, 70
Higgs Field, 53
high-stakes case, 5
Howard, Christopher, 166
Hubble sphere, 93
humility-inspired openness, 103
Huxley, Thomas, 1

inconclusive evidence, 208
inconsistency criterion, 8, 12, 34, 39, 41, 48, 52, 57, 79
inconsistent attitudes explanation, 18–19, 21
Incurvati, Luca, 63
indecision, 33, 51
inquiring mental stance, 57
inquiring state of mind, 83
inquiry-entails-agnosticism thesis, 84
inquiry-opportunity, 46
Insufficient Positive Evidence, 78, 111
interrogative complement, 62

judging that p, 61

knowledge-ascriptions, 72

Less Reliable Alternative Standard, 186
Lilly, Whitney, 2, 70
Litmus Test, 196

Lizard Case, 176, 179
Lord, Errol, 2, 87, 126, 156

Markman, Art, 13, 15, 17
Masny, Michal, 1–2, 41, 44, 46
Masny's metacognitive account, 49
McGrath, Matthew, 2, 107, 156, 205
mental compartmentalisation, 14, 17–18, 22, 88
mind-as-hallway model, 15, 18
mind-as-warehouse model, 15
misleading evidence, 174
missing attitudes explanation, 19, 21
mongrel concept objection, 126
More Reliable Alternative Standard, 187
Morgenbesser, Sidney, 138

Nagel, Jennifer, 156
negative justification, 110
negative neutrality, 119
neutrality criterion, 32, 40–42, 48–49, 53, 57, 80
Nickel, Philip, 175–176
  adequate evidence, 176
  conclusive evidence, 175
non-agnostic indecision, 35–38
non-attitudinal accounts, 12
non-belief, 34
non-belief views, 7–8, 11
non-epistemic reasons, 12
non-evidential reasons, 163
non-existence thesis, 3
normatively commitment-involving, 60–61

omitting judgement, 113
open-ended questions, 64, 66
optional inquiry norm, 102

Palmira, Michele, 4, 84, 172, 189, 197
parity failure objection, 62
parity thesis, 66
peer disagreement, 4, 172, 188
  agnostic disagreement, 4
  agnostic response, 4, 172, 189, 197–198
  conciliationism, 188
  equal fallibility requirement, 189
  evidence of peerhood requirement, 191
  evidence of relative-reliability requirement, 195
  independence, 193, 195
  one way rationality, 198
  steadfastness, 189
permissivism, 4, 171, 173
  agnosticism-involving, 173
  clear-eyed, 183
  negative, 171, 175, 183, 201
  positive, 171, 181

Positive Evidence of Equiprobability, 78
positive justification, 110
positive neutrality, 120
pragmatic reasons, 3, 5
pragmatism, 151
 agnosticism-directed, 151, 155, 166
praxistic attitude, 135, 206
prescriptive thesis, 92
proper picking, 140
proposition-directed, 66

question-directed attitude, 83
question-directed attitude account, 56, 59
questioning-attitude account, 2, 59
questioning mental stance, 59, 75, 80–83

Radioactive Isotope, 162
Raleigh, 31
Raleigh, Thomas, 1–2, 25, 31, 41, 77
Raleigh's Metacognitive Account, 50, 52
rational agnosticism constraint, 155
rationally appropriate, 38, 179, 202
Raz, Joseph, 109
refraining from belief, 119
refraining from judgement, 3
research agenda, 84
Revised Litmus Test, 199
Revision Criterion, 32, 34, 38
Roeber, Blake, 163–164
Russell, Bertrand, 2, 9, 41
Russell's Metacognitive Account, 41–43

sceptical questioning, 67
Schoenfield, Miriam, 171–172, 180
Schroeder, Mark, 152, 158
 sufficiency principle, 158
Schultheis, Ginger, 183
Shah, Nishi, 59, 152
Shoe Box, 45
Sosa, Earnest, 180
spontaneity criterion, 9, 40–41, 49, 53, 57, 80
Staffel, Julia, 35, 37

Steglich-Petersen, Asbjørn, 166
strong cognitivism, 132
sui generis account of agnosticism, 1–2, 54, 57, 71, 75, 81
suspending whether p, 75
suspension of belief, 119
suspension of judgement, 3, 6
suspension permissibility norm, 102
Suspicious Samantha, 153
Suspicious Susan, 112

Temporary Impairment, 109, 115, 119, 125
Temporary Visual Impairment, 116
termination criterion, 11, 40–41, 49, 53, 57, 80
that-clause, 62
toggling attitudes explanation, 19, 21
Train Case, 176
transparency, 166
 agnosticism, 153, 166
 belief, 152–153
tripartite account of neutrality, 108

Ullmann-Margalit, Edna, 138
uniqueness theory, 4, 167
 evidential uniqueness, 168
 reasons uniqueness, 168
unusual proposition cases, 177
unusual situation cases, 177

Velleman, David, 59, 152

Wagner, Verena, 2, 6, 32–33, 36, 39, 41, 50–51, 54–55
 Wagner's Criteria, 33, 41
 Wagner's endorsed-indecision account, 52–53
Way, Jonathan, 153
whether-clause, 62, 71
White, Roger, 180
withholding judgement, 3, 6

yes-or-no questions, 64, 83

For EU product safety concerns, contact us at Calle de José Abascal, 56–1°,
28003 Madrid, Spain or eugpsr@cambridge.org.

www.ingramcontent.com/pod-product-compliance
Ingram Content Group UK Ltd.
Pitfield, Milton Keynes, MK11 3LW, UK
UKHW020700060925
462614UK00020B/412